Six Sigma Statistics using Minitab® 19

Green Belt Edition
(Black & White Version)

By Rehman M. Khan

Chartered Chemical Engineer

& Six Sigma Master Black Belt

ISBN- 9798600792234

DEDICATION

For Mum & Dad, Mahwish, Iqra, Humzah and Raeesa.

CONTENTS

Acknowledgements

Detailed Contents

ACKNOWLEDGEMENTS

I want to thank God for giving me the ability and circumstance to put pen to paper and complete this book.

I want to thank my family for being patient with me while I completed this work. Even though this is an update, it still takes time and effort to ensure the book is continually improved. There is a lot of patience required on the part of my family, as I use some of my annual leave and weekends to write the books.

I would like to thank Sigma Pro for helping me achieve a greater understanding of Six Sigma and becoming a Master Black Belt.

I would like to thank the great people at Minitab for supporting me.

And thanks for your great feedback because it has driven me to get this edition completed.

1 INTRODUCTION

1.1 Introduction

'The capacity to learn is a gift; the ability to learn is a skill; the willingness to learn is a choice.' Welcome and thank you for buying this book. You have made the choice, and now it is up to me to teach you how to use Minitab for Six Sigma Statistics.

I am assuming you have already done your Green Belt training and you have your course notes. What you need is support in understanding how to use Minitab for those common topics that all Green Belts should cover. This book is focussed on Minitab 19. It is the updated version of my Minitab 17 book. If you have that, already I don't recommend you buying this book.

I wrote my first book, Problem Solving and Data Analysis using Minitab, after deciding that there was not enough support for Six Sigma Practitioners following the initial training, especially on Minitab. I felt the soft tools could be understood following the initial training, but as most people had not covered statistical tools before they needed more support. This book follows on in the same fashion but focuses on the needs of Green Belts.

There are two levels of Minitab book that I have written and will continually update. There is this one, and in October 2019 I completed 'Six Sigma Statistics using Minitab 18, Black Belt Edition'. I have included the full contents of that book at the back of this book. I hope that you like the style of this book sufficiently so that you go on to buy that book.

1.2 What to expect

Confucius said "I hear and I forget. I see and I remember. I do and I understand". I still love this Confucius quote as it describes what I want to achieve with the book. This book is a teaching companion, not a reference book or a textbook.

This book aims to teach the reader how to use Minitab to perform Six Sigma statistics at the Green Belt level. The non-statistical tools of Six Sigma are not covered and indeed there is not much coverage of completing DMAIC projects. However, if you work through this book, it should improve your ability to use Minitab and make decisions based on your analysis, which is the most challenging element of Six Sigma when you start.

The order of the chapters is selected deliberately to build the understanding of the reader so that by the end of the book, the reader is using fairly sophisticated Six Sigma tools such as Multiple Regression. They are not in the order you would use the tools in DMAIC. This is what we will be covering

Chapter 2, Minitab Boot Camp- we learn the basics like opening files and navigation between the different windows. A lot has changed in Minitab 19, and I think for the better.

Chapter 3, Data Manipulation- we learn how to handle data by using techniques that allow us to extract and concentrate relevant information

Chapter 4, Generating Graphs- we learn how to produce several graphs and build on what we learned in Boot Camp.

Chapter 5, Core Statistics- we review the core statistics that you should understand.

Chapter 6, An overview of Hypothesis Testing- A lot of the statistical decision making within Minitab is done using Hypothesis Tests. Therefore, it is beneficial to understand what is happening at a basic level. Having a good understanding of Hypothesis Testing is the key to furthering your knowledge of Six Sigma statistics.

Chapter 7, Hypothesis Testing- we learn how to conduct the simple statistical tests that are collectively known as Hypothesis Tests.

Chapter 8, ANOVA- we build on the simple Hypothesis Testing that we learnt in the previous chapter. Chapter 7 was about testing either one sample against a target or two samples against each other. Chapter 8 is about testing more than two samples against each other.

Chapter 9, Control Charts- we learn how to assess whether our process is stable or whether there are uncontrolled forces disrupting our key variables. Producing control charts at the start and end of a project is a good way of demonstrating improvement when there are stability issues.

Chapter 10, Process Capability. These are a set of tools used to assess how your process performs against the customer requirements, which are usually set in specifications. Conducting capability studies at the start and end of a project is a good way of demonstrating improvement against a specification limit.

Chapter 11, Measurement System Analysis (MSA)- This is a fundamental tool that is used early on in a project to understand whether we can measure our key parameters. If we are weak on this step we may conduct a lot of abortive work just because we assumed we could measure with accuracy and precision when we could not.

Chapter 12, Regression Tools are a set of statistical tools used to assess the link between input variables with output variables mathematically. You will get to see the new magical Multiple Regression routine within the Assistant. Minitab has done a fantastic job to make it easy and accessible. I believe that Green Belts will benefit from this new routine whereas in the past it might have been left to the Black Belts.

Chapter 13, Design of Experiment is very much like Regression, but you spend more time on the initial design of the study. The payback is an optimised number of experimental runs to make a conclusion. Again Minitab has done a fantastic job on the routine in the Assistant. When I did my Green Belt training we were not even taught DOE as it was thought to be beyond Green Belts, However, the sequential DOE routine that Minitab has delivered here is a marvel and should be used by Green Belts.

Chapter 14, A detailed contents list of the Black Belt Edition is presented, so when you are ready to get to the next level, you will have the right support materials.

When I started this book, it was 2019 and the version I used to write the book was 19.2. Therefore, I was up-to-date at the time of release. However, with future updates, the look of Minitab will change so you might notice minor differences between my screenshots and the ones you get from Minitab. On Occasion, I edit the screens within Minitab before I capture the shot to clarify the message. This will also result in minor changes to the screenshots that you will see in your version of Minitab.

1.3 How to use the Book

As stated in the previous section, the aim of this book is to teach how to use Minitab. Most chapters will start with a simple explanation of the statistical tool being taught and will then go into an example. At the end of the chapter, there will usually be a number of exercises for the reader to try. A detailed solution for each of the exercises is available from the website so the reader can check that the topic has been understood.

All of the data for the examples and exercises can be downloaded at www.rmksixsigma.com.

I would strongly advise that you download all the data files and put them on your desktop for easy access. Then work through each chapter in turn, first going through the worked example. When you can go through the worked example without looking at the book, later try the associated exercise. Finally, review the answer to the exercise to ensure you got the same result as on the website.

1.4 Target Audience

Six Sigma uses a system of coloured belts to describe the individuals level of proficiency as seen in martial arts. Many years ago, I used to do Tae Kwon Do (TKD) where the increasing level of the belts are described as a plant taking root and gaining strength.

I have given the TKD belt descriptions below and inserted Six Sigma where appropriate.

Yellow represents the earth where the seed of Six Sigma is planted as the foundation of Six Sigma is being laid.

Green represents the plant growing as the skills of Six Sigma develop.

Black: The opposite of white, therefore signifying a maturity and proficiency in Six Sigma. It also indicates the holder's imperviousness to darkness and fear.

The analogy works well for Yellow and Green belt and although a Six Sigma Black Belt won't make you 'impervious to darkness and fear' you should be a much more experienced and knowledgeable practitioner. The point is that at Green Belt, you are still within the development process. To help you develop this book focuses on methods within Minitab that make the statistical tools more natural to use. Minitab uses two systems of conducting tests within the program. One is the traditional method which relies on text and graphical outputs to convey test results. However, interpretation is totally up to the user. The traditional method tends to be preferred by experienced users who prefer flexibility and a greater number of options.

The other method, which Minitab is continuing to develop, is the Assistant. This appeared in Minitab 16. The tools within the assistant are easier to use for beginners. For test commands the Assistant produces multi-page reports which provide graphical advice on the test procedures and also help with interpretation. I remember one person on the Minitab course I was delivering saying 'Why would anyone not use the Assistant?'. For these reasons, the Green Belt edition will focus on the Assistant and the Black Belt edition will focus on the Traditional Menus.

2 MINITAB BOOT CAMP

2.1 The Initial layout

Start your copy of Minitab 19 by double-clicking on your Minitab Icon or running the program from the Start menu.

The first screen that you will see will look like the one shown below. There are quite a few changes to the layout to improve ergonomics, compared to the previous versions of Minitab.

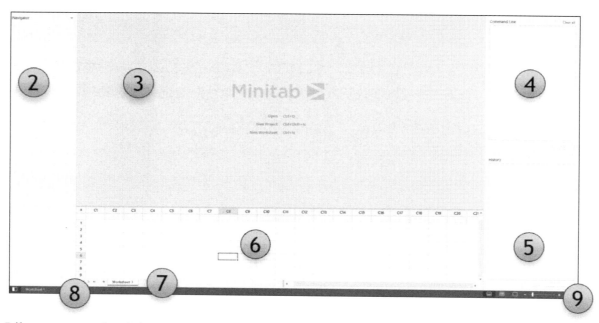

Like most productivity programs, Minitab has a number of drop-down menus at the very top of the screen. It also has several buttons for quick access to essential commands or tools.

Below that we have a number of sub-windows, 2-9, which are used data input, analysis output, displaying historical commands, re-sizing windows etc. There functional will feel familiar even if they are new to the Minitab main screen. Let's breakdown the function of each sub-window by their designated number.

2- The primary function of the Navigator is to tell the story of your analysis in chapter headings. As you proceed through the project you can easily refer back to graphical outputs you have proceed and the result of the analysis you have conducted. The Navigator also has edit functions for these types of output.

3- This is the Output Pane, when analysis/graphs are produced or selected in the Navigator they are displayed here.

4- This is the History Pane it works with the Command Line Pane,5. We will cover these with example data in the next chapter. Items 4 & 5 can be hidden from the View menu if required.

6- This data pane displays the active worksheet. This is where the user enters their data for Minitab to analyse.

Items 7,8 & 9 have been magnified for ocular comfort. 8 & 9 together are the Status bar.

7- This is a navigation bar for worksheets. Additional worksheets can be adding by clicking the plus sign.

8- This section of the Status Bar displays the active worksheet and has a button for hiding the Navigator, [□]. If screen size is not limited, I would recommend that you keep the navigator open and not hide it.

9- The right side of the Status Bar has some useful buttons for sizing the Active Worksheet and Output Pane.
[□] - Extends and displays only the Output Pane.
[⊞] - Extends and displays only the Active Worksheet.
[⊟] - Splits the display between the Output Pane and Active Worksheet. The ratio of the sizes of the windows can be changed by dragging the dividing bar.
There is also a slider that can be used magnify whichever is active out of the Output Pane or Active Worksheet. Clicking on either area will activate it.

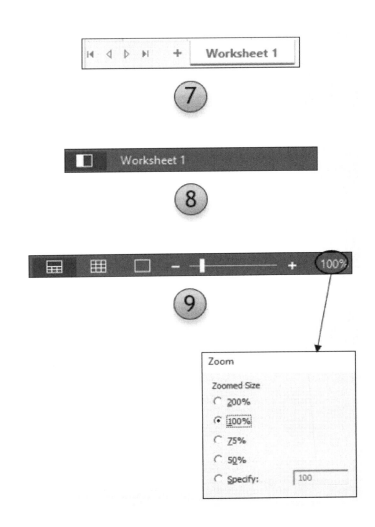

2.2 Working Alongside the Text

In my first Minitab book, I asked the trainee to enter commands from both the text frames and graphically. However, I now feel there will be more benefit in terms of saving space if I give you the command I want you to complete in the text frame. For example,

1. Click **Stat<<BasicStatistics<< Graphical Summary.**

If the trainee wants to work along with the example I want them to left-click on the

Stat Menu and then select the next two sub-commands and then left-click again on 'Graphical Summary'. Please do this now.

If you did it correctly, the Graphical Summary menu box will open. Just press cancel for now or I should say

2. Click on the **Cancel** button.

2.3 Opening a File

If you are working along with the book or even one of the Youtube videos, you will need to download the support files for the chapter from www.rmksixsigma.com. Please do that now and store all the files in an easily accessible file local.

First, we are going to open the Minitab project file called 02 Minitab Boot Camp.MPX. Where the MPX file extension refers to a Minitab 19 project file. Worksheets have the following Minitab file extensions .MTX. In Minitab 19 Graphs are no longer supported as stand-alone Minitab documents.

By the way, newer versions of Minitab are always backward compatible, but not forward compatible. So your copy of Minitab 19 will open .MPJ project files for Minitab 17 or 18 but those versions won't open .MPX project files.

If you want you can simply navigate to the required folder and double click on any of the Minitab file types and Minitab will be launched with your chosen file. The other way is to do the following

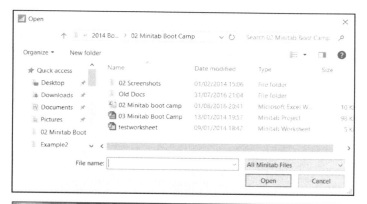

3.   Launch Minitab and click **File<<Open.**
4.   Navigate to where you have stored 02 Minitab Boot Camp.MPX and select the file. The type of each file can be seen within the menu window. Note, we have a filter on the bottom left of the menu. This can be used to restrict the type of items seen within the menu.
5.   Click the **Open** button.
Minitab will open the project for you.

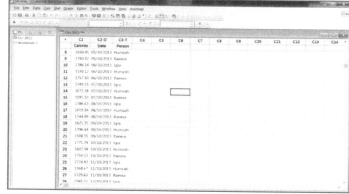

If you are working along with the book or even one of the Youtube videos, you will need to download the support files for the chapter from www.rnksixsigma.com. Please do that now and store all the files in an easily accessible file local.

First, we are going to open the Minitab project file called 02 Minitab Boot Camp.MPX. Where the MPX file extension refers to a Minitab 19 project file. Worksheets have the following Minitab file extensions .MTX. In Minitab 19 Graphs are no longer supported as stand-alone Minitab documents.

By the way, newer versions of Minitab are always backward compatible, but not forward compatible. So your copy of Minitab 19 will open .MPJ project files for Minitab 17 or 18 but those versions won't open .MPX project files.

Method 1 (from within Windows Explorer)- navigate to the required folder and double click on the 02 Minitab Boot Camp.MPX and Minitab will be launched, and it will automatically open your file.

Method 2 (from within Minitab 19)

6. Click **File<<Open.**

7. Navigate to where you have stored 02 Minitab Boot Camp.MPX and select the file. Click the **Open** button, and Minitab will open the project for you.

Minitab only lets you have one project open at a time. If you try and use the **File<<Open** with another project file Minitab will close the active project first and then open the new project. However, you can open additional worksheets. They will be added to the current project as additional worksheets.

8. Try this now by using **File<<Open.** Then open the worksheet called Testworksheet.MTX.

We don't need this right now so we are going to close testworksheet.

9. Right-click on the worksheet name and

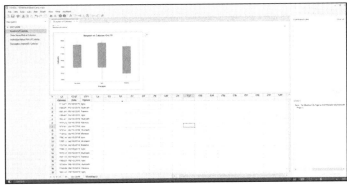

↓	C1	C2	C3	C4	C5	C6
	Type1	Type2	Result			
2	0.97162	18.2804	12.9716			
3	3.49401	19.7060	15.4940			
4	7.91583	16.6765	*			
5	4.94245	16.2431	16.9425			
6	5.34789	12.7306	*			
7	3.81062	16.4601	15.8106			
8	7.25851	18.3253	*			
9	5.15095	14.3953	*			
10	7.88454	19.0217	*			
11	4.61413	13.1964	16.6141			

| ◄ ◄ ► ►I | + | Oct 2019 | Worksheet 2 | testworksheet.mwx |

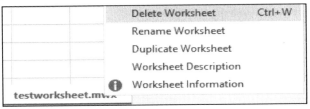

		Delete Worksheet	Ctrl+W
		Rename Worksheet	
		Duplicate Worksheet	
		Worksheet Description	
testworksheet.mwx		ⓘ Worksheet Information	

then select 'Delete Worksheet'.

If you have a project already open within a Minitab program and then double click on a Minitab project file from the windows environment, a second instance of a Minitab program will be opened. It is possible to have multiple instances of Minitab open at the same time.

2.4 Importing Data from an Excel Spreadsheet

I hope that you are working along with the book and as you do this you will find that the data-sets for the examples and exercises are mostly in Microsoft Excel spreadsheets. There are two straightforward ways to bring you data into Minitab, which we are going work-through using a spreadsheet called 'Excel Spreadsheet.xlxs'.

	A	B
1	Calories	Person
2	139.13	Carrot
3	135.96	Lettuce
4	140.63	Broccli
5	137.03	Carrot
6	134.90	Lettuce

Method 1

10. Open the spreadsheet.

11. Select cells A1 to B49. Press Ctrl+C to copy the cells.

12. Go to Minitab and open a new worksheet.

13. Paste the data at the top of the worksheet in the first two available columns. A common mistake is to paste the column names into the numbered rows of Minitab. This is okay to do in Excel, but Minitab works with columns of data and putting the column headings with the data messes things up.

	C1	C2-T
	Calories	Person
1	139.127	Carrot
2	135.957	Lettuce
3	140.632	Broccli
4	137.033	Carrot
5	134.898	Lettuce
6	141.200	Broccli

Method 2

14. Click **File<<Open.** Navigate to where you have stored the files and then select and open 'Excel Spreadsheet.xlxs'.

15. A dialogue box opens which gives details of the data being imported. Note that Minitab checks the data type of each column and we have the opportunity to change it. There will be more on Minitab column data types very soon. Click OK to complete the import.

16. And to tidy up before we go onto the next session, use the **File<<Open** method to open a fresh copy of 02 Minitab Boot Camp.MPX.

Open Excel File - Excel Spreadsheet.xlsx

First row to import: 1

Last row to import: 49

☑ Data has column names

	☑ A	☑ B	☐ C
	Numeric ▼	Text ▼	▼
1	Calories	Person	
2	139.13	Carrot	
3	135.96	Lettuce	
4	140.63	Broccli	
5	137.03	Carrot	
6	134.90	Lettuce	

2.5 Navigating within the Main Window

Now that we have started afresh we should all be faced with this view, or something close to it. To explore this project, there are two main areas we need to know and understand.

Area 1- is to navigate between the worksheets

Area 2- is to navigate to different graphs and text-based statistical outputs from Minitab, those that used to be in the Session Window in older versions.

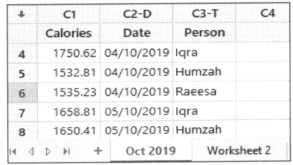

Navigator		Boxplot of Calories ▾ ×
Boxplot of Calories		OCT 2019
Time Series Plot of Calories		Boxplot of Calories
Individual Value Plot of Calories		
Descriptive Statistics: Calories		

↓	C1	C2-D	C3-T	C4	C
	Calories	Date	Person		
1	1719.01	03/10/2019	Iqra		
2	1768.45	03/10/2019	Humzah		
3	1561.44	03/10/2019	Raeesa		
4	1750.62	04/10/2019	Iqra		
5	1532.81	04/10/2019	Humzah		

Oct 2019   Worksheet 2

Let's start by looking at Navigation between worksheets.

The active worksheet is called Oct 2019, and we can see some of the data within the worksheet. The tabs below the data tell us that the project has another worksheet, which is called 'Worksheet 2'. This is a generic name and we cannot see the data within that worksheet at this time.

↓	C1	C2-D	C3-T	C4
	Calories	Date	Person	
4	1750.62	04/10/2019	Iqra	
5	1532.81	04/10/2019	Humzah	
6	1535.23	04/10/2019	Raeesa	
7	1658.81	05/10/2019	Iqra	
8	1650.41	05/10/2019	Humzah	

Oct 2019   Worksheet 2

To have a look at the contents of the other worksheet do the following.

17. Click on the "Worksheet 2" tab.

18. Have a look at the data within Worksheet 2 and then return to the first worksheet by clicking on the "Oct 2019" tab.

You may have noticed that Worksheet 2 contains data that relates to November 2019. It would be a good idea to rename the worksheet to follow the same nomenclature as the first worksheet.

19. Right-click on "Worksheet 2" and select 'Rename' from the drop-down list.

20. Change the name to Nov 2019 and then press enter. It should look like the screenshot shown.

21. When we changed the worksheet name, you may also have noticed a selection called 'Worksheet information'. Right-click and select that for the 'Nov 2019' worksheet.

↓	C1-T	C2-D	C3-T	C4
	Calories	Date	Person	
1	R1669.52	03/11/2019	Iqra	
2	1631.48	03/11/2019	Humzah	
3	1687.58	03/11/2019	Raeesa	
4	1644.4	04/11/2019	Iqra	
5	1618.77	04/11/2019	Humzah	

Oct 2019   Worksheet 2

a	Delete Worksheet
mzah	Rename Worksheet
eesa	Duplicate Worksheet
a	Worksheet Description
mzah	ⓘ Worksheet Information
Worksheet 2	

↓	C1-T	C2-D	C3-T	
	Calories	Date	Person	
1	R1669.52	03/11/2019	Iqra	
2	1631.48	03/11/2019	Humzah	
3	1687.58	03/11/2019	Raeesa	
4	1644.4	04/11/2019	Iqra	
5	1618.77	04/11/2019	Humzah	

Oct 2019   Nov 2019

Congratulations. You have conducted your first analysis that appears in the Navigator and Output Pane. There are 4 previous pieces of analysis that came with the project file.

22. Click through each of them and look at the corresponding analysis in the output pane. Finish with the Boxplot of Calories.

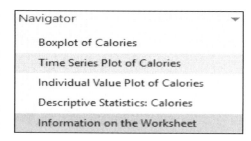

You may have noticed that the page you produced was the first relating to worksheet 'Nov 2019'. The previous 4 pages are related to 'Oct 2019'. If you are doing a lot of analysis across different worksheets the Navigator can be modified to show results by Worksheet. Let's set this up now.

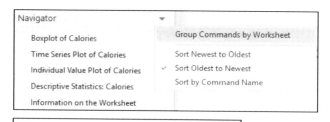

23. Click on the small down-arrow in the top left of the Navigator sub-window and then select 'Group Commands by Worksheet'.

Now Commands are ordered by Worksheet, and we can even minimise the commands of a particular worksheet. My preference is having Commands are ordered by Worksheet as it is much easier to find information when you get deep into a project.

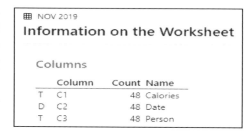

Using the Navigator go back to the Box Plot of Calories, that is associated with the Oct 2019 Worksheet. Occasionally it is useful to zoom into a graph examine an anomaly in detail.

24. Ensure the graph is selected.
25. Use the magnifying slider on the right of the status back to increase the size of the graph.

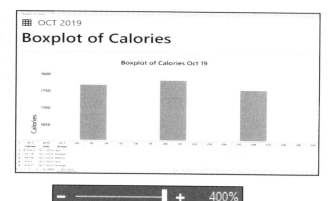

26. Select the Data Pane by clicking on it. Use the magnifying slider to increase the size of the Data Pane as well.
27. Return both to normal size.

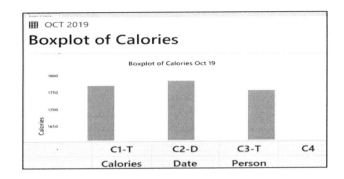

A lot of the time, it helps to be able to look at the analysis side by side for any combination of graphical and text-based results.
Using the Navigator go back to the Box Plot of Calories, that is associated with the Oct 2019 Worksheet.

28. Right-Click on 'Descriptive Statistics:Calories' and then select 'Open in Split View'. Both Windows will appear side by side.
29. Do the same for 'Time Series Plot of Calories'.

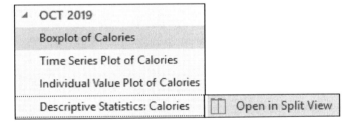

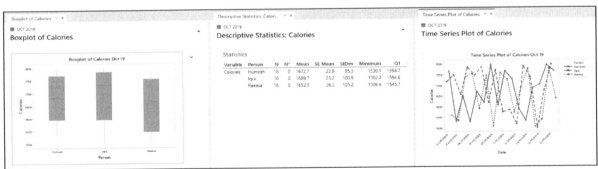

Individual views can be quickly closed by clicking on the cross in the tab for each of the commands.

2.6 Column Formats

We are going to discuss the column formats that Minitab uses.

30. Maximise the data pane for worksheet Oct 2019 and look at the top section of the columns.

Minitab uses the 1st Row to denote the column number, C1, C2, C3 etc, and the data type used within the column. Minitab only allows one type of data within each column.

In Worksheet Oct 2019 there are 3 columns, and each has one of the 3 different column data types used by Minitab.

T indicates the **Text** data type within the column.

D indicates a **Date/Time** data type within the column.

No letter after the column number indicates a **Numeric** data type.

Go to worksheet Nov 2019 and look at the top of the worksheet at the data formats used within the columns.

We can see that there has been an error of some sort and that C1 is not formatted as numeric data but text data. This needs to be corrected, or Minitab won't let us carry out any of the tests used on numeric data.

31. Place the cursor in Row01, C1. Then double click within the cell. You can now edit the contents using the cursor. Remove the 'R' from in front of '1669.52' and press enter.

We can see that removing the 'R' does not change the formatting of the column, it is still a Text Column. We must change the format manually, even though all the data in the column is now actually numeric.

32. To change the column format, click **Data<<Change Data Type.**
33. Select Calories as the column to be modified.
34. Then click OK and the format will be corrected.

If you are copying and pasting data from any spread-sheeting program into Minitab, make sure it is correctly formatted, with the data in columns and without mixing data types, before you copy it to Minitab.

Oct 2019

C1	C2-D	C3-T
Calories	Date	Person
1719.01	03/10/2019	Iqra
1768.45	03/10/2019	Humzah
1561.44	03/10/2019	Raeesa

Nov 2019

C1-T	C2-D	C3-T
Calories	Date	Person
R1669.52	03/11/2019	Iqra
1631.48	03/11/2019	Humzah
1687.58	03/11/2019	Raeesa

Nov 2019

C1-T	C2-D	C3-T
Calories	Date	Person
1669.52	03/11/2019	Iqra
1631.48	03/11/2019	Humzah
1687.58	03/11/2019	Raeesa

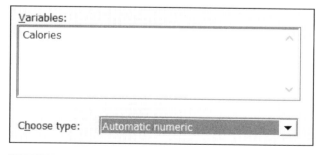

Variables:

Calories

Choose type: Automatic numeric

C1	C2-D	C3-T
Calories	Date	Person
1669.52	03/11/2019	Iqra
1631.48	03/11/2019	Humzah
1687.58	03/11/2019	Raeesa

A useful function to know in Microsoft Excel is the Transpose function as it can be used to turn your data by 90 degrees in Excel. If you have never used it before, use the Help menu in Excel to find out how to use it.

2.7 Sending Minitab Outputs to Microsoft Office Programs

Most people use Microsoft Office products for report writing so this section reviews how to transfer Minitab outputs to Word, Excel and Powerpoint.

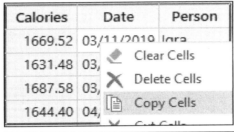

35. To transfer data from the Data Pane highlight the area you wish to transfer and then right-click and then click on 'Copy Cells'. The selection can then be pasted into Office. Depending on which program has received the data, it will be in cells or text boxes and can be edited.

36. To transfer Outputs from the Navigator right-click anywhere on the required title and then select 'Send Section to ....'.

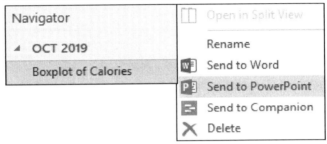

37. To transfer Outputs from the Output Pane click on the down arrow and select 'Send Section to ....'.

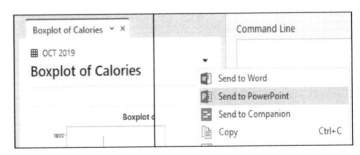

2.8 File Security

We are not going to go into saving our files apart to say that save your files as Minitab Projects (.MPX) if you want to keep all the information. If you wish to save only the Data Pane, save your work as a Worksheet (.MTX).
If you wish to add a layer of security to your project, you can set a password, which will be required to open the project again. So if you decide to set a password, don't forget the password!
To set a password
38. *Click File>>File Security.*
You can then set your password.

3 DATA MANIPULATION

3.1 Introduction to Data Manipulation

This chapter aims to teach you how to manipulate data within the worksheet window. It is advantageous to have these skills so that you can reduce a large worksheet into a much smaller and focused one. This helps to focus the mind and reduce errors. So these skills will come in useful early on in a project when you are required to sanitise your data before applying your analysis skills.

We will only be working with data in the worksheet window, and we will be using a single example throughout the chapter.

This can be found in the file 03 Data Manipulation.xlsx. When you are ready, copy the data from that file into a new worksheet within Minitab. Have a look at the data in the worksheet window. Get a feel for the type of data in each column and the type and magnitude of the data elements.

↓	C1-T	C2	C3	C4	C5	C6-D
	Factory	A Conc	A Feeder2	B Conc	Product Code	Reaction Time
1	UK	54.6	2.02375	75.7652	903	12:03:01 AM
2	Nigeria	63.5	2.92875	80.9307	106	12:00:48 AM
3	Spain	74.0	0.57250	88.7614	605	12:00:45 AM
4	Dubai	86.3	1.94000	89.3517	903	12:04:39 AM
5	Nigeria	87.9	1.80375	75.9439	605	12:04:46 AM
6	UK	65.8	3.81250	86.4065	903	12:03:43 AM

In this example, you have been asked by a company to analyse how reaction time of a product varies with the concentration of two additives called A & B. The company are only interested in data from their UK site and their Low Fat product. As you can see from the screen-shot, they have supplied data from several sites and for all the product range. Additionally, the product range is listed in terms of the company's own internal codes. Also, they have two feeders for ingredient A and they both carry out the same function.

We are going to learn how to use a number of functions within Minitab to focus our data on what we feel are the relevant parameters. We are also going to make the data easier to interpret. By that I mean we will change the format of the Reaction Time column into a numeric column and we will only display a single figure which will be in units of seconds only. Although Minitab will allow us to use the

Date/Time format as shown within calculations I would much rather see this converted to number of seconds only.

3.2 Splitting a Worksheet

The first thing we are going to do is to isolate the UK data into a separate worksheet.

1.   Click *Data<<Split Worksheet.*
2.   Select Factory as the variable to be used to split the worksheet.
3.   Click OK. This action will leave our original worksheet intact and form four new worksheets. These will be split by the four factory locations that were listed in the 'Factory' column.
4.   Click on the Worksheet window icon. This will tidy-up all those worksheets.
5.   Ensure that the worksheet relating to the UK data is active by clicking on it.

We now have 5 worksheets. The original and one each for each of the different countries, although we are only interested in the one for the UK.

	C1	Factory	By variables:
	C2	A Conc	Factory
	C3	A Feeder2	
	C4	B Conc	
	C5	Product Code	
	C6	Reaction Time	

☐ Include missing as a BY level

| Worksheet 1 | Worksheet 1(Factory = Dubai) | Worksheet 1(Factory = Nigeria) |

| Worksheet 1(Factory = Spain) | Worksheet 1(Factory = UK) |

↓	C1-T	C2	C3	C4	C5	C6-D
	Factory	A Conc	A Feeder2	B Conc	Product Code	Reaction Time
1	UK	54.6	2.02375	75.7652	903	12:03:01 AM
2	UK	65.8	3.81250	86.4065	903	12:03:43 AM
3	UK	64.1	1.09000	83.5307	903	12:04:35 AM

3.3 Using Code

We are now going to change the data within the Product Code column to make it more user-friendly. Presently, it contains four numbers which represent the products that the company makes. These are

106→Herbal
109→Organic
605→Sugar Free
903→Low Fat

We will make this conversion on the worksheet.
6.   Click *Data<<Recode<<To Text.*
7.   Under 'Recode values in the following columns' select the Product Code column.
8.   Under Method select in 'Recode individual values' from the drop-down list.
9.   Enter the text as shown against each of the product codes.

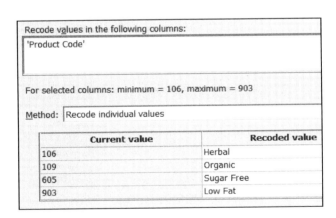

Recode values in the following columns:

'Product Code'

For selected columns: minimum = 106, maximum = 903

Method: Recode individual values

Current value	Recoded value
106	Herbal
109	Organic
605	Sugar Free
903	Low Fat

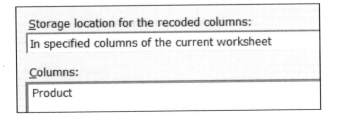

Storage location for the recoded columns:

In specified columns of the current worksheet

Columns:

Product

10. Minitab is then asking us where we want to put our converted data. We are going to tell it to put the data into a specified column. We tell it to put the converted data into a new column called 'Product'. As the column does not exist, Minitab will create it. Complete this section as shown.

11. Click OK. Minitab creates the data column in C7.

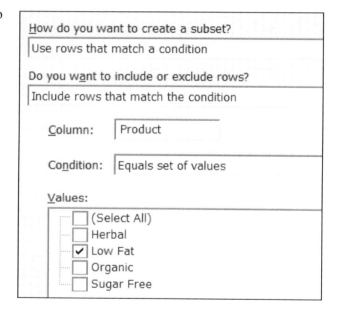

3.4 Sub-setting the Worksheet

We used the 'Split Worksheet' command to produce worksheets specifically for each country. We then started working on the UK worksheet. We will now use the 'Subset Worksheet' command to draw out data only for the Low Fat product. 'Subset Worksheet' only produces a single worksheet unlike 'Split Worksheet'.

12. Click **Data<<Subset Worksheet.**
13. Leave the default selection in the first two drop-down lists. This sets the selection so we include rows that match a specific condition.

14. Next, we need to specify the column that will be used to split the worksheet. Under Column enter Product.

15. Now we need to specify that whenever the value in the Product column is equal to Low Fat put that row into the new worksheet. Under Condition select 'Equals set of values' from the drop-down list. Then select 'Low Fat'.

16. At the bottom of the menu, we have the option of specifying a new worksheet name but we are going to leave that blank.
17. Click OK to generate the new worksheet.

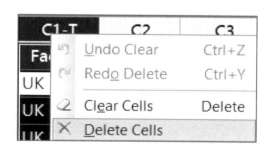

18

18. Delete columns 1,5 & 7, **Factory, Product & Product Code,** by clicking in the cell where the column headers (C1 etc.) are to select the column and then right-click and select **Delete Cells**. This will leave 4 columns in the worksheet.

↓	C1	C2	C3	C4-D
	A Conc	A Feeder2	B Conc	Reaction Time
1	54.6	2.02375	75.7652	12:03:01 AM
2	65.8	3.81250	86.4065	12:03:43 AM
3	64.1	1.09000	83.5307	12:04:35 AM
4	60.3	4.08250	78.4096	12:02:54 AM

3.5 Extract numeric data from a cell with Date/Time format

19. Rename the active worksheet UK Low Fat.

20. The remainder of the worksheets can now be deleted.

Reaction Time is our response, it should be in C4. The formatting is not very appealing. It would be better if it were displayed in minutes and seconds as per the original Excel file or just in seconds. We are going to change the format, so the response is the total number of seconds.

C4-D
Reaction Time
12:03:01 AM
12:03:43 AM
12:04:35 AM

Original Excel File

Reaction Time
0:03:01
0:00:48
0:00:45

21. Click on ***Data<<Date/Time<<Extract to Numeric.***

22. Select Reaction Time as the target column and enter **Mins** as the name of the column that we will store the number of minutes within.

23. In the selection box at the bottom of the menu, specify 'Minute' as the data to be extracted.

24. Click OK.

Minitab will create a column with the minute data from our Reaction Time column.

We will now extract the number of seconds from our response data.

25. Click on the Edit Last Dialog Box icon or press Ctrl+E. **This is a good tip,** Press F3 to clear the menu. It is useful to know as it clears all sub-menus as well. It is very useful if you are using the same menu repeatedly for different inputs.

Extract from date/time column:	'Reaction Time'
Store numeric column in:	Mins

Specify at least one component to extract from date/time

☐ Year		☐ Hour
◉ Four Digit		☑ Minute
○ Two Digit		☐ Second
☐ Quarter		☐ Tenths
☐ Month		☐ Hundredths
☐ Week		☐ Thousandths
☐ Day of month		
☐ Day of week		

26. Enter **secs** as the name of the column that we will store the number of seconds within.

Store numeric column in:	secs

27. In the selection box at the bottom of the menu, specify Second as the data to be extracted.

28. Click OK.
Minitab will create a column with the second data from our Reaction Time column.

☐ Hour
☐ Minute
☑ Second
☐ Tenths
☐ Hundredths
☐ Thousandths

With a bit of mathematics, we can convert our two new columns into a single column that contains only the total number of seconds.

Reaction Time	Mins	secs
12:03:01 AM	3	1
12:03:43 AM	3	43
12:04:35 AM	4	35

3.6 Using the Calculator

29. Click **Calc<<Calculator.**

In Excel, a mathematical operation would be initiated in the worksheet by putting ' = ' in front of the instruction. In Minitab, we use the calculator, the difference is that Minitab works with columns of data but it conducts the operations across the rows of data.

1. We tell Minitab to store the results here.

2. We enter the mathematical expression here. Expressions can also use logic functions.

3. We have the option of using the buttons in this area to enter the expression.

4. This is a function selector that can be used to quickly select functions. If a function is selected the required formatting is shown underneath the selector.

5. This is an optional tick box for assigning the expression as a formula. We will learn more about this in the next section.

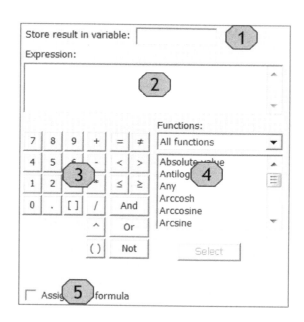

30. Enter **Time** as the name of a new column that will be used to store the results.
31. Enter the following under Expression **Mins*60+secs** . This will give us the total number of seconds. Remember, when you come across a column name you don't have to type it all in. You can double-click on the column name in the column select menu. Click OK.
Minitab will produce the new column called Time, and it will contain the reaction time in terms of seconds.
32. Delete the columns that we don't need any more; Reaction Time, Mins and secs. These should be C4, C5 & C6.

Store result in variable:	Time
Expression:	
'Mins'*60+'secs'	

At the start of this example, we said that the company uses 2 feeders for component A. We are going to simplify the worksheet by adding the two columns together. This is an excuse to demonstrate how to Assign a Function. In the real world, we might want to handle the two feeders independently.

A Conc	A Feeder2	B Conc	Time
54.6	2.02375	75.7652	181
65.8	3.81250	86.4065	223
64.1	1.09000	83.5307	275
60.3	4.08250	78.4096	174

3.7 Assigning a Function

The menu for Assigning a Function looks very similar to that for the Calculator. The only difference is that the Assign Function menu does not ask you for a storage location. The storage location for the results of the expression is set by placing the active cursor before you assign a function.

33. Move the active cursor to any cell within C5.
34. Click on the Assign Function button.
35. Enter the expression **A Conc + A Feeder2**.
36. Click OK.
37. Rename C5 as **Total A**.

Expression:	
'A Conc' + 'A Feeder2'	

Notice the green tick within the title cell of C5. This signifies that Assign Function has been used to generate this column of data and also that it will be updated if any values in the parent columns change. When the Calculator is used there is no automatic update of the calculated column as there is with Assign Function.

C5 ✓
Total A
56.6238
69.6125

If you hover over the green arrow with your mouse pointer, Minitab will show you the formula that has been used to generate that particular column.

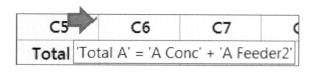

If you try and delete one of the parent columns, the warning shown will be displayed, don't do this now but if you do delete one of the parent columns the values in the **Total A** column will no longer update.

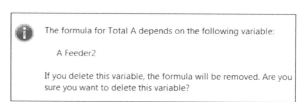

3.8 Setting the Decimal Places & Rounding Values

Let's say that I did not want to display the value in C5 to 4 decimal places (dp). I could format the column to only show 2 dp.
38. Place the active cursor on any cell within C5.
39. Right-click and select *Format Column*.
40. Under Choose type change the selection to **Fixed decimal.** Then change the number of Decimal places to **2**.
41. Click OK.

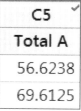

The values to 4dp still exist, but now C5 is only displayed to 2 dp. We also have the option to round the number and this will mean that the number to 4 dp will no longer exist.
42. Change the display back to 4 dp for C5 by using the Format Column command again.

We can also use a function command to round the number of decimal places. Rounding is different to changing the display as it will change the value that is stored in the cell, whereas, in the last section we only changed the display.

43. Move the active cursor to any cell within C5.
44. Click on the Assign Function button. The existing expression is **A Conc + A Feeder2** .

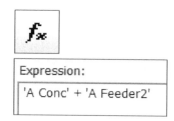

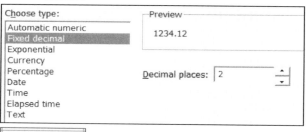

45. Select 'Round' from the function selector. The basic form is shown here. Our expression will replace 'number' within the basic form. Change the expression as shown.

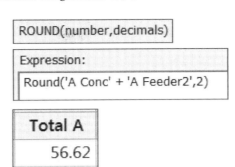

ROUND(number,decimals)

Expression:

Round('A Conc' + 'A Feeder2',2)

46. Click OK.

Total A
56.62
69.61
65.19

47. Take a look at C5. It has been rounded to 2 dp.

3.9 Deleting Data

48. Right-click on the Worksheet tab and select 'Worksheet Information'. This will display information on the columns within the active worksheet window. The information will be displayed in a separate project manager window. We can see the headings for each of our columns and the number of rows of data that they contain. We see that within the **Time** column, there are 5 missing data elements. 'Type' indicates the column format. We spoke about the three data types used in Minitab in the last chapter.

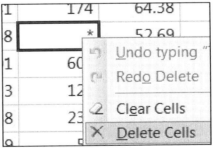

+ UK Low Fat   ⓘ Worksheet Information

Columns

Column	Count	Missing	Name
C1	56	0	A Conc
C2	56	0	A Feeder2
C3	56	0	B Conc
C4	56	5	Time
C5	56	0	Total A

78.41	174	64.38
75.48	*	52.69
81.01	600	76.29

49. Look at row 5 in the Time column. As a default, Minitab uses the '*' to denote a cell with no data.

50. We will delete the empty cell by moving the active cursor onto the cell and then right-clicking and selecting **Delete Cells**.

1	174	64.38
8	*	52.69
1	60	
3	12	
8	23	

↶ Undo typing "
↷ Red̲o Delete
✐ Cle̲ar Cells
✕ Delete Cells

Deleting a single cell can cause significant problems as demonstrated here. The missing cell is deleted but then all the cells below it are moved up one space. This means that the data within the row is not all related to one instance in time or one event as it was before the deletion.

78.41	174	64.38
75.48	600	52.69
81.01	127	76.29

51. Click on the **Undo** icon. If we want to delete the cell, we must delete the complete row to stop the misalignment of data.

52. Left-click on the row number for row 5. This highlights the complete row.
53. Right-click in the same position. Then select **Delete Cells.** Notice that this action deletes the complete row.
54. Initially, there were 5 missing cells in the **Time** column, so that means there are 4 left to delete. Let's pretend that the data set is really long, thousands of rows, and we want an easy way to locate the row numbers of missing data cells. We need a better method of deletion for this scenario.
55. Place the active cursor in C4 Row1.

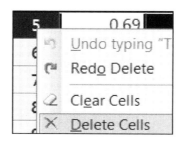

56. Click *Editor<<Find and Replace<<Find*
57. Type in the asterisk symbol in the **Find What** menu box.
58. Then click on the **Find Next** button on the same menu. Minitab will move the active cursor to the next occurrence of ' * '. Make a note of the row number.
59. Keep clicking on the **Find Next** button until you get to the bottom of the column. Row 19, 39, 41 and 54 should contain the missing data. Close the Find pop-up box.
60. To delete the data from these rows in one step click *Data<<Delete Rows.*

61. Enter the 4 rows of data into the menu with a space between each number. Then select all the columns in the next menu box. An easy way to select all the columns you want is to highlight them all, just by starting at the top then holding the left mouse button and dragging all the way down, and then pressing select. Then click OK.

The missing data and the rows associated with that data should have been deleted.

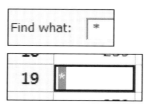

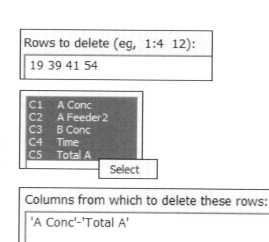

3.10 Conditional Formatting

Conditional Formatting was introduced in the 17.2 update. It is a handy tool with lots of sub-options. I will give you a brief introduction but you should have a play and explore session yourself.

62. Click **Data<<Conditional Formatting<<High/Low<< Highest Percentage**

63. Select Time as the column that we will format.

64. Leave the Percent selection as 10. This means that the highest 10% of the Time data will be formatted. As there are 51 rows of data, that means 5 cells will be formatted.

65. Under Style choose 'Red' as the formatting style.

66. Click OK and check the worksheet. Cells in row 5, 12, 20, 40 & 43 of the Time column should be highlighted.

67. Repeat the steps shown above to format the lowest 10 percent with a yellow background.

68. Click **Data<<Conditional Formatting<<Manage Rules**. Don't' make any changes at this point.

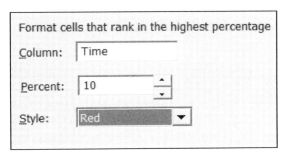

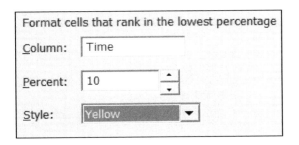

This menu allows us to manage the rules that we created for conditional formatting and to some extent, it will enable editing. There is a drop-down menu at the top to select the appropriate column if you have formatted more than one column. Below that are the rules that you created. They are order specific. You can delete rules and change their order.

At the bottom of the menu, there is a Format button. This allows you to edit the formatting and gives you more options than in the original menu.

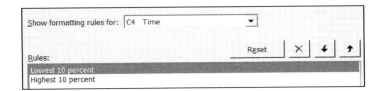

3.11 Using the Command Line to Execute Historical Commands

Let's say you show the spreadsheet to the boss and they say 'I don't like the highlighting, please remove it'. As a conscientious employee, you comply using the following step.

69. Click **Data<<Conditional Formatting<<Clear Rules**.

Then later the same day, the boss say's 'I have had a stunning idea, why don't you highlight the top 10 percent of times in red and the bottom 10 percent of times in Yellow.

As you haven't logged out of the project in Minitab re-applying the yellow is easy. You would do the following

70. Click on the Edit Last Dialog Box icon or press Ctrl+E. Then click OK.

There is a reasonably easy way to repeat older commands as well.

70. Examine the History and locate the code where the first highlight command occurred.

71. Copy all of that code into the Command Line and Click Run.

The Edit Last Dialog Box is limited to just the previous command. Using the command line, we can execute older commands within the project or even import them. After a bit of practice, it is not that difficult to find the command you need and it's parameters.

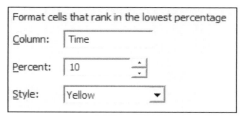

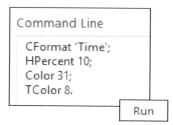

4 GENERATING GRAPHS

4.1 INTRODUCTION TO GENERATING GRAPHS

The starting point for all analysis should be to have a look at the data in a way our minds can understand. A graph allows our minds to draw out patterns from thousands of data points.
This chapter starts you off on how to create, manipulate and analyse data using graphs.
This subject could easily produce a book in itself, but I want to keep it reasonably brief so we can get down to the hardcore statistics. To keep things brief we will only be covering the more useful graphs for Green Belts. I will completely miss out some of the ones like Stem & Leaf because I have never found them helpful. We will cover several graphs within the chapter but we will also be learning more about graphical analysis as we work through the statistical modules. For example, Multi-Vari-Plot, Main Effects Plot and Interactions Plot will be covered in the ANOVA module. Also, as the book focuses on the Assistant many graphs will be shown within the reports generated by the Assistant so they won't be covered in this chapter.
We will be covering the Boxplot, Dotplot, Individual value Plot, Bar Chart, Time Series Chart and a couple of new charts for this edition. Then we will show you how to manipulate these graphs and that will apply to all other graphs which are generated without the Assistant.

4.2 BOXPLOTS AND THE MENU SYSTEM

1.   The data that we are going to be using in this module is in the Excel file 04 Generating Graphs.xlsx. Open this file and transfer the data from Sheet 1 into a worksheet within a new Minitab Project.

We are working with a similar data set as the one used in Chapter 4, where we investigated product data for a company. Our numerical response data is called reaction time. We then have two columns of numerical data for the Concentration of A and B. There are two columns of categorical variables also. These are the Product Code and the Factory, and then we have the 'Fact-Prod' column which is a concatenation of the two. The 7th column is Defects% produced by the Fact-Prod combination.

2.   To produce the first Boxplot click *Graph<<Boxplot.*
The first choice that we need to make is whether we want to display one variable or more than one variable. As we only want to show one variable without breaking it down into groups we select the **One Y, Simple** option on the top left of the four boxes, this is the default selection anyway.

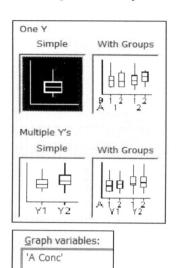

3.   For this example, select **A Conc** as the variable to be plotted. Then click OK.
A simple boxplot is produced, which shows the distribution of A Conc data. The top of the box on the boxplot is at the 75th percentile and the bottom of the box is at the 25th percentile. The horizontal line in the box represents the median. The asterisk at the top denotes an outlier.

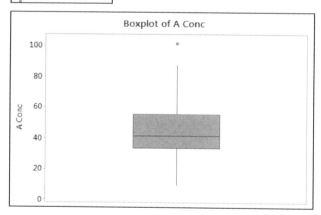

A simple boxplot is produced, which shows the distribution of A Conc data. The top of the box on the boxplot is at the 75th percentile and the bottom of the box is at the 25th percentile. The horizontal line in the box represents the median. The asterisk at the top denotes an outlier.

4.   We will investigate the outlier within the data. Hover the mouse over the outlier on the graph. Minitab tells us that the data for the outlier is within Row 11. We will now pretend that the data was incorrectly recorded and the value for **A Conc** in Row 11 should be 61.3 and not 101.3.
5.   Correct the value for **A Conc** in row 11.

10	UK	44.4
11	Nigeria	61.3
12	Spain	38.7

6. Go back to and look at the message at the top of the Output Pane. It is telling us that the graph that is being displayed no longer matches the data that we used to generate it. We have 3 options; 1) do nothing, 2) update the current graph or 3) keep the graph we have and make a new one with the updated data.

7. We have the option to update the Boxplot. Click on '**Update these results**'.

8. If you know that you want your graphs always to be current, you can enable automatics updates for individual graphs by clicking on the down arrow at the top right of the Output Pane and then selecting 'Update Results Automatically'.

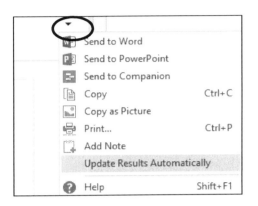

We are going to produce a 1Y simple boxplot with groups.

9. Click *Graph<<Boxplot.* Then, Click on the selector for **1Y with Groups**. Click OK.

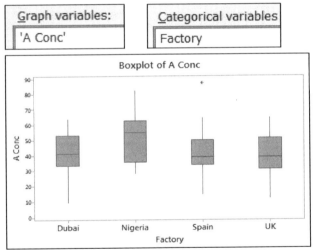

10. Again the 1Y that we are going to investigate is A Conc. Select 'A Conc' as the Graph Variable. If we want to split the groupings further, we can add more than one categorical variable. Select 'Factory' as the Categorical Variable.

11. Click OK to produce the Boxplot. Using this Boxplot, we can compare the 'A Conc' variable across different sites. We need to remember that there is a product range made by each site and this may change any conclusions we make regarding the variable we are investigating.

As a mini exercise produce a Boxplot using the Multiple Y's with Groups options as shown.

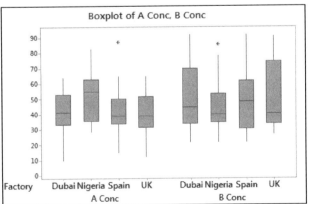

4.3 Editing Graphs

We are now going to learn how to edit the graph and change its physical appearance. The appearance of the graph can be changed considerably by editing it. Every area of the graph can be transformed and the appearance modified.

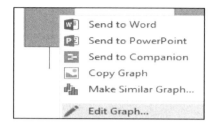

12. To Open the Graph Editor either double click on an editable region of the graph or right-click on the graph and then select 'Edit Graph'. The appearance of the graph can then be modified either using the toolbars and drop-down menu's or by double-clicking on editable regions. For the features, I have circled and have a quick look at each menu in turn.

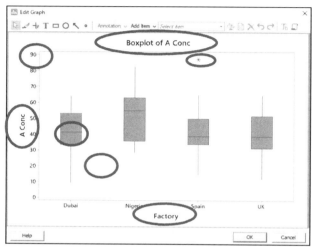

Below the graph, I have shown the editing menu for the Y-Scale. You can see the number of tabs that are available for the different characteristics of the Y-scale that can be amended.

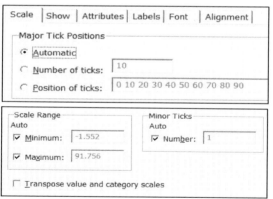

The tabs and the menu options are self-explanatory, so I won't try and go through all the options within the book. I would suggest that you go through the menu's yourself and make some changes and observe their effects on the graph.

4.4 Duplicating Graphs

Here's one I made earlier. I have made quite a few changes to the graph. If I wanted to keep my formatting consistent over several graphs, I would have to remember what changes I made and then make them each time. Thankfully there is an easier way of producing more graphs with the same formatting.

In this case, I have the 1Y with Groups plot; my Y variable is 'A Conc' and my categorical variable is Factory. I want to keep the formatting but I want to produce another graph where 'Product Type' is the Categorical variable.

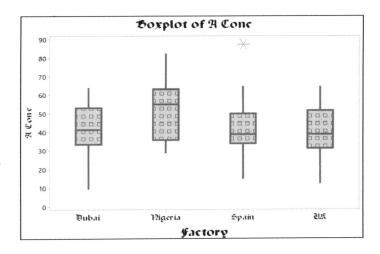

13. Ensure the graph shown is selected.

14. Right-Click on the graph and select 'Make Similar Graph'.

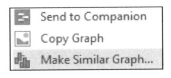

15. In the menu that opens change the Categorical Grouping from Factory to Product Type.

16. Click OK to produce the new graph.

In the new graph, change the following variables:		
Role	**Original Variable**	**New Variable**
Categorical grouping	Factory	Factory
Y	'A Conc'	'A Conc'

We have made our new graph and retained the formatting that would otherwise have taken a fair amount of time to put into place.

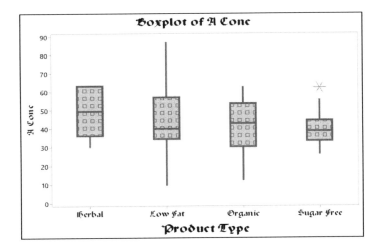

4.5 The Individual Value Plot

When I am conducting graphical analysis, which involves looking for trends within groups, I will start with boxplots and then change to Individual value plots when I have seen a pattern and want to see the real data in the trend.

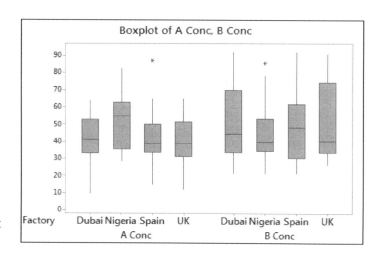

Have a look at the two charts shown here. The underlying data and the groupings are exactly the same. Even with the same data, both charts look very different. This is a good reason not to rely on one type of chart when you are conducting graphical analysis.

To produce this Individual Value Plot
17. Click *Graph<<Individual Value Plot*

18. Click on the selector for **Multiple Y's, with Groups**. Click OK.

19. Select 'A Conc' and 'B Conc' as the graph variables.

20. Select 'Factory' as the Categorical variable for Grouping.

21. Click OK to produce the plot.

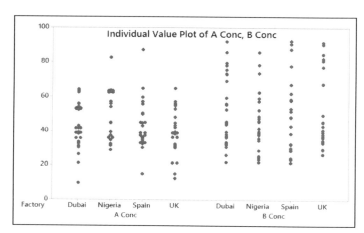

4.6 The Dot Plot

The Dotplot is an interesting graph as it comes with additional optional presentations using Stacking. Stack groups is another option for displaying the data points similar to a cumulative frequency plot.

To produce this Individual Value Plot

22. Click *Graph<<Dotplot*

23. Click on the selector for **Multiple Y's, Stack Groups**. Click OK.

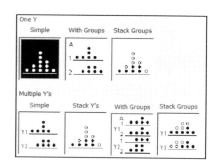

24. Select 'A Conc' and 'B Conc' as the graph variables.

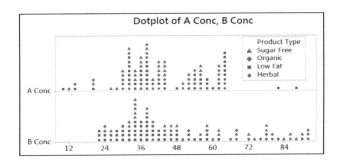

25. Select Product Type as the Categorical variable for Grouping.

26. Click OK to produce the plot.

4.7 The Bar Chart

Even though Excel is very good at producing Bar Charts, it is worth knowing how to form them in Minitab as well, especially when you want to bring statistical calculations into the mix.
To produce a simple Bar Chart
27. Click **Graph<<Bar chart**

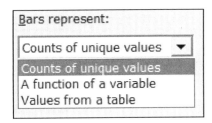

The Bar Chart options menu opens, and the first thing we need to decide is what the Bars represent. This menu is for the numerical side of the chart and relates to the Y-axis. The next thing that we determine is what the X-axis will look like and this refers to the categorical variables that we use. The options for the X-axis are Simple, Cluster and Stack.
There are 3 main options for the Y-axis and 3 options for the X-axis; that makes 9 combinations altogether. (I'm not counting the Multiple Y versions of the Bar Chart). The examples shown in this section will cover only 3 combinations but use all the options for each category.

28. From the Bar represents drop-down menu select 'Counts of unique values'.

29. Select Simple then Click OK. The sub-menu opens for this type of Bar Chart.

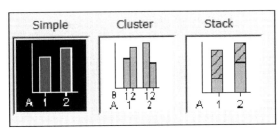

30. Select Factory as the Categorical Variable.

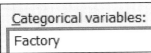

31. Click OK to produce the Chart.

The Bar Chart gives a count of the number of times each factory appears in the data. Hence the name 'Counts of unique values'.

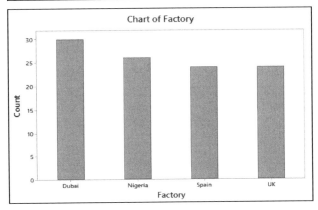

'Function of a variable' is much more interesting. It offers to carry out stats functions through menu selections for a limited number of functions.

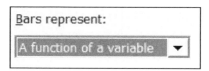

32. Click *Graph<<Bar chart*

33. From the Bar represents drop-down menu select 'A function of a variable'.

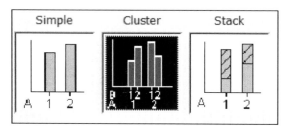

34. Select Cluster under the One Y heading then Click OK. The sub-menu opens for this type of Bar Chart.

35. Select 'StDev' from the function drop down menu. There are 9 other available functions.

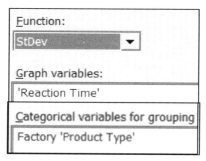

36. Select 'Reaction Time' as the Graph variable.

37. Select 'Factory' and 'Product Type' as the Categorical Variables for grouping.

38. Click OK to produce the Chart.

The Bar Chart gives us the values of StDev for Reaction Time with the data broken down by factory and then product.

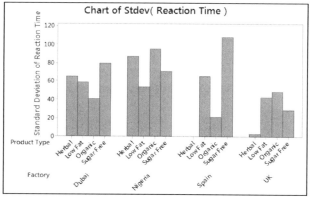

The final option is 'Values from a table'. This is simply the sum, or total, of the data of the selected categorical variables. It produces the same graph as using the Sum function when using the 'Functions of a variable' option from the drop-down list.

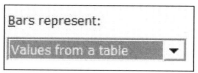

39. Click *Graph<<Bar chart*
40. From the Bar represents drop-down menu select 'Values from a table'.

41. Select Stack under the One Y heading then Click OK. The sub-menu opens for this type of Bar Chart.

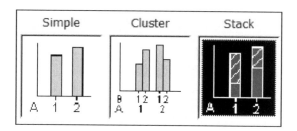

42. Select 'Reaction Time' as the Graph variable.

43. Select 'Factory' and 'Product Type' as the Categorical Variables for grouping.
44. Click OK to produce the Chart.

The Y-axis for the produced chart is the sum of Reaction Time within each of the categories.

Notice that for every other graph that we produced, as a default, Minitab ordered the Categorical variables in alphabetical order, but it did not do this on this occasion.

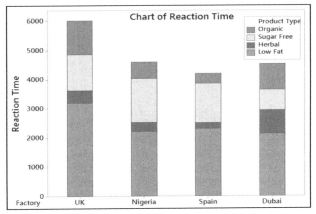

4.8 Changing the order on a Categorical Axis

Learning how to change the order on a categorical axis is something that not many people know how to do. Once you learn it, you will be able to impress your colleagues with your understanding of Minitab. I must admit that I don't know why the last Bar Chart has not selected alphabetical order for the X-axis but has defaulted to order of appearance in the spreadsheet. Let's correct that now. This only works on graphs produced using the Classic Menus and not on graphs produced using the Assistant.

45. Place the active cursor in the column that you wish to correct, we want to change column C1, Factory.
46. Right-click and select **Column Properties<<Value Order**
47. Using the radio buttons at the top of the menu select 'User-specified order'.
48. The box for Define an order should pre-populate with the alphabetical list but if it does not type it in.
49. Click OK.
The graph produced will have the X-axis categorical variables in alphabetical order. Did you notice that there is a radio button for 'Alphabetical order', but I opted not to use that. It does not work for this graph on my copy of Minitab.

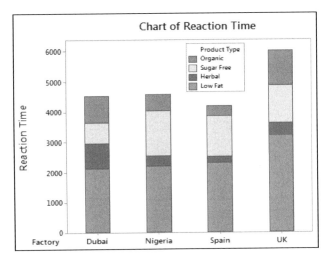

4.9 The Time Series Plot

Time series plots are very valuable for looking for patterns in time-ordered data. Your goal might be to look for complete randomness in the data and no trends, you might want to look for cyclic trends or merely increasing or decreasing trends.

For this example, we are going to use the data on worksheet 'Sheet2'. This has 3 columns of data. The first column is time in 10 minute intervals and the second and third are the feed rate of two components called C and D.

50. Please load the data from 'Sheet2' into a new Minitab project worksheet.

51. Click **Graph<<Time Series Plot**

52. For the grouping options, select Multiple. Click OK.

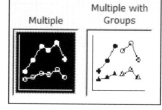

53. For the Series, select Feed C and Feed D.
54. Click on the **Time/Scale** button.

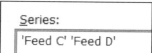

55. Click on the radio button for 'Stamp' and select the Time column as the Stamp Column. This will replace the X-axis with the data stored in the time column.

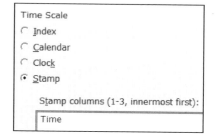

56. Click OK and OK again to produce the chart.

A quick examination of the chart indicates that Feed D is following Feed C.
Adding the Time Stamp is only available on graphs produced via the classic menus.

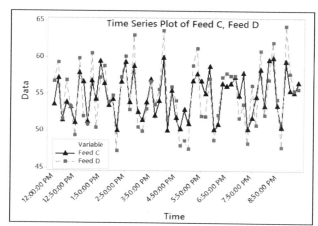

36

4.10 The Pareto Plot

The Pareto plot is placed with the Quality Tools and not with the other graphs. It is very handy in identifying the most significant losses so that you can prioritise projects.

57. Click ***Stat<<Quality Tools<<Pareto Chart***

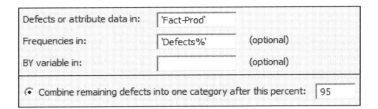

58. Select the 'Fact-Prod' column as the Defect or attribute data. This column is my factory names and product names joined together or concatenated.

59. For each combination of Factory and Product we have the amount of defects produced as a percentage of total production, this column is called Defect%. Enter this as the Frequencies variable. If we don't enter this variable, our Pareto Chart will be made up of counts of the 'Fact-Prod' column.

60. Click OK to produce the chart.

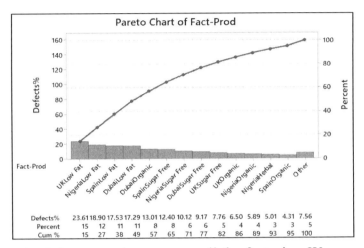

The chart is telling me that the Low Fat product is giving us an issue across all the factories. We probably need to launch a project across the factories.

We can also make a descending Bar Chart that is similar to a Pareto chart.
61. Click *Graph<<Bar chart*

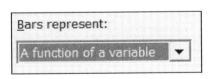

62. From the Bar represents drop-down menu select 'A function of a variable'.

63. Select 'Simple' under the One Y heading then Click OK. The sub-menu opens for this type of Bar Chart.

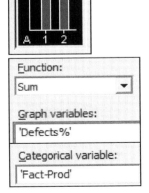

64. Select 'Sum' from the function drop down menu. There are 9 other available functions.

65. Select 'Defects%' as the Graph variable.

66. Select 'Fact-Prod' as the Categorical Variables for grouping.

67. Click on the Chart Option Button. Select 'Decreasing Y' as the order for the main X group.

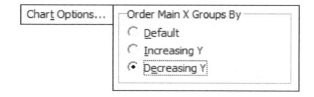

68. Click OK to produce the Chart.

The Bar sizes for this chart as the same as the Pareto Chart but there is no cumulative data line.

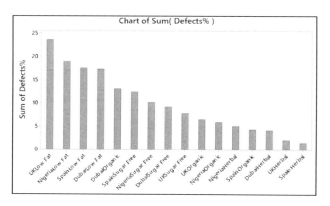

4.10 The Scatter Plot

The scatter plot is usually covered in the Regression Module, but as we use the Assistant predominantly in that Module, it won't be included in the Regression chapter.
Following on from the Time Series Plot we just produced and found that Feed D was following Feed C we can create a Scatter Plot and check the variables against each other.

69. Click *Graph<<Scatter Plot*

70. For the type of plot select With Regression. This option will add the line of best fit onto the plot.

71. Click OK

72. Under Y variable select 'Feed C' and under X variable select 'Feed D'.

73. Click OK to produce the chart.

The general pattern of the dots is in a cloud that is going diagonally upwards. This indicates that the variables are correlated. We would use the equation for the line of best fit if we wanted to mathematically explain how Feed D and Feed C were related.

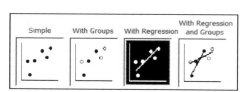

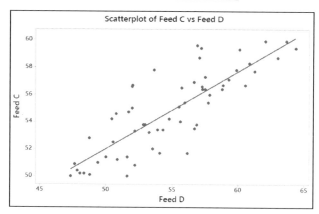

4.12 The Marginal Plot

We have just seen the Scatter Plot, so a good plot that builds on this is the Marginal Plot. At the core is the Scatter Plot but additional we get a secondary graphic showing the linear distribution of data along the X-axis and Y-axis. We the option of choosing how the secondary information is displayed. It can be done using a histogram, dot plot or box plot.

74. Click *Graph<<Marginal Plot*
75. For the type of plot select 'With Histograms'.
76. Click OK to produce the chart.

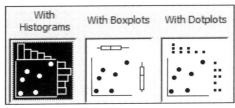

The general pattern of the dots is in a cloud that is going diagonally upwards. This indicates that the variables are correlated. We would use the equation for the line of best fit if we wanted to mathematically explain how Feed D and Feed C were related.

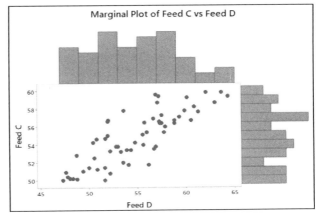

4.13 The Bubble Plot

A scatter plot displays 2 continuous variables against each other. If we want to add another variable, we get into the 3-D plot. Another option is to use a Bubble Plot. I like the idea of the Bubble plot but I must admit I have never really found that useful. This is because you need to have just the right amount of data. Too little and the chart looks sparse, too much and it is difficult to see the trends.

77. Return to Worksheet 1

78. Click *Graph<<Bubble Plot.* For the chart type select 'With Groups'.

79. Enter the variables as shown. Note that the Bubble Size will be calculated from our Defects% data. And the Categorical Variable is Factory, which is the different colours of the bubbles.

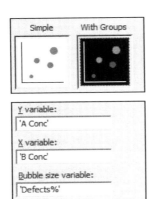

80. Click OK to produce the chart.

The initial plot is a bit too bubbly! We can do something about this

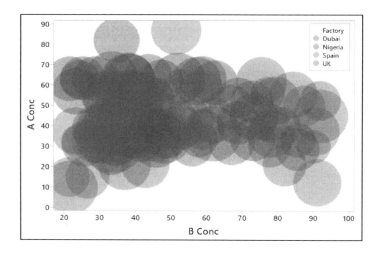

We can either manually adjust the bubble size or use the continuous variable directly.

81. Double-click on the Bubble Plot to open the editor.
82. Double-click on the bubbles to open the Edit Bubbles menu.
83. Using the drop-down for Bubble size select 'Bubble size variable contains the sizes'.
84. Click OK

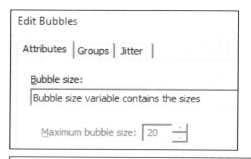

The Bubble Plot is now usable, and we have a chance of finding trends within the plot. One issue is still that bubble size is based on a variable that does not have that much variation, which means the bubble sizes will again look quite similar to the human eye.

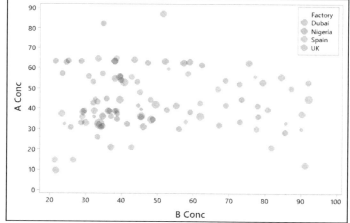

5 CORE STATISTICS

5.1 Introduction.

We know Six Sigma uses the DMAIC methodology to solve problems. As the team goes through the DMAIC process decisions, have to be made. A lot of these decisions involve statistics so we use Minitab to ensure our decisions are sound and based on statistics rather than our own opinions. Minitab changes our data into information so we can make decisions.

In this book, we don't cover the mechanics of statistical calculations. However, there is a requirement to understand some elementary statistics as this will help the reader to

1) Understand the limits and assumptions of the tools.
2) Communicate with peers.
3) Understand what the tests are telling you.
4) Understand the risk of being wrong.

I think of the understanding of core statistics being similar to owning and driving a car. You don't need to know precisely how the engine works but having an idea will probably help.

5.2 Types of Data

What is data? It is any information we care to collect about a system. As Six Sigma Practitioners, we probably expect our data to be numerical but there is categorical data as well. Categorical data is pieces of information that are not numerical e.g. the product names used in the primary example of chapter 3, Low Fat, Organic, Herbal & Sugar Free.

Statistical value refers to the number of data points required to make a statistically significant decision. In terms of statistical value per unit of data, continuous data has the most value. We will be covering both continuous and attribute data in the book, and you can make a rough comparison of the number of data points required to make the same sort of decisions using the different types of data.

If you are working with modern technology, you will more than likely be working with numerical data. However, if you have a system that uses attribute data, then try to convert your attribute data system into a numerical one. As you will experience a leap in the statistical value from your data.

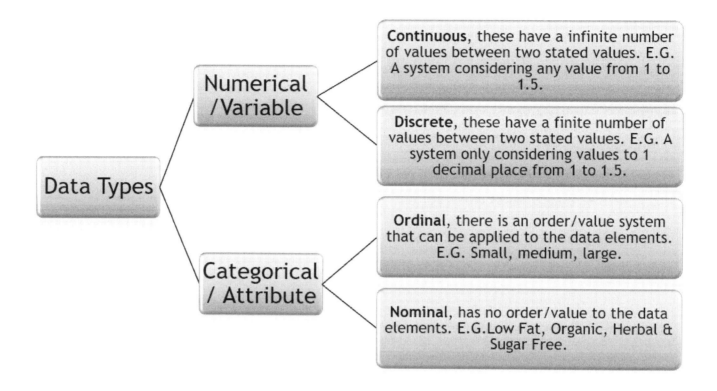

5.3 Measuring the Centre of a Data Sample

For illustration purposes, we are going to use the 8 number list, shown on the left, as our population of data.

When we want to examine a data set, we often want to know what the central value is in that data set and also the spread of the data. There are 3 prevalent measures for measuring the central value. These are the mean, the mode and the median.

Mean is the most useful measure of the central value; it is the sum of the data set divided by the number of elements in the data set.

5.5
7.3
6.1
4.2
6.2
7.5
5.5
6.7

$$Mean = \frac{5.5+7.3+6.1+4.2+6.2+7.5+5.5+6.7}{8} = 6.125$$

The mode is the data element that occurs the most often. In this case, it is 5.5, as it occurs twice in the list and no other data element is repeated.

The median relates to the number in the central position if we were to order our list from the smallest value to the largest.

Order	1st	2nd	3rd	4th	5th	6th	7th	8th
Value	4.2	5.5	5.5	6.1	6.2	6.7	7.3	7.5

As we have an even number of elements in our data set, we don't have one value at the centre. Therefore we must take the mean of the two central values, 6.15 (As 6.15= (6.1+6.2)/2).

In summary, depending on which method of calculating the average that we choose, we may get three different values.
For our data set,
> the mean is 6.125
> the mode is 5.5
> the median is 6.15

5.4 Measuring the Variation of a data sample

There are several ways we can look at the variation within our data set. The most common methods use the mean as the centre point and consider the spread of data around the mean. There are methods which take the median as the centre point and there are methods which use no centre point at all.
Range returns the difference between the highest value in the data set and the lowest value in the data set.

Range= 7.5-4.2= 3.3

The interquartile range (IQRange) is the difference between the first quartile (Q_1) and the third quartile (Q_3). The second quartile being the median. Q_1 is the value which is equal to or greater than 25% of your data, or the 25th percentile. The calculation gets messy as it usually involves interpolation. If we look at our ordered data again, where we have 8 elements, n=8.

Order	1st	2nd	3rd	4th	5th	6th	7th	8th
Value	4.2	5.5	5.5	6.1	6.2	6.7	7.3	7.5

If we want to calculate IQRange, then we must first calculate an interim value which I am going to call R.
> R(Q1)=(1+n)/4= (1+8)/4=2.25

I am going to split R into its integer value and decimal value; I am going to call these I & D respectively, where I=2, D=0.25.

Our formula for finding Q1 is
> $Q1 = X_I + D(X_{I+1} - X_I)$

Where $X_{(2)}$ is the 2nd element in our data series.
> $Q1 = X_2 + D(X_3 - X_2)$
> $Q1 = 5.5 + 0.25(5.5 – 5.5)$
> $Q1 = 5.5$

Our method for finding Q3 changes slightly
> R(Q3)=3(1+n)/4= (1+8)/4=6.75   now I=6 & D=0.75

$Q3 = X_I + D(X_{I+1} - X_I)$
$Q3 = X_6 + 0.75(X_7 - X_6)$
$Q3 = 6.7 + 0.75(7.3 - 6.7)$
$Q3 = 7.15$

We can now calculate the Interquartile range.
$$IQRange = Q3 - Q1 = 7.15 - 5.5 = 1.65$$

When a boxplot of our data set is displayed, we see that the box is the Q1 to Q3 values with the line in the middle as the median value. So the IQRange is the length of the box. The whiskers at the end of the box extend to the minimum and maximum values in the data set as long as they are within 1.5 x IQRange from Q1 or Q3 respectively. If not they are shown as '*' and deemed to be outliers.

It is worth being aware that as the calculations for the median and IQRange will not use outliers, they are a better measure of central tendency and spread for highly skewed data than the mean and standard deviation.

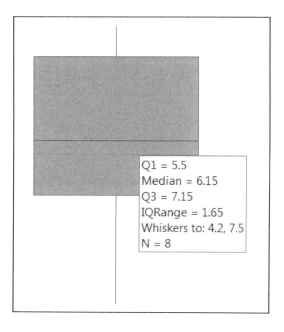

Q1 = 5.5
Median = 6.15
Q3 = 7.15
IQRange = 1.65
Whiskers to: 4.2, 7.5
N = 8

Variance and Standard Deviation are both expressions of variation about the mean value. We are now going to look at how they are both derived. By the way, I hate typing out Standard Deviation so you will see it abbreviated to StDev throughout this book.

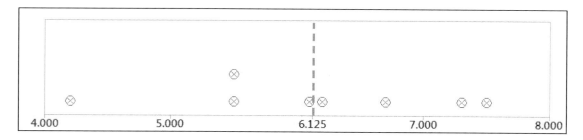

Let's start by looking at how our data sits around the mean. We can take each point in turn and have a look at its distance from the mean value.

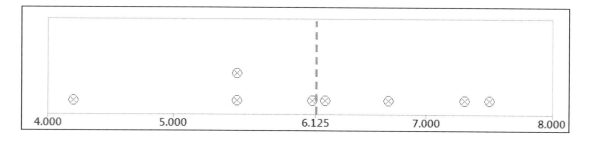

The distance from the first point to the mean is 4.2-6.125 = -1.925. This is called the deviation. If I wanted to add up all the deviations, I would write

Sum of Deviations= $(X_1 - \mu) + (X_2 - \mu) + (X_3 - \mu) + (X_4 - \mu) + (X_5 - \mu) + (X_6 - \mu) + (X_7 - \mu) + (X_8 - \mu)$

Where μ is the population mean. For convenience, we write the above equation in the following form.

$$\text{Sum of Deviations} = \sum_{i=1}^{N}(Xi - \mu)$$

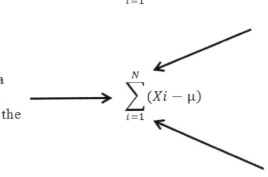

N is the symbol for the number of elements in the population. In our case it is 8. Meaning there will be 8 terms in the series.

The capital Sigma means add up the repeated terms in the series.

This means that you start the series from i=1, the first data element.

If we compute our Sum of Deviations, we will get zero. If you don't that means the mean is wrong. In order to get some value from deviations we can take the sum of deviations squared. As an equation, this looks like

$$\text{Sum of Deviations Squared} = \sum_{i=1}^{N}(Xi - \mu)^2 = 8.095$$

Dividing the Sum of Deviations squared by N, the number of elements in the population gives us the population variance.

$$\text{Variance} = \frac{\sum_{i=1}^{N}(Xi - \mu)^2}{N} = 8.095/8 = 1.0119$$

Finally, the Variance square rooted is the population standard deviation, σ. You now know how we calculate the variance and StDev of a set of numbers.

$$\sigma = \sqrt{\left(\frac{\sum_{i=1}^{N}(Xi - \mu)^2}{N}\right)} = 1.0059$$

You might have noticed that we talked about the population variance and population StDev. However, on most occasions, you won't have the entire population you will only have a sample from the population. Minitab will actually calculate sample statistics by default. There is more about population and samples in the next section.

The main difference between population variance and population StDev and their sample equivalents is that the denominator is changed to n-1 for the sample statistics. This makes the calculated statistic larger when the sample size is small but makes little difference when the sample size is large.

$$\text{Sample Variance} = \frac{\sum_{i=1}^{N}(Xi - xbar)^2}{n - 1}$$

$$\text{Sample StDev} = \sqrt{\left(\frac{\sum_{i=1}^{N}(Xi - xbar)^2}{n-1}\right)}$$

This is where I need to apologise and say that I am using 'Xbar' to represent $\bar{x}$, the sample mean.

5.5 Populations and Samples

The next two topics are strongly linked. They are also the key to understanding the statistics we do at this level and why we do it. The population is the data set from which we are going to be drawing our sample data. The term population represents all the possible data elements related to a parameter. It may even be the case that not all of the data regarding the population has been recorded. As populations can be so large we usually try and take a smaller and more manageable data sample. And of course, when taking a sample we try and take a random sample so we don't influence our results.

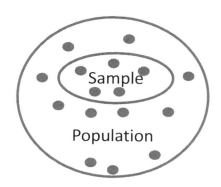

To help explain the issues surrounding samples and populations, I am going to use an example Excel macro that I have written within a macro-enabled spreadsheet. The worksheet is called 'Multiple Processes' and it is within the Excel spreadsheet called '05 Core Stats.xslm'.The data for the remainder of this chapter is also in this spreadsheet.

Exercise 5.5.1 Multiple Processes

Your boss has given you the task to purchase a factory, and your boss has shortlisted three possible candidates for you to consider. As the price is the same for all three factories, you are only going to review the yield from each factory. The three factories have submitted their last 500 batch yields. These are listed in the spreadsheet. As your career is in the balance, you wisely decide to hire a consulting firm to analyse the data. Rather than decide for you, they provide you with a macro. When you press the button, the macro takes 10 random data samples and gives you the mean. Using the means of the samples you must make the decision as to which factory should be purchased.

1. Open the spreadsheet '05 Core Stats.xlsm'
2. Ensure you have the Multiple Process tab selected.
3. Press the ***Take Sample*** button for each factory. Note, if there is an error please press 'end' on the dialogue box and continue as normal.
4. Use the macro buttons to take repeat

Factory A	Factory B	Factory C
72.8	87.2	73.6
76.5	61.9	88.4
64.2	74.2	67.6
76.9	84.4	72.4
62	63.9	68.3
79.2	61.1	60.9
61.2	75.3	63.8
68.9	60.8	63.7
80.8	83.5	74.6
87.5	76.3	84
70	76.5	66.4
83.7	60.9	88.9
88.4	84.2	70.5
78.4	80.9	79.1
61	61	70.4
69.3	82.5	83
88.8	61.9	60.2

Factory A — Take Sample — Mean of Factory A=

Factory B — Take Sample — Mean of Factory B=

Factory C — Take Sample — Mean of Factory C=

samples until you are happy with your conclusion.

The consultants have also submitted their data. They have found that Factory B delivers the highest mean yield and this is the factory that should be purchased.

Note-this macro used 'sampling with replacement'. This means that if an element was selected to make up the mean, it was immediately replaced into the population giving it the chance to be chosen again.

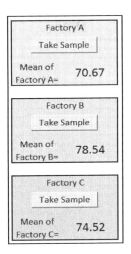

Once you start taking more repetitive samples for each factory, it becomes tough to decide which factory is the best. However, this is a process that we do every day without thinking about whether our sample mean matches the population mean. And this process of sampling not only applies to means but it can apply to medians & standard deviations (StDev) etc. In summary, when we analyse a sample to infer a property of the population, there is a chance that we will be wrong. I am referring to the 500 pieces of data as the population as this is the data set from which we are going to be drawing our sample. Incidentally, we are going to discuss making the wrong conclusion about the population in the next chapter called Hypothesis Testing.

The answer to Exercise 5.5.1 is that all three factories are the same.

Example 5.5.2 Single Process

| 32.8 |
| 38.7 |
| 35.5 |
| 50.6 |
| 43.8 |
| 40.6 |
| 55.2 |
| 41.1 |
| 59.9 |
| 48.2 |

Take random samples & calculate means

Sample Size	Mean of Sample	Mean of Population
1		44.926
2		44.926
5		44.926
10		44.926
30		44.926
100		44.926
200		44.926
400		44.926
500		44.926

The next example is on the 'Single Process' tab of the 05 Core Stats.xlsm spreadsheet; please go to that tab now. On this worksheet, we have a data set from a different factory which also happens to contain 500 elements; the mean of the population is 44.926 to 3 decimal places (dp). When the macro is executed, it will randomly take a sample and calculate the mean of the sample. The sample size is shown in the first column of the table. The other difference is that this macro samples without replacement so that the same element is never used repeatedly.

Sample Size	Mean of Sample	Mean of Population
1	59.500	44.926
2	50.300	44.926
5	38.900	44.926
10	51.990	44.926
30	42.963	44.926
100	43.186	44.926
200	44.762	44.926
400	44.914	44.926
500	44.926	44.926

Give it a go and click on the 'Take random samples…' button. I have shown the results that I obtained; however, your results will be slightly different. In my results, we see that as the sample size increases the sample mean converges on the population mean.

When the sample size is the same as the population, the means must match.

I will summarise the key learnings from 5.5.1 & 5.5.2.

1)   When we analyse a sample to infer a property of the population, there is a chance that we will be wrong.

2) As we increase the sample size, we will converge on the population parameter.

3) The only way to calculate the population parameter exactly is to analyse the entire population.

What we need to do is manage the risk of the sample statistic, not reflecting the population parameter. This is where confidence intervals come in.

5.6 Confidence Intervals

As seen in the last section, we need to manage the risk of the sample parameter not reflecting the population parameter. And I said this is where confidence intervals come in. We are not going to learn how to calculate confidence intervals as we want Minitab to do the maths for us. We need to appreciate what they mean to us in terms of samples and populations. We are going to do this by producing a Graphical Summary, which is a really useful starting point for most statistical analysis.

Example 5.6.1 Confidence Intervals on a Graphical Summary.

1.   Open the spreadsheet '05 Core Stats.xlsm'.
2.   Ensure you have the Single Process tab selected.
3.   Copy the first 20 cells from column A and transfer them to a Minitab worksheet.
4.   Label the column as **Factory.**
5.   Click *Stat<<Basic Stats<<Graphical Summary.*
6.   In the menu box that opens select the Factory column as the Variable to be investigated.
7.   Click OK to produce the Graphical Summary.

↓	C1
	Factory
1	32.8
2	38.7
3	35.5
4	50.6

Variables:

Factory

Let's have a look at the data table within the Graphical Summary, shown on the page below. We are going to look at the Normality Test next so I will leave section 1 alone for now.

In section 2, we are given sample parameters, so we know the actual sample of 20 data points has a mean of 43.85 and sample StDev of 9.07. Skewness is a measure of how much a distribution is leaning to one side, skewed. Kurtosis is a measure of how sharp or flat a distribution is compared to the normal distribution.

In section 3, we are given data related to the range and median of the sample data.

In section 4, we get to the Confidence Intervals. In section 2, we were told that the sample had a mean of 43.85 and here we are told that Minitab is 95% sure that the population mean is between 39.605 & 48.095. If you remember back to the spreadsheet the population mean was listed as 44.926. Minitab got it right that time but remember 95% confidence means being wrong 1 in 20 times.

	Anderson-Darling Normality Test	
1	A-Squared	0.43
	P-Value	0.280
2	Mean	43.850
	StDev	9.070
	Variance	82.269
	Skewness	0.39293
	Kurtosis	-1.03810
	N	20
3	Minimum	31.900
	1st Quartile	35.775
	Median	42.450
	3rd Quartile	50.125
	Maximum	59.900
4	95% Confidence Interval for Mean	
	39.605	48.095
	95% Confidence Interval for Median	
	36.671	48.582
	95% Confidence Interval for StDev	
	6.898	13.248

The confidence interval is made up by adding & subtracting half the confidence interval width to the sample mean. The confidence interval width is a function of the following
   1) The confidence level that you want to state, usually 95%.
   2) The sample StDev, S.
   3) The reciprocal of the square root of the sample size.
If the following actions were all carried out independently, they would increase the width of the confidence interval
   1) increasing the confidence level
   2) increasing the sample StDev
   3) reducing the sample size.

Exercise 5.6.2 Confidence Intervals

Here's one for you to do. Go back to 05Core Stats.xlsm and go to the Multiple Processes tab. Take the top 20 data elements, cells A2:A21, for Factory A and produce a Graphical Summary. What is the 95% Confidence Interval (CI) for the mean? Is the population mean likely to be 80.

Answer. We see that the 95% CI for the population mean is from 70.169 to 78.421. The population mean is unlikely to be 80. Using confidence intervals, we are putting forward the best guess as to the population parameter while stating that there is a chance that we could be wrong using our sample data.

95% Confidence Interval for Mean	
70.169	78.421
95% Confidence Interval for Median	
68.994	79.012
95% Confidence Interval for StDev	
6.705	12.877

5.7 The Normal Distribution

Knowing the normal distribution is foundational knowledge for statistics. Understanding the normal distribution helps us further our understanding of the assumptions that were made when the statistical test we use were developed. However, we now know the having normal data for many of the tests we use is not that important as long as the sample size is sufficient and we don't have special causes acting on our data. You can read about this yourselves in the development papers for Minitab, The normal distribution plotted on a frequency plot can be described by several generic rules.

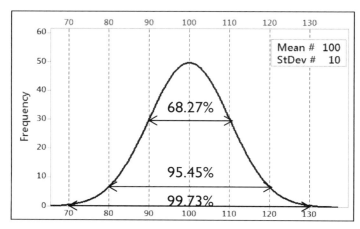

- 68.27% of all data appear 1 StDevs from the mean
- 95.45% of all data appear 2 StDevs from the mean
- 99.73% of all data appear 3 StDevs from the mean
- It can be described by its mean and standard deviation.
- The tails extend to ± infinity.
- All observations appear under the curve.
- The Curve is symmetrical.
- The mean, mode & median are almost equal.

Bernoulli...	Chi-Square...
Binomial...	Normal...
Geometric...	F...
Negative Binomial...	t...
Hypergeometric...	Uniform...
Discrete...	Beta...
Integer...	Cauchy...
Poisson...	Exponential...
	Gamma...
	Laplace...
	Largest Extreme Value...
	Logistic...
	Loglogistic...
	Lognormal...
	Smallest Extreme Value...
	Triangular...
	Weibull...

Although we spend the majority of our time discussing the normal distribution, we must remember that many other distribution models exist. Minitab can model 8 different discrete distribution models and 17 different continuous distribution models.

To test for normality, we use the Anderson-Darling (AD) Normality test. The AD test starts by assuming that your data was normally distributed and then checks for a lack of normality. Again, we are analysing a sample to make the normality assumption about the population. Therefore, in order for the test to be reliable, we must have more than 20 data points; otherwise, the test can indicate normality incorrectly.

Example 5.7.1 Testing for Normality

1.   Open worksheet Normality and transfer the data into a new Minitab Worksheet. This file contains two columns of data. Column 'Example1' has a sample size of 25, which is above our safe limit and Column 'Example2' which has a sample size of 100.

2.   Click **Stat<<Basic Stats<<Normality Test.**

3.   For the variable to be tested enter 'Example1'.

4.   Note the radio buttons for the type of Normality test we are going to be using. The Anderson-Darling test is selected by default.

5.   Click OK, and the Probability Plot is produced.

6.   Find the P-value for the AD test, if it is above 0.05, we can assume that the sample came from a normally distributed population.

7.   Another very rough and ready test is called the 'Fat Pencil Test, ' which is primarily used to test residuals. If you can cover the data points on the Probability Plot with a fat pencil, you can assume normality. Remember the Fat Pencil test mainly applies to residuals and you will learn more about testing residuals for normality in later chapters.

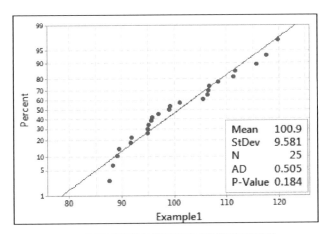

Example 5.7.2 Testing for Normality

In this example, we are going to look at the AD P-value on the Graphical Summary again and also look at the minimal case where the AD normality test doesn't work very well.

1.   Click **Stat<<Basic Stats<<Graphical Summary.**

2.   For the variable to be tested enter 'Example2'.

3.   Then click OK and examine the results.

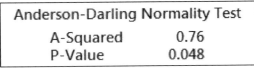

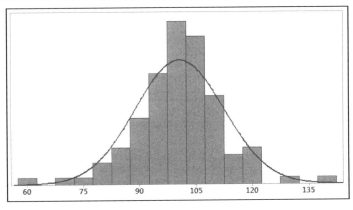

The P-value of the AD Normality test indicates that there is sufficient evidence to conclude the population is not normally distributed. When we look at the histogram and the fitted curve, it seems as though we have a normally distributed sample. However, it is known that the AD test does not work very well when outliers are extending the tails of the distribution. This can be seen in the histogram but more so in the boxplot. We can use one of the other normality tests that are better suited to this type of sample, the Kolmogorov-Smirnov (KS) test.

4.   Click *Stat<<Basic Stats<<Normality Test.*
5.   For the variable to be tested enter 'Example2'.
6.   On the radio buttons for the type of Normality test select the KS test.
7.   Click OK, and the Probability Plot is produced.

The P-value for the KS test is >0.15 and therefore indicates that the sample came from a normally distributed population. As good Six Sigma practitioners, we should be thinking about the outliers that are visible on the Probability Plot and why they were generated.

Occasionally, our data will try to trick us. One particular trick that I want you to be aware of is the bi-modal distribution. This is when something changes in the process while we are collecting data and we end up collecting data from two separate distributions thinking they are one. Take a look at the histogram it is made of two distributions but this only really becomes apparent when we look at the control chart on the Diagnostics Report if using the Assistant. The problem is that the results of any hypothesis test that we are conducting become useless when we treat two separate distributions as a single distribution.

If you are not using the Assistant, always check your process stability using a control chart. Bi-modal distributions are much harder to spot on histograms than they are on control charts.

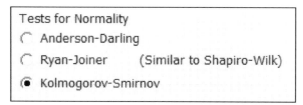

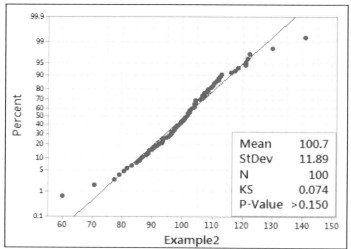

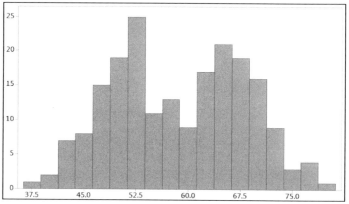

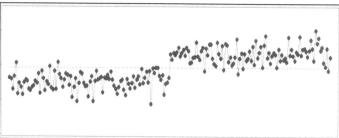

5.8 The Central Limit Theorem

The Central Limit Theorem, CLT, states that if you repeatedly take a sample and build up a distribution of means, let's called that the child distribution. Then the child distribution will be more normally distributed and have a narrower distribution than the parent. Even if you start with a very non-normal distribution and repeatedly take a set sample size and calculate the mean of the sample. Then build up a distribution of those means that will result in a more normal and narrower distribution. It has been stated that setting the sample size at 30 will ensure the child distribution is normal. Another benefit is that the child distribution will have the same mean as the parent.

The equation shown below supports the CLT. It indicates that the StDev of the child distribution will be reduced by a factor of $\sqrt{N}$, where on this occasion, N is the size of the sample that you are going to take repeatedly.

$$S = \frac{\sigma}{\sqrt{N}}$$

Where S=sample StDev, σ= population StDev
Let's take a look at a demonstration of the Central Limit Theorem.

I have generated a random population of 250 elements and called it 'Original'. My σ (population StDev) is 28.44, and you can see that the distribution is fairly flat.
Now I am going to start taking 2 random samples from 'Original' (N=2) and calculating their mean. I am using sampling with replacement because I want to conduct my calculation many times. I do it 150 times to build a distribution.
You can see from the 'N=2' distribution that it is more normal looking and narrower than Original. Let's now look at increasing N and see how that changes the look of the distribution.

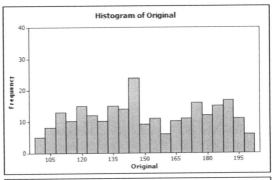

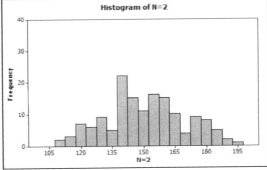

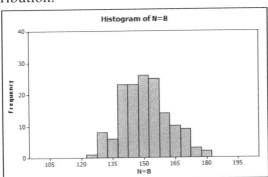

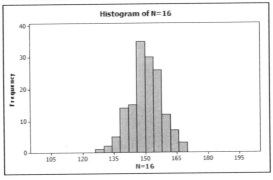

As a reminder, N is the number of samples I am taking and using to calculate their mean.
As I increase N the distribution displays a lower variance and becomes more normal looking.

The table shows the numbers generated by the equation and in practice by the demonstration. There is a slight difference between the calculated and actual S values which is probably due to my predetermined limit of taking 150 sets of samples.

N value	$\dfrac{\sigma}{\sqrt{N}}$	Calculated S	Actual S from example	AD P-value
1	28.44			<0.005
2	$\dfrac{28.44}{\sqrt{2}}$	20	19.1	0.25
4	$\dfrac{28.44}{\sqrt{4}}$	14.2	13.1	0.39
8	$\dfrac{28.44}{\sqrt{8}}$	10.1	11.5	0.467
16	$\dfrac{28.44}{\sqrt{16}}$	7.1	7.5	0.892

6 AN OVERVIEW OF HYPOTHESIS TESTING

6.1 What is Hypothesis Testing.
6.2 Understanding the Procedure

6.1 What is Hypothesis Testing

.

In a Six Sigma project, we are usually trying to understand a loss so that we can reduce or eliminate it or we are trying to make something better. If it is a data-driven project, we want to be able to use data to make decisions that will improve our understanding and will eventually help us achieve an improvement. At its simplest level Hypothesis Testing (HT) is a method that is generically used to help us make decisions about our data.

Hypothesis Testing (HT) is a formal procedure used when we want to solve a statistical problem. As a Green Belt, you need to have a good understanding of the process and be able to use it. However, as you become more experienced, you conduct the procedure by reflex rather than formally. This chapter is written to teach you the formal way so you can start using the statistical tests. Before this starts to sound tiresome, know that the rest of the book assumes you will conduct the procedure by reflex.

There are two parts to HT, the procedure and the statistical test. We will be focusing on the procedure in this chapter. The statistical tests start from the next chapter onwards. There is a lot of terminology in hypothesis testing, and you need to understand all of it.

6.2 Understanding the Procedure

The procedure for HT can be broken down into a number of generic steps.

I used to call step 1 'The Problem Statement'. However, I now feel that 'problem' is not the right word and probably more negative than it needs to be. I now call it an 'investigation statement'.

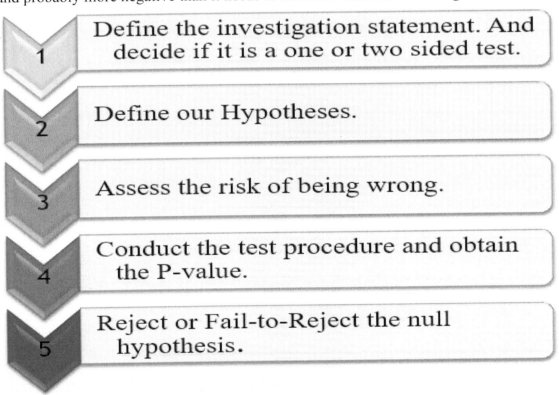

1. Define the investigation statement. And decide if it is a one or two sided test.

2. Define our Hypotheses.

3. Assess the risk of being wrong.

4. Conduct the test procedure and obtain the P-value.

5. Reject or Fail-to-Reject the null hypothesis.

1 — Define the investigation statement. And decide if it is a one or two sided test.

To start the process off, we should have a clear idea in our minds what the information is that we are looking for. Ideally, there should be one investigation statement for one hypothesis test. Note, some statistical procedures in Minitab will have more than one hypothesis test associated with them. Being able to formulate this investigation statement helps us to focus on the problem at hand and it should make us ask 'if this information is really going to help with the project?'. But only you can answer that.

The investigation statement should be a single line question that has the following properties
   1) It should only have two possible results to the investigation
   2) It should indicate to a Six Sigma practitioner which test is applicable
   3) It should be concise.

We don't need to include data types, even though this would have a bearing on the test used. It is inferred that the data type will be known.

Let's have a look at an example investigation statement.

Is the mean of Group Carb the same as the mean of Group Protein, or is it different?

Let's go through our check-list.

   1) The answers can only be Carb has the same mean as Protein, or Carb has a different mean to protein.
   2) A Green Belt should be able to conclude that the test is comparing the means of two groups of data. Therefore, a 2 sample T test is required.
   3) The statement is concise and to the point.

So that we learn the terminology, let's consider if our test is going to be one sided or two sided.
For our example investigation statement, 'Is the mean of Group Carb the same as the mean of Group Protein or is it different?' we use the word 'different'. 'Different' means that it can be 'less than' or 'greater than' and we are not really bothered. As 'different' has two outcomes we call this a 'two sided test'.
However, we may only be interested in knowing if the mean of carb is greater than protein. We now have two choices in terms of test options. Choice 1 is to use the standard two way test and then interrogate the data and graphs to figure out if it was actually greater than. Choice 2 is to use a one way test. For this we need to modify our investigation statement.

Is the mean of Group Carb equal to or less than the mean of Group Protein, or is it greater than the mean of Group Protein?

As we are now only interested in 'or is it greater than' as the alternative, this is called a one sided test. The benefit of opting for a one sided test is that it is better at spotting the difference between your two investigation statement options than a two sided test, when a difference exists.

2 Define our Hypotheses.

In this step, we state which of our two outcomes of our investigation statement is the null hypothesis, H_o, and which is the alternate hypothesis, H_a. The null is always given to the result which implies 'no change', ' difference' or even 'the population is normally distributed' for the AD normality test. The alternate is given to the outcome which implies 'there is a difference' or 'something has changed.'

Let's look at our two sided example again,

Is the mean of Group Carb the same as the mean of Group Protein, or is it different?

The null hypothesis would be 'there is no difference between the means of Carb and Protein populations'
Mathematically, $H_o : \mu_{carb} - \mu_{protein} = 0$.

The alternate hypothesis would be 'there is a difference between the means of Carb and Protein populations '
Mathematically, $H_a : \mu_{carb} \neq \mu_{protein}$

And our one sided example again,

Is the mean of Group Carb equal to or less than the mean of Group Protein, or is it greater than the mean of Group Protein?

The null hypothesis would be 'the population mean of Group Carb is equal to or less than the population   mean of Group Protein '
Mathematically, $H_o : \mu_{carb} \leq \mu_{protein}$

The alternate hypothesis would be 'the population mean of Group Carb is greater than the population mean of Group Protein'
Mathematically, $H_a : \mu_{carb} > \mu_{protein}$

Remember, if we wanted, we could set up the H_a to be based around 'less than.'

3 Assess the risk of being wrong.

We learned in the Core Statistics chapter that as we are taking a sample and then making inferences about a population, then there is always a chance that we are going to be wrong. In this section, we are going to discuss how to handle the risks involved. The risks are there because our sample size is smaller than the population size. And if it were the same, then there would be no point using Minitab for hypothesis testing. We could use a calculator to make decisions.
We are going to start to put together a hypothesis testing truth table. On the Y-axis, we are going to put reality. As we don't know reality there are two possible states for reality; there is 'No Difference' or that

there is a 'Difference.' To make things easier to understand we are just going to look at 'No Difference' to start with.

At the end of the test procedure, we will learn how to make our decision about whether there is a difference or not. And in the next chapter, we will learn about selecting the appropriate test so don't worry about that now.

If my decision is 'No Difference' and in reality there is no difference then I will be correct. Unfortunately, as I will never know reality I will never truly know if I am right or wrong. All I can do is calculate the risks to start with and try to ensure the odds are sufficiently in my favour before I start the process.

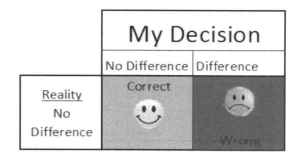

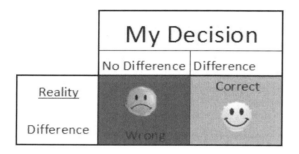

The other way things can work out is if in Reality there is a difference. My decision will still have the same options but I will only be correct if the test detects a Difference.

Now we bring the two halves of the table together. In terms of my decision, there are only two things that I can decide. But there are four outcomes when we bring Reality into the table as well. We know already that if I have a larger sample size, I can improve my chances of being 'Correct.' There may be other factors that can help me be 'Correct' as well.

		My Decision	
		No Difference	Difference
Reality	No Difference	Correct	Wrong
	Difference	Wrong	Correct

'Null Hypothesis' was the name we gave the state when there was no change, or there was no difference. Therefore, if we want, we can substitute the word 'Reality' for 'Null Hypothesis'. This does not change the table at all but improves our statistical terminology.

My Decision now relates to whether I 'Failed to Reject' or 'Rejected the Null Hypothesis. Notice the term 'Failed to Reject' is being used instead of Accepted; this will be explained later in this chapter.

		My Decision	
		Failed to Reject	Rejected
Null Hypothesis	TRUE	Correct	Wrong
	FALSE	Wrong	Correct

I have added the names of the different types of risk we associate with the matrix. I have split the matrix back up again as I want to look at the two states of reality separately.

If we are looking at the case when there is no difference (or the null hypothesis is correct) the probabilities of me deciding 'No Difference' added to probability of me deciding 'Difference' will equal 1 or 100%.

1=Confidence + Significance

$1=(1-\alpha) + \alpha$

We call the probability of correctly saying there is no difference the Confidence. You have probably heard that we use 0.95 or 95% as the default value for confidence. We call the probability of incorrectly saying there is a difference when there is none the Significance, α. This can also be called the producer's risk or a Type I error.

My Decision		
	No Difference	Difference
Reality No Difference	Correct 😊 Confidence, $(1-\alpha)$	Wrong 😞 Significance or producer's risk, α Type I error

Let's now look at the other state of reality when there is a difference. We call the probability of correctly saying there is a difference the Power. You may have heard of that term. Most practitioners will want a Power of typically between 80-90%. Several factors affect the power of a test and it is essential to have sufficient Power in any procedure you carry out.

The probability of incorrectly saying there is no difference is called the Consumers Risk or β. It is also known as a Type II Error.

My Decision		
	No Difference	Difference
Reality Difference	Wrong 😞 Consumers Risk, β Type II Error	Correct 😊 Power, $(1-\beta)$

Let's say that we conducted a HT test and concluded that there was no difference without establishing the Power before performing the test. Well, was there really no difference or did we incorrectly conclude there was no difference when there really was? Without knowing the Power we have no idea which is more likely. But if we have the right conditions to obtain a Power of 90% and then we concluded 'no difference' we know we can be much more confident in our conclusion. Therefore, before we start any procedure, we want to know that we have sufficient Power and Confidence. The Confidence is set by default at 95% but can usually be changed in the options settings of the test menus. Power can be calculated in a separate process known as Power & Sample Size (PSS) or it is calculated within the Assistant. There are probably quite a few occasions where you would want to know you have sufficient Power before you conduct a test e.g. when getting a large enough sample size is an issue. In those instances, using a separate procedure before the Assistant becomes necessary. During Minitab courses, I have found that a fair number of beginners like to skip over this step but for the reasons explained above that could lead to disaster. We are now going to learn how to use the PSS procedure. At this point, we need to know the type of HT test we would be using but we don't need to know anything further about the test at this point.

Example 6.2.1 PSS for 1 Sample t test.

Curran Cycles make a 50cm frame. They want to test whether the mean of the 50cm frame is 50cm and for this, they know that they need to conduct a 1 sample t test. They know that the difference that they are interested in being able to detect is 0.3cm and they know that historically they get a StDev=0.45cm in the 50 cm cycle frames. Explore the Power that would be obtained if they sample 20, 25 & 30 frames for a two-sided test and then a one-sided test. No data file is required for this example.

1.   Click *Stat<<Power and Sample Size<<1 Sample t*

2.   For this test, we must specify our estimate of the population Stdev. Enter '0.45' for this in the menu.

3.   We want to know the Power so we will leave that section blank. Enter all three samples sizes that we are interested in. Leave a space between each number.

Specify values for any two of the following:	
Sample sizes:	20 25 30
Differences:	0.3
Power values:	
Standard deviation:	.45

4.   Enter the difference we are interested in.

5.   Click OK to execute the procedure.
6.   Examine the Power curve graph.

On the Power curve graph, we have Difference as the X-axis and Power as the Y-axis. We have 3 curves displayed one for each sample size. For each of the curves, we can see how changing the detectable difference would change the Power or vice versa. Hovering the mouse pointer over each of the dots displays the exact value of Power.

Above the Power Curve, the individual results are listed against each of the sample sizes.

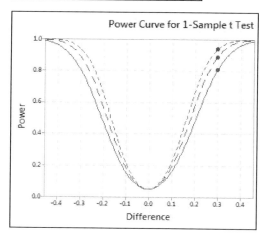

Results

Difference	Sample Size	Power
0.3	20	0.807292
0.3	25	0.892017
0.3	30	0.941576

For the two-sided 1 sample t Test with 20 samples and this particular set of conditions
- Estimated population Stdev of 0.45
- Detectable difference of 0.3
- 95% Confidence

We get a power of 80.7%. This means that if the population mean of the 50cm cycle frames was different by 0.3cm we would have an 80.7% chance of detecting a difference. You can see that increasing the sample size increases the Power.
We are going to change to a one-sided 1 sample t Test and assess the Power that results for the same conditions. In the actual test, our H_a would change from the two-sided test to a one-sided alternate hypothesis.

7. Click *Stat<<Power and Sample Size<<1 Sample t*

8. If it is not already there, enter the data as shown.

9. Click on the *Options* button.

10. Under Alternative Hypothesis, select the radio button for 'Greater than.' As you can see, we can also change the Significance level within this menu.

11. Click OK twice. Examine the Power curve graph. The Power curves are now one-sided.

12. Navigate to the Session window and find where the Powers are listed against each of the sample sizes.

For the one-sided 1 sample t Test with 20 samples, we get a power of 89.0%. This has increased by around 8% from the two-sided test.

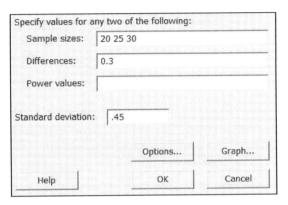

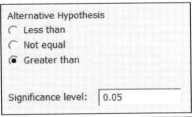

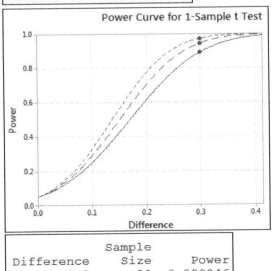

Power Curve for 1-Sample t Test

Difference	Sample Size	Power
0.3	20	0.890246
0.3	25	0.944343
0.3	30	0.972541

The next graphic shows the factors that affect the Power of a HT Test.

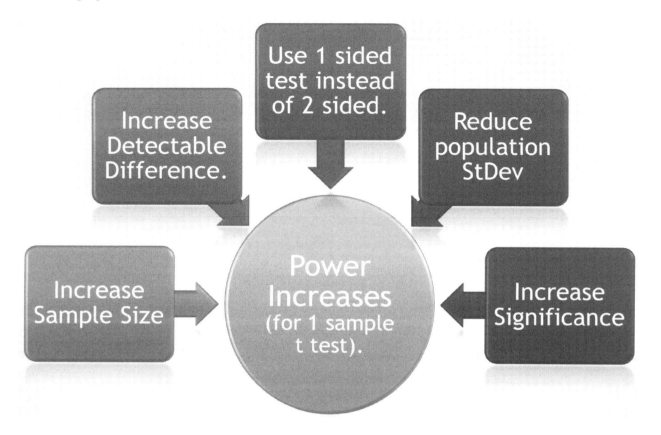

Exercise 6.2.2 PSS for 1 Sample t test.

For a two-sided 1 sample t Test with a StDev of 4 and a difference of 1 how many samples would you need to get a Power of 90%?

Note when entering Power into the menu, it is entered as a decimal.

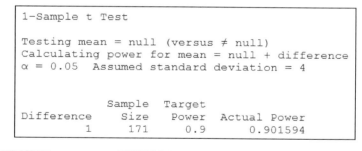

```
1-Sample t Test

Testing mean = null (versus ≠ null)
Calculating power for mean = null + difference
α = 0.05  Assumed standard deviation = 4

                   Sample  Target
Difference          Size   Power   Actual Power
         1           171    0.9       0.901594
```

 Conduct the test procedure and obtain the P-value.

 Reject or Fail-to-Reject the null hypothesis.

HT procedures are going to be taught in the next chapter using the Assistant. The Assistant interprets the analysis for you to provide you with a conclusion regarding the data. If we use the classic method, we must run the test and then find the P-value in the session window. We then decide to Reject or Fail-to-Reject the null hypothesis based on the P-value. Most people learn the rhyme 'If the P is low, the null must go'. This means that if the P-value is below the significance level, then reject the null hypothesis. If that is all, you want to know then skip the rest of this section. If you want to know more about what we are doing when we decide to Reject or Fail-to-Reject the null then read on.

Let's start with the P-value. What is the P-value?

'It is the probability of getting your sample results, including results that are more extreme, given that the null hypothesis is true.'

Therefore, we need a method of working out probabilities for getting specific samples (or events) if the null hypothesis is true, or when there is no effect/change. To do this, we use something called a null distribution which gives us a distribution of outcomes when there isn't any effect i.e. the null is true. Let's see how we might put together our own null distribution.

Example 6.2.3 P-value.

Develop a method for testing whether a single dice (note, it is permissible to call a single die a dice in modern English) is likely to have been tampered with to give a high score. Once you have developed your test method, you will be given 3 dice to test.

For my method of testing, I am going to work out the null distribution for the cumulative score of a single dice thrown 4 times. I am using four throws as this increases the resolution of the data. Just having 1 throw would limit me to the score 1 to 6.
With 4 dice the probability of scoring a 4 or 24 is the same and is

$$\frac{1}{6} \times \frac{1}{6} \times \frac{1}{6} \times \frac{1}{6} = \frac{1}{1296} = 0.000772 \quad \text{or} \quad 0.0772\%$$

Working out the values in between 4 & 24 is a bit harder. However, I am not going to calculate the probabilities because I have run a simulation in Excel 10,000 times. Below are my results in graphical form.

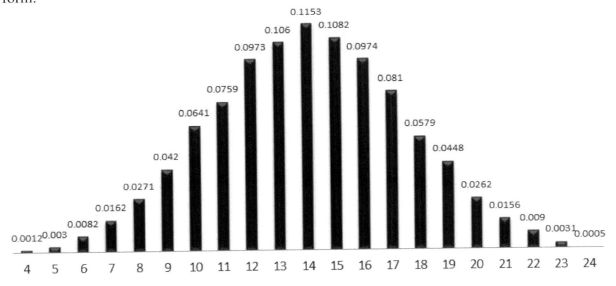

Cumulative Score of Throwing Four Dice Vs Probability of Score.

As you can see from the graph, I obtained a probability of getting a score of 24 as 0.0005 in my simulation. And I got a probability of getting a score of 4 as 0.0012. Both of these scores are different from the theoretical value of 0.000772 but we will still go with the simulation. We see that rolling a score of 14 has the highest probability of 0.1153, meaning a score of 14 would be expected 11.53% of the time.

If we wanted to we could work out the probability of getting a range of scores by adding the individual probabilities together. The probability of getting a score of 10, 11 or 12 is $0.0641 + 0.0759 + 0.0973 = 0.2373$ or 23.7%.

Similarly, we could ask what is the probability of getting a score of 7 or less. The probability of getting a score of 7, 6, 5 or 4 is $0.0162 + 0.0082 + 0.003 + 0.0012 = 0.0286$ or 2.86%.

Carrying on with the example, I now need to set a cut-off for when I am going to conclude that the dice has been tampered with. I decide to consult my youngest daughter, who is a prolific cheat at every game. She suggests that I should use 3% as my significance level for this test; I go with that. I am now ready to start testing the dice and as I am demonstrating hypothesis testing, I will use the procedure.

Investigation Statement – Will the test dice deliver a higher score over four rolls than a normal dice? As we are only interested in a higher score, we know that this is a one-sided test.

Hypothesis - H_o = The test dice delivers the same score or less than a normal die.
          H_a = The test dice delivers a greater score than a normal die.

Assess the Risk- I have set my significance to 0.03 or 3% on advice from my daughter.

Conduct the Test –
For Dice 1, I get a score of 12. This gives me a P-value of 0.7623, these are the cumulative probabilities from 12 to 24.
For Dice 2, I get a score of 20. This gives me a P-value of 0.0544, these are the cumulative probabilities from 20 to 24.
For Dice 3, I get a score of 21. This gives me a P-value of 0.0282, these are the cumulative probabilities for 21 to 24, $0.00156 + 0.009 + 0.0031 + 0.0005$.

Accept the null or alternate.

We can only reject the null if we have 'sufficient evidence.' The 'evidence' is that the results we obtained are extremely unlikely given the null is true i.e. the P-values. Sufficient means the level of evidence exceeds our significance level in terms of improbability.

For Dice 1, we have a P-value of 0.7623 in terms of improbability it does not exceed $\alpha = 0.03$. Therefore, we do not have sufficient evidence to reject the null. Which means we accept dice 1 as a good dice.

For Dice 2, we have a P-value of 0.0544 in terms of improbability it does not exceed $\alpha = 0.03$. Again, we do not have sufficient evidence to reject the null. Which means we accept dice 2 as a good dice.

For Dice 3, we have a P-value of 0.0282 in terms of improbability it does exceed $\alpha = 0.03$. On this occasion, we have sufficient evidence to reject the null and accept the alternate hypothesis.

We can see that there is a cut off when getting a score of 20 and 21. With 20, we deem the dice to be fair but a score of 21 and the dice is deemed unfair. However, on occasion, we may want to have a zone for 'undecided' as there can be grey areas. Also, we never really know if the dice was unfair; we just assume that the event was so unlikely that the alternate hypothesis has to be true. This was a demonstration, in real life, we would have a larger sample i.e. more than 4 throws and would have used a test where we could have used Minitab to calculate the Power of the test.

This whole exercise is something similar to what Minitab is doing when it calculates a P-value in any test.

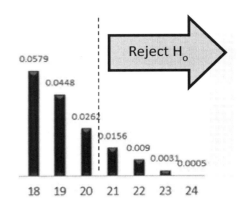

7 HYPOTHESIS TESTING

7.1 Introduction to Hypothesis Testing.

Tests Comparing One Sample to a Target
7.2 1 Sample T
7.3 1 Sample Stdev
7.4 1 Sample % Defective
7.5 Chi-Square Goodness of Fit

Tests Comparing Two Samples with Each Other
7.6 2 Sample T
7.7 Paired T
7.8 2 Sample Stdev

Tests Capable of Comparing more than Two Samples
7.9 Chi-Square % Defective
7.10 Chi-Square Test for Association

7.11 Hypothesis Testing Exercises

7.1 Introduction to Hypothesis Testing.

Previously it was said that there are two parts to Hypothesis Testing, the procedure, and the tests. In chapter 6, you covered the process in detail. If not, please go back and cover the chapter as you need to know terms like Confidence, Power, Null, Alternate, one-sided test & P-value.

In this chapter, we are going to start learning how to use these tests via the Assistant. You will see how these tests take your sample data and give you information about your population. They will be predominantly used in the Analyse phase of DMAIC but could also be used in control for showing that a change has been achieved.

The way the Assistant carries out HT is much more accessible to beginners than the classic menus. Additionally, some of the test procedures have also been changed to remove complexity. However, there are still general prerequisites for the tests. For instance, if the sample size is sufficient, the normality of the data is not an issue. Also, you will see the warning repeatedly that 'unusual data points can have a strong influence on the results.' This means that if there is a lot of special cause variation acting on your data, the results may not be repeatable. Therefore, checking that your process is in control before hypothesis testing is always wise.

Note that all the data for this chapter is in Excel file 07 Hypothesis Testing.xlsx, which can be downloaded from WWW.rmksixsigma.com. The answers for the exercises are also available from the same site.

1. Click *Assistant<<Hypothesis Tests*
This will open up the main page for hypothesis testing. There are 3 boxes that contain the tests and these have been subdivided by your objective; compare one sample with a target, compare two samples with each other and compare more than two samples. Clicking on any of the tests will take you to the test menu. However, if you click on 'Help Me Choose' above any of the boxes, it will take you to a decision tree.

2. Click '*Help Me Choose'* above the 'compare one sample with a target' box.

The decision tree asks two questions to help you decide which of the four tests to use. The first question is about the data type. Do you have Continuous or Attribute data?

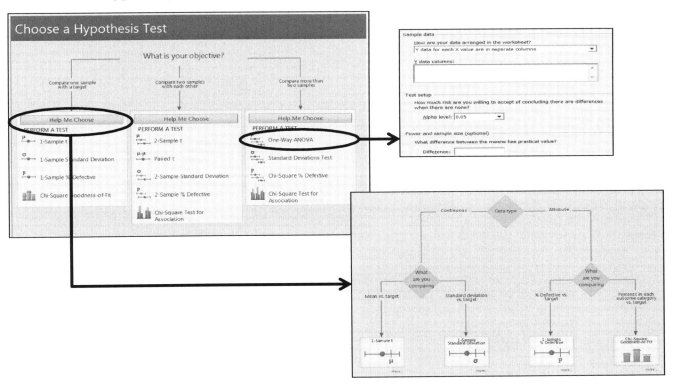

If you need further information to answer the question, you can click on the diamond.
3. Click on the diamond for '*What are you comparing.'*

This opens up another page that informs us about the differences between the two tests. There is even an example of how the test could be used.

4. Click on the *Back* button. Then click on '*more*' which is below the button for the 1-Sample StDev Test. This opens up a page that gives the requirements for the test conditions. Each one of the sub-menus can be opened to obtain more details on the data requirements.

Now that we understand a bit more about the menu system, we are going to start looking at how to use the tests.

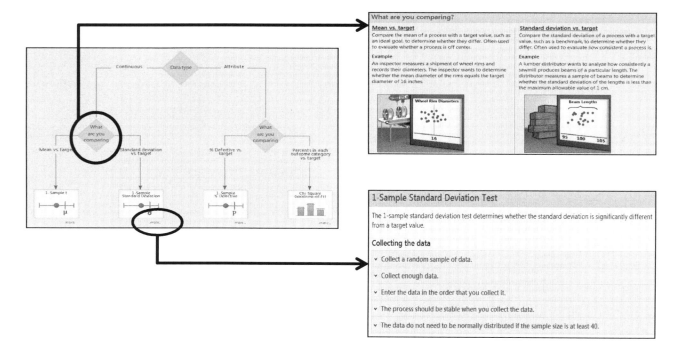

Tests Comparing One Sample To A Target

7.2   1 Sample t test

1 Sample t test	
Function	Tests whether the mean of a population is at a target level given a sample of data.
Sample Size	20 data points are required for the normality of the population that the sample is drawn from not to be an issue. More samples may be required to obtain a reasonable power (>80%) depending on the difference you wish to detect.
Data type & Format	Continuous data which is time ordered from a uni-modal distribution.
Considerations	The process must be stable.

Example 7.2.1 Bursting Discs

Bursting Discs Specialists (BDS) make the Raptor bursting disc, which is rated at 15bar. A bursting disc is a safety device that is added to a pressure vessel. If the pressure in the vessel gets too high the disc will rupture and the pressure will be relieved to a safe area.

BDS wants to check whether their Raptor Discs actually burst at 15 bar pressure. But as the discs are expensive, they want to limit the number they use for testing. They feel they want to be able to measure a difference of 0.15 bar. From tests conducted previously, they know that they can use 0.2 bar as an estimate for the population StDev. What is the minimum number of discs they must sample to get a power of 90%?

Then test the sample data provided in worksheet Bursting Disc to establish whether BDS can claim that the population bursting pressure of the Raptor Disc is correctly rated.

As we need to know the number of samples we require before conducting the t test we need to perform the separate Power & Sample Size (PSS) procedure within the classic menus.

1. Click **Stat<< Power and Sample Size<<1 Sample t**

2. We need to establish the sample size, so leave that box blank. Enter the remaining data that was given in the question, then click OK.

3. Check the Results table and Power graph in the Output Pane.

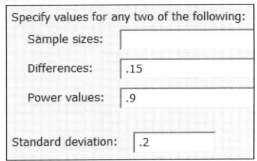

We see that we need a sample size of 21 to achieve a Power of 90%. This means that if there is a difference of greater than 0.15, we will have a 90% chance of detecting it. If you remember, the Confidence is set within the test menu usually at a default value of 95%.

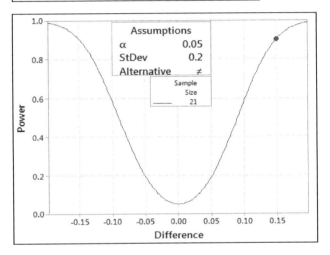

Let's have a look at the second part of the question using our Hypothesis Testing Procedure that we learned in chapter 6. After all, there was a reason we did a whole chapter on it.

Our Investigation Statement is ' Is the mean of the population bursting pressure of the Raptor disc 15bar, or is it different?

From the Investigation Statement, we can form our Null & Alternate Hypothesis.

H_o : Mean bursting pressure is 15 bar for the Raptor.
H_a : Mean bursting pressure is not 15 bar for the Raptor.

We have already assessed the PSS, and we are happy with the Power achieved so we can conduct the test.

BDS takes a sample of 25 discs over some time and checks the bursting pressure. The data is recorded in time order in spreadsheet 07 Hypothesis Testing.xlsx in the worksheet Bursting Disc.

4. Transfer the single column of data into Minitab. Remember to copy the title row of the data into Minitab's title row.

5.   Click *Assistant<<Hypothesis Tests*

6.   Click on the *1 sample t Test* box within the **Compare one sample with a target** group.

7.   The test menu opens. Select 'Burst_Press' as the sample data. We are testing to see if your population is different to 15, so enter '15' as the target. Below the Target section, you will see the radio buttons used to select whether we use a 'one-sided' or 'two-sided' test. Select the bottom radio button for the 'two-sided' test.

8.   At the bottom of the menu, we tell Minitab the difference between the mean and the target that has implications for us. Minitab will use this and the sample StDev to calculate the power. Enter '0.15'as the Difference.

9.   Click OK to run the test.

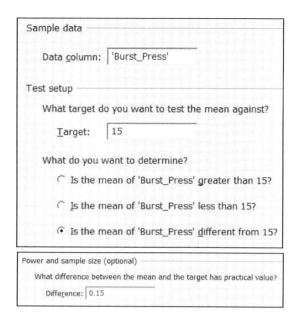

The Assistant produces a 3 page report that is within the Output Pane. Scroll down to see all 3 pages and, if necessary, resize the Output Pane to be able to see a single full page of the report at a time. The 3 pages that are produced for a 1 sample t Test are the Summary Report, the Diagnostic Report and the Report Card.

Please navigate to the Summary Report. In the top left corner, we get the answer to our Investigation Statement.   The question ' Does the mean differ from 15?' is asked and the answer is given on the sliding scale as 'No.' We see that we have a P-value of 0.346   and   as   this   was   above   our Significance level of 0.05, we did not have enough evidence to reject the null. We can see that the Assistant has a zone for P-values between 0.05 and 0.1. The Assistant deems   a   P-value   in   this   zone   to   be inconclusive. Our P-value is far outside the marginal zone so we don't have to worry about that.

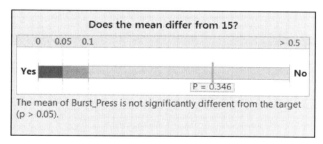

Below that, we see our sample data displayed on a histogram, the calculated 95% confidence interval for the population mean is shown and we see that the value 15 sits   within   the   confidence   interval. Therefore,   we   cannot   say   that   the population mean is different to 15.

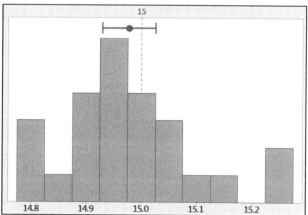

Also, check the actual distribution. The test only works if it is a single distribution not two distributions joined together. Refer back to module 5.7 to see the discussion on bi-modal distributions.

On the top right of the Summary Report, we have our sample statistics. We see the sample mean and the upper and lower limits of the confidence interval. Note that the sample StDev is calculated to be 0.116. The Assistant uses this value for its Power calculations. Previously, we used 0.15 as our population estimate.

Please navigate to the Diagnostic Report.
At the top, we see a basic control chart showing our sample data. We have no unusual data points that need to be explored.

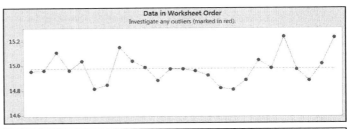

At the bottom of the Diagnostic Report, we get the analysis of Power. We get a power that is rounded up to 100.0%. This is much higher than our estimate as the sample size is larger and the StDev used here is from the samples and lower than our initial population estimate.

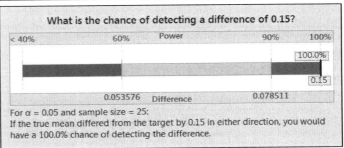

Finally, go to the Report Card. This gives us a summary of the validity of our test. We are told
1)   That there were no unusual data points that could make our test results unreliable.
2)   Normality of our data was not an issue due to our sample size.
3)   Due to our sample size there was a high Power value for the test. This was important as the test concluded there was 'no difference.' Therefore, the high Power value reduces our chances of getting a Type II error.

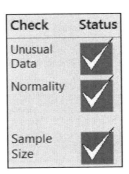

Example 7.2.2 Tablet

Parky wants to measure the power draw from his new quad-core tablet and compare it to the power draw figure supplied by the manufacturer. It's the best time to do this as the tablet has only just come out of the box. Parky sets up his power measuring system to take a reading every minute and sets up the tablet so it doesn't go into

a screen saver mode. Help Parky work out if the actual population of the power draw of this tablet is different from 12.4 watts. For the purposes of calculating the Power (1-β) Parky decides that a difference of 0.4 watts would be the smallest significant difference to him.

Parky takes 142 data samples. The data is recorded in time order in spreadsheet 07 Hypothesis Testing.xlsx in the worksheet Tablet.

1. Transfer the single column of data into Minitab.
2. Click *Assistant<<Hypothesis Tests*
3. Click on the *1 sample t Test* box within the **Compare one sample with a target** group.
4. The test menu opens. Select 'Tablet' as the sample data. We are testing to see if the population mean is different to 12.4, so enter '12.4' as the target.
5. Select the radio button for the 'two-sided' test.
6. At the bottom of the menu, we tell Minitab the difference between the mean and the target that has implications for us. Minitab will use this and the sample StDev to calculate the power. Enter '0.4'.
7. Click OK to run the test.

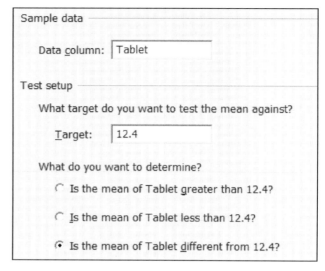

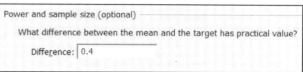

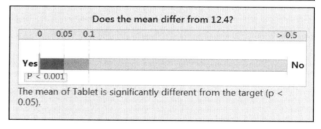

Minitab produces a three page report in the Output Pane. Please navigate to the Summary Report page of that report. In the top left corner, we get the answer to our Investigation Statement. The mean of the population is likely to differ from 12.4.

Below that, we see our sample data displayed on a histogram. The calculated 95% confidence interval for the population mean is shown and we see that the value 12.4 sits below the confidence interval for the population. The shape of the distribution does not look great. There could be issues that need further investigation.

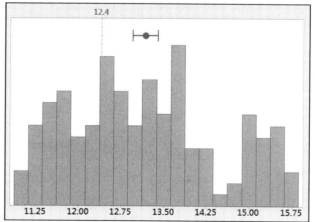

On the Diagnostic Report, we see the control chart of our data. It does not show any unusual data points but it does show a shift in the mean level of the data.

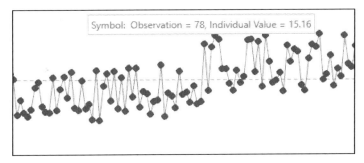

Hover your mouse pointer over any data point in the chart, the position and value of the point will be shown. Hover over the first data point where the level increases. It will reveal the position of that data point, it is observation 78 out of 142.

Parky wonders what could have changed on the tablet and then asks his son if he had used the tablet. He replies that he installed the Candy Squash app and left it running.

That explains why the power usage changed. It also demonstrates that the histogram we saw earlier was indeed a bi-modal distribution. As illustrated, it is far harder to spot on a histogram than a control chart.

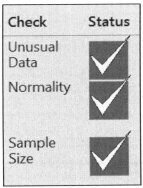

Don't feel bad if you didn't spot the bi-modal distribution the Report Card did not detect it either. It just shows that even though the Assistant is doing a lot of the work, you always need to be on your toes.

If Parky still wants to test his tablet, he must repeat the whole experiment or isolate the relevant data.

7.3 1 Sample StDev

1 Sample StDev	
Function	Test whether the StDev of a population is at a target level given a sample of data.
Sample Size	The results of this test could be invalid if there is more data in the tails of the population distribution than expected in a normal distribution. A sample size of at least 40 is required to test for this condition. More data points may be required to obtain a reasonable power or if the distribution you took your sample from has heavy tails.
Data type & Format	Continuous data which is time ordered from a uni-modal distribution.
Considerations	The process must be stable.

Example 7.3.1 Internet Speeds

Compo is telling his friends that the average UK broadband internet speed is reported to be 8.5Mbps when precisely on a 2 mile radius of a telephone exchange. Additionally, the StDev of the broadband speeds is reported to be 0.6Mbps ±0.2Mbps.

We have collected the relevant data, is Compo's statement about StDev true?

To be able to complete this test with a relatively small sample size, 40, and the requirement to have a reasonable power, we need to set a limit in our difference of interest that is a fairly large proportion of our target.

If we were to set the difference of interest to 0.1 instead of 0.2Mbps the sample size requirement would increase dramatically.

We have Compo's sample data, which consists of 40 data elements. The data is recorded in time order in spreadsheet 07 Hypothesis Testing.xlsx in the worksheet called 'Mbps.'

1. Transfer the single column of data into Minitab.

2. Click *Assistant<<Hypothesis Tests*

3. Click on the *1 sample StDev* box within the **Compare one sample with a target** group.

4. The test menu opens. Select 'Mbps' as the sample data. We are testing to see if the population is different to 0.6, so enter '0.6' as the target.

5. Select the bottom radio button for the 'two-sided' test which tests for a difference whether higher or lower than the target level.

6. At the bottom of the menu, we tell Minitab the difference between the mean and the target that has implications for us. Enter '0.2'.

7. Click OK to run the test.

Minitab produces a 3 page report which is accessible from the Navigator and will be displayed in the Output Pane. We will go through each of these pages in turn and look at the crucial areas.

Please navigate to the Summary Report within the Output Pane.

In the top left corner, we get the answer to our Investigation Statement. 'Does the standard deviation differ from 0.6?' is asked and the answer is given as 'Yes.'

We see that we have a P-value of <0.001. As this is below our Significance level of 0.05, we have strong evidence to reject the null. The probability of getting the results that we did given that the null hypothesis was correct are deemed to be very low.

Below that, we see the calculated 95% confidence interval for the population StDev against the target value, the population of Broadband speeds will likely have a higher StDev than our target.

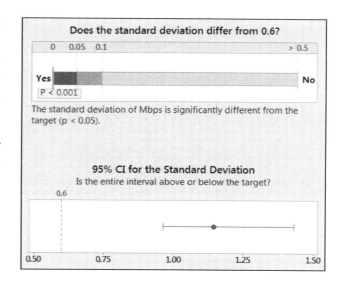

On the top right, we have our sample statistics. We see the sample mean and StDev. We are given the upper and lower limits of the confidence interval for StDev. This test tells us that Compo was wrong with his statement about broadband speed StDev. You could use the 1 sample t Test to check if he was right about the mean level.

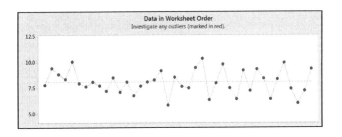

Statistics	
Sample size	40
Mean	8.0908
Standard deviation	1.1440
95% CI	(0.96247, 1.4299)
Target	0.6

Please navigate to the Diagnostic Report.
On the top, we see a basic control chart showing our sample data. We have no unusual data points that need to be explored.

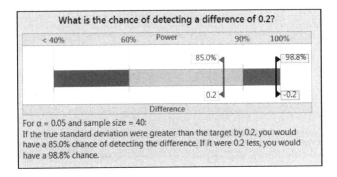

Data in Worksheet Order
Investigate any outliers (marked in red).

At the bottom of the Diagnostic Report, we get the analysis of Power. We have two different Power values. If the difference we wanted to explore was greater than the target by 0.2 our Power would be 85%, which it was for our data.

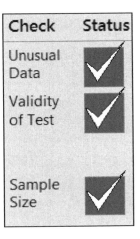

What is the chance of detecting a difference of 0.2?

For α = 0.05 and sample size = 40:
If the true standard deviation were greater than the target by 0.2, you would have a 85.0% chance of detecting the difference. If it were 0.2 less, you would have a 98.8% chance.

Go to the Report Card. This gives us a summary of the validity of our test. We are told
1) That there were no unusual data points that could make our test results unreliable.
2) The results of this test could be invalid if there were more data in the tails of the population distribution than expected in a normal distribution. A sample size of at least 40 was required to test for this condition. Our sample did not show this condition.
3) Due to our sample size we had a good Power for the test.

Check	Status
Unusual Data	✓
Validity of Test	✓
Sample Size	✓

7.4 1 Sample % Defective

1 Sample % Defective	
Function	Test whether the defect rate of a population is at a target level given a defect rate from a sample of data.
Sample Size	The sample size must be sufficient to give a reasonable Power when trying to detect the difference that is meaningful to the user.
Data type & Format	Counts of attribute data.
Considerations	The sample must be representative of the process. Each item tested must have the same chance of being defective as any other item. Samples must be randomly selected.

Example 7.4.1 Blades

Hannan works for a company that produces directionally cast single crystal turbine blades for supersonic engines. The internal trigger level for defective blades is 27%, if above this value, the casting department would be required to start an improvement initiative to reduce the defect rate. Up to now, the department has always reported that the defect rate is not greater than 27%.

Hannan reviewed the reporting guidelines and found that the company check 100 blades every month. Last month they found 30 defective blades but again, they reported that the defect rate was not greater than 27% to the Operations Director.

Help Hannan assess whether the casting department is using the correct methodology when reporting to the Operations Director. If it is not correct, assess the data using the right methodology.

This example does not require us to use a data set.

Hannan looks at last month's data and wonders if the assessment is correct as initially 30 defects in 100 samples is 30% and 30% is higher than the target of 27%. However, Hannan understands Six Sigma Statistics and decides to run the 1 Sample % Defective test in Minitab.

1. Click *Assistant<<Hypothesis Tests*
2. Click on the *1 sample % Defective* box within the **Compare one sample with a target** group.
3. The test menu opens. We are going to name the item that we tested as 'Blades'. We also have the option of using the generic name 'Test Items'.
4. Enter '100' as the number of items tested and '30' as the number found to be defective.
5. We enter our target of '27' as the percentage defective parts we wish to test against. On this occasion, we want to use a one-sided test as we are only interested in finding out if our %defective within the population is greater than 27%. To do this, ensure the top radio button is selected under 'What do you want to determine?'.

Sample data

Name of items tested: Blades

Total number of items tested: 100

Observed number of defectives: 30

What target do you want to test the % defective against?

Target: 27 %

What do you want to determine?

◉ Is the % defective of Blades greater than 27?

6. On this occasion we have not been told what difference the company wants to be able to detect, so we will assume it is 1%. Enter '1' for Difference.

7. Click OK to run the test.

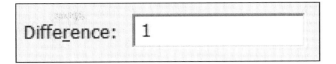

Please navigate to the Summary Report within the Output Pane.

In the top left corner, we get to see why the casting department is reporting that their defect rate is not higher than 27%. It is because the P-value does not provide sufficient evidence to reject the null hypothesis.

Below that, we see the confidence interval for the population defect rate and the target value is well within the confidence interval.

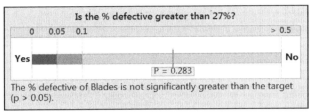

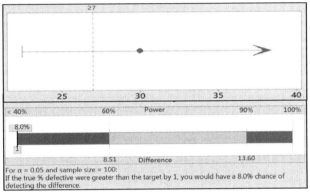

In the Diagnostic Report, we see the analysis of the Power of the test. For this test, we wanted to detect a difference of 1 but for a sample size of 100, we only get an 8% Power. This means that if a difference did exist, we only had an 8% chance of detecting it. This suggests that we could easily suffer from a Type II error.

Hannan realises that he needs to increase the sample size and uses the table on the diagnostic report to decide on the sample size required. He opts for a sample size of 15,000 which should give him a Power between 80 & 90%.

What sample size is required to detect a difference of 1?	
Sample Size	Power
7124	60%
9326	70%
12280	80%
17048	90%

Hannan finds that there were 4150 defective blades in the 15,000 that were used as his sample.

8. Rerun the test but this time use '15,000' as the number of items tested and '4150' as the number of defectives.

Please navigate to the Summary Report.

On this occasion, we see a different answer. We have a P-value of 0.034 and this does provide sufficient evidence to reject the null hypothesis. We can say that the population defect rate is greater than 27%.

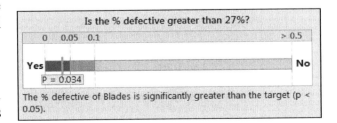

We see the confidence interval for the population defect rate is greater than the target value.

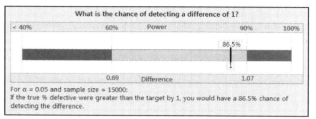

In the Diagnostic Report, we see that the Power achieved was 86.5%. This is a much more reasonable value to use than the 8% Power they had before.

Additionally, the Report Card indicates that the sample size was adequate for the test.

Hannan must now advise the casting department that they need to begin an improvement initiative to reduce the defect rate.

7.5 Chi Square Goodness of Fit

Chi Square Goodness of Fit	
Function	Data is categorised into three or more categories. The split of the data is compared to a target split. Categories that are different to their target value are identified.
Sample Size	There must be a minimum 5 samples in each category. However, as sample size increases the accuracy of the test will increase.
Data type & Format	Counts of attribute data.
Considerations	Samples must be randomly selected. Samples must be easily categorised without any overlap between categories.

Example 7.5.1 Budget

The Government has published figures on a national survey they conducted where they asked a number of households to state what was the single most difficult item to purchase for their monthly household budgets. The results were 12% said Food, 20% said Council Tax, 24% said Motoring, 34% said Mortgage and 10% said Energy.

A local council decided to check if their constituents felt the same way. They received the results of 339 questionnaires and checked the local results against the national results.

Is there any difference between the local and national results?

If there are any differences in which categories are they?

The data is recorded in spreadsheet 07 Hypothesis Testing.xlsx in the worksheet called 'Budget.'

1.   Transfer the three columns of data into Minitab. The Counts column represents the survey results received by the council. The Proportions column is the split we are testing the council results against, in this case, the national results.

2.   Click *Assistant<<Hypothesis Tests*

3.   Click on the *Chi-Square Goodness-of-Fit* box within the **Compare one sample with a target** group.

4.   The test menu opens. We have the option of using the generic name for our process, but we are going to use the name **Budget**.

5.   We have 5 categories, so change Number of Outcomes to '5'.

6.   We have the option of entering our data manually into the menu, or we can ask Minitab to pick up the data from the Worksheet Window by selecting the column headings. The second way is far easier so we will use that.

Use the drop down icon next to Outcome Name and select column 'C1 Household Budgets'.

Use the drop down icon next to Sample Count and select column 'C2 Counts'. Use the drop down icon next to Target Percent and select column 'C3 Proportions'.

The final frame shows the complete table within the test menu.

7.   Click OK to run the test.

Please navigate to the Summary Report within the Output Pane.

In the top left corner, we are answered our Investigation Statement; do any of the local categories differ from the national results? As the P-value is less than the significance level, we have sufficient evidence to reject the null hypothesis. Therefore, at least one of the local categories is different from the national result. At this time, we do not know which category is different.

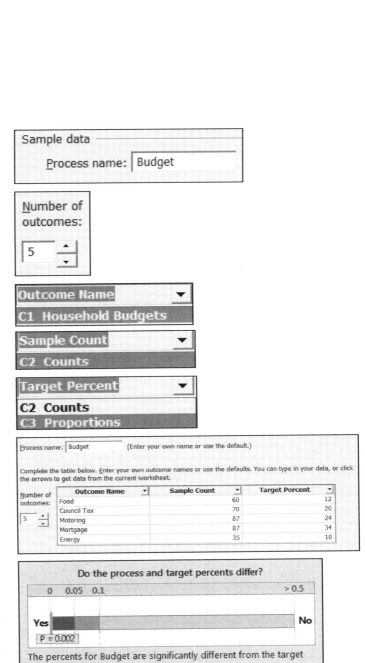

Also, on the Summary Report, we see a Bar Chart showing the percentages of each category with the sample against the target. The greatest difference is in the categories of Food and Mortgage. The sample for Food was greater than the target but it was the other way round for Mortgage. However, we do not know if the categories are statistically significant.

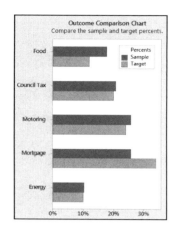

On the top right of the Summary Report, we are told which Categories differed from the targets. We are told that the Food Category and Mortgage Category did differ from the targets and we are told in which direction they differed.

Outcome	Sample Percent	Target Percent	Differ
Food	17.7	12	Higher
Council Tax	20.6	20	No
Motoring	25.7	24	No
Mortgage	25.7	34	Lower
Energy	10.3	10	No
	Total count = 339		

Please navigate to the Diagnostic Report.
At the top, we see a chart that shows the magnitude of difference between sample and target and the direction of difference. We see that the Food category has the greatest percentage difference. That chart is not shown here.

At the bottom of the Diagnostic Report, we get a table showing the summary of results. We can see confidence intervals for each category.

Outcome	Target Percent	Sample Percent	Individual 95% CI
Food	12	17.7	(13.6, 21.8)
Council Tax	20	20.6	(16.3, 25.0)
Motoring	24	25.7	(21.0, 30.3)
Mortgage	34	25.7	(21.0, 30.3)
Energy	10	10.3	(7.1, 13.6)

Go to the Report Card. This gives us a summary of the validity of our test. We are told that our sample size was sufficient to ensure the validity of the test and the confidence intervals.

Check	Status
Validity of Test	✓
Validity of Intervals	✓

The next section is the 'Compare two samples with each other group'. We cover the 2 sample t test, paired t test and the 2 StDev tests but we are not going to cover the attribute tests in this section. This is because in terms of test set-up and interpretation of results, they are very similar to tests for comparing more than two groups and those tests are covered later.

Tests Comparing Two Samples With Each Other
7.6   2 Sample t Test

2 Sample t test	
Function	Test whether the means of two populations differ given a sample of data from each population.
Sample Size	15 data points are required for the normality of the population that the sample was drawn from not to be an issue. More samples may be required to obtain a reasonable Power (>80%) depending on the difference you wish to detect.
Data type & Format	Continuous data which is time ordered from a uni-modal distribution.
Considerations	The process must be stable. Unlike the classic method the method used within the Assistant does not need to know if the groups have equal variances.

Example 7.6.1 Factory Outputs

Iqra works for a famous chocolate bar manufacturer and wants to find out which of the two factories has the highest sugar yield. She takes 62 random samples from each factory and analyses them for sugar content and then knowing the sugar that went into each bar she can work out the sugar yield. Help Iqra work out which factory has the highest sugar yield.

The 2 Sample t test is probably the most commonly used test in hypothesis testing as it covers the comparison of the means of two populations. It is therefore used to measure whether a change of state has occurred or whether two populations are different. In this example, we must establish if the two factories are different from each other.

The data is recorded in time order in spreadsheet 07 Hypothesis Testing.xlsx in the worksheet 'Sugar yield.'

1.   Transfer both columns of data into a new Minitab project file.

2.   Click *Assistant<<Hypothesis Tests*

3.   Click on the *2 sample t Test* box within the **Compare two samples with each other** group.

4.   We need to tell Minitab how the data is arranged in the worksheet. In our case, the two samples are in two separate columns; this is known as 'unstacked.' If the data were 'stacked' the data would be in one column and there would be a column carrying the data headers. Select 'Each sample is in its own column' and then select the column names.

5.   We want to determine only if there is a difference between the two factories, so select the bottom radio button.

Sample data

How are your data arranged in the worksheet?

Each sample is in its own column

Sample 1: Phobos

Sample 2: Demios

What do you want to determine?

○ Is the mean of Phobos greater than the mean of Demios?

○ Is the mean of Phobos less than the mean of Demios?

● Is the mean of Phobos different from the mean of Demios?

6. At the bottom of the menu, we tell Minitab the difference between the two means that has an implication for us. We don't have a value for this but after consulting with Iqra, we will use a value of 1.

7. Click OK to run the test.

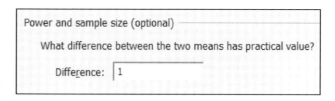

Please navigate to the Summary Report. In the top left corner, we get the answer to our Investigation Statement. The question ' Do the means differ ?' is asked and the answer is given on the sliding scale as 'Yes'. The P-value is 0.019 which means we have sufficient evidence to reject the null.

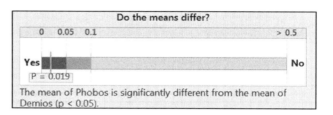

Below that, we see the 95% confidence interval for the difference between the means. This can be positive or negative depending on which order we selected our samples in the test menu. We also see that zero is not within the confidence interval. This indicates there is a difference between the groups.

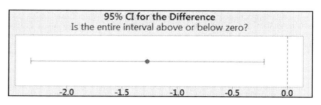

Below that, we see our sample data displayed on two histograms with the calculated 95% confidence interval for the population means overlaid. It is interesting to note that the two confidence intervals overlap very slightly and yet Minitab has detected a difference.

On the top right we have our sample statistics. We see the sample mean and the upper and lower limits of the confidence interval. We are given -1.27 difference based on the mean values but the real difference between the populations could be anywhere between -2.32 and -0.21.

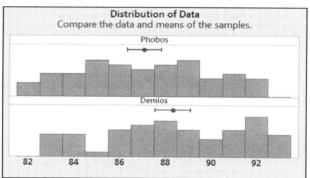

Statistics	Phobos	Demios
Sample size	62	62
Mean	87.065	88.337
95% CI	(86.32, 87.81)	(87.570, 89.104)
Standard deviation	2.9205	3.0209

Statistics	*Difference
Difference	-1.2716
95% CI	(-2.3281, -0.21516)

*Difference = Phobos - Demios

Please navigate to the Diagnostic Report.
At the top, we see two basic control charts showing our sample data; I have only shown one of them here. Any unusual data points would be marked in red on this chart.

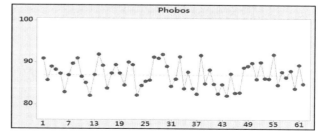

If a data point stands out from the rest of the data by a long way, it should be investigated. It is possible to get 2-3% of data points shown as unusual and it would be nothing to worry about.

The Assistant identifies a data point as unusual if it is more than 1.5 times the interquartile range beyond the lower or upper quartile of the distribution. The lower and upper quartiles are the 25th and 75th percentiles of the data.

At the bottom of the Diagnostic Report, we get the analysis of Power. We are told that with our present sample with a requirement of detecting a difference of 1 we would only have a 46.0% chance of detecting a difference if one existed. But we know that we discovered a difference so we don't have to worry. It would have been a different story if we had conducted the Power test on its own before conducting this analysis in the Assistant.

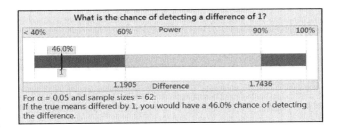

We are also given examples of the sample size required in each group to obtain a specific Power. We can see that if we wanted a Power of 90%, then we would need 187 samples in each group.

Please go to the Report Card. This gives us a summary of the validity of our test. We are told
1) That there were no unusual data points that could make our test results unreliable.

2) Normality of our data was not an issue due to our sample size.

3) The sample size was sufficient to detect a difference between the means.

4) We are told that as the Assistant uses a different calculation method to the classic menus, we do not need to worry whether the groups have equal variances or not.

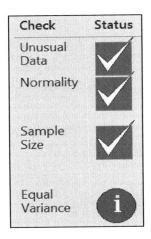

7.7 Paired t Test

Paired t test	
Function	Test whether changing a specific condition between dependant observations has an effect on a population.
Sample Size	20 data points are required for the normality of the population that the sample is drawn from not to be an issue. More samples may be required to obtain a reasonable Power (>80%) depending on the difference you wish to detect.
Data type & Format	Continuous data which is time ordered.
Considerations	The process must be stable. As each element is tested under two conditions the data for each element must be in the same row.

Example 7.7.1 Darts

Aman Darts Specialists want to demonstrate the improvement that there new spinning titanium shaft gives over standard nylon shafts. They run a demonstration with 50 volunteer darts players of varying abilities who use standard nylon shafts. After allowing them to warm up, they take their total score using 9 darts. The players are then given the new titanium rotating shafts which they fit into their darts replacing the nylon shafts. After another warm-up period, their scores from 9 darts are recorded again. Establish if the titanium shaft is better than the nylon shaft. A difference of a score of 9 is deemed to be the minimum difference of interest to Aman Darts.
The two scores for each player are recorded in a separate row of the spreadsheet.

A paired t test is different from a 2 Sample t test as it is used for two dependent populations, whereas a 2 Sample t test is used for two independent populations. Let's take the example of the darts demonstration. Aman Darts could have scored the nylon darts with one set of players and then tested the titanium shafts on a second set of players and then compared the scores. This would be two independent populations. However, there might be a problem if most of the good players went into one of the groups. To get around the possibility of all the good players going into one group, only one group is used, and they test both types of shaft. This gives us the two dependent populations.
A Paired t test is the same as calculating the difference of the dependent values and then using a 1 sample t test against a target difference of zero.
The data is recorded in time order in spreadsheet 07 Hypothesis Testing.xlsx in the worksheet 'Darts.'

1. Transfer both columns of data into a new Minitab project file.
2. Click *Assistant<<Hypothesis Tests*
3. Click on the **Paired t** box within the **Compare two samples with each other** group.
4. Enter the sample data in the order shown. As we only want to know if Titanium is better, this is a one-way test. We select the appropriate radio button under Test set-up.
5. At the bottom of the menu, we tell Minitab the difference between the two means that has implications for us. Enter '9' for the difference.

Sample data
Measurement 1: Titanium
Measurement 2: Nylon

Test setup
What do you want to determine?
⦿ Is the mean of Titanium greater than the mean of Nylon?

Power and sample size (optional)
What difference between the two means has practical value?
Difference: 9

6.   Click OK to run the test.

Please navigate to the Summary Report.
In the top left corner, we are told the answer to the question 'Is Titanium greater than Nylon ?' and the answer is 'Yes.' The P-value means we have sufficient evidence to reject the null that there is no effect. This means the players did get a statistically significant better score with the Titanium shafts.

Below that, we see a histogram showing the values of the actual differences between the scores for each person. We see how some people had a worse score, others stayed the same but mostly, there was an increase in scores. We can see the Confidence Interval (CI) for the mean difference in the score and how this was greater than zero.

On the top right of the page, we have our sample data. We see that the mean difference in scores was 19.56. You might also notice that Minitab is using a 90% CI where a 95% CI is expected. This is because Minitab uses a 90% CI for a one-way test.

Please navigate to the Diagnostic Report.
At the top, we see a control chart showing both sets of data and the associated difference. Unusual data points would be shown in red and these might affect our results. Luckily we don't have any in this study.

At the bottom of the Diagnostic Report, we get the analysis of Power. We are told that with our present sample with a requirement of detecting a difference of 9 we would only have a 68.2% chance of detecting a difference if one existed. But we know that we detected a difference so we don't have to worry.

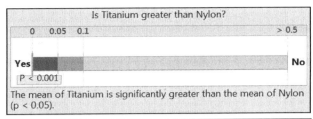

The mean of Titanium is significantly greater than the mean of Nylon (p < 0.05).

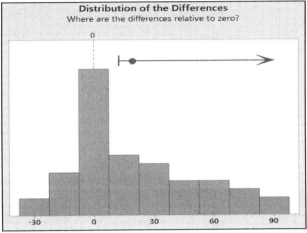

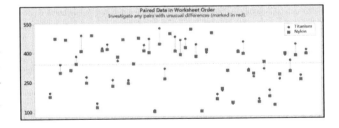

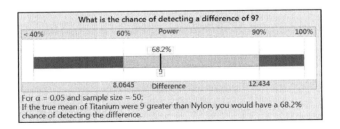

For α = 0.05 and sample size = 50:
If the true mean of Titanium were 9 greater than Nylon, you would have a 68.2% chance of detecting the difference.

Please go to the Report Card. This gives us a summary of the validity of our test. We are told

1)   That there were no unusual data points that could make our test results unreliable.

2)   Normality of our data was not an issue due to our sample size.

3)   The sample size was sufficient to detect a difference between the means.

Check	Status
Unusual Data	✓
Normality	✓
Sample Size	✓

7.8   2 Sample StDev

2 Sample StDev test	
Function	Test whether the StDev's of two populations differ given a sample of data from each population.
Sample Size	20 data points are required for the normality of the population that the sample is drawn from not to be an issue. More samples may be required to obtain a reasonable Power (>80%) depending on the difference you wish to detect.
Data type & Format	Continuous data which is time ordered.
Considerations	The process must be stable. The method of calculation used within the Assistant differs from the classic method. This means that normality is not an issue as long as the sample size is at least 20.

Example 7.8.1 Feeders

Woody wants to settle the age-old argument regarding which type of feeder gives less feeder variation, The corimass feeder or the belt feeder. He collects feed rate data from both feeders when running at the same feed rate. Woody wants to be able to detect a difference of 10%. Even though this sounds quite large, Woody knows that a lot of data points will be required to achieve a good Power for this test. Collecting a lot of data is not an issue as the control system logs all the required information.

Help Woody settle the age-old question and calculate if there is a difference between the two types of feeder in terms of feedrate StDev.

The data is recorded in time order in spreadsheet 07 Hypothesis Testing.xlsx in the worksheet 'Feeders.'

1.   Transfer both columns of data into a new Minitab project file.
2.   Click *Assistant<<Hypothesis Tests*
3.   Click on the *2 sample StDev* box within the **Compare two samples with each other** group.

4.   Select 'Each sample is in its own column' and then select the column headers.

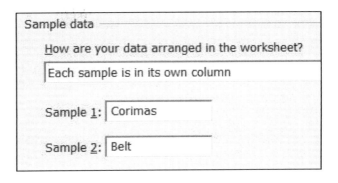

5.   We want to determine only if there is a difference between the two feeders, so select the bottom radio button. This is a two-way test.

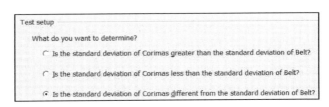

6.   At the bottom of the menu, we tell Minitab that Woody is interested in detecting a difference of 10%. This is the value that would have practical implications in selecting new feeders in the future.

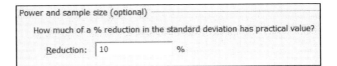

7.   Click OK to run the test.

Please navigate to the Summary Report. In the top left corner, we get the answer to ' Do the standard deviations differ ?' and the answer is 'No.' The P-value is 0.144 which means we do not have sufficient evidence to reject the null that there is no effect. This means that Woody must conclude that there is no difference in terms of variation between the two types of feeders.

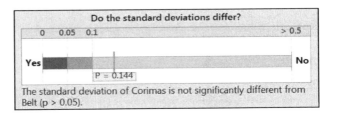

Below that, we see a plot showing 95% confidence intervals for the two StDevs. As the confidence intervals overlap and the P-value is 0.144, we can conclude there is no difference between the StDevs.

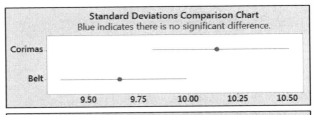

Below that, we see our sample data displayed on two histograms. It is interesting to see the type of distributions that we get. This may become relevant in a future project.

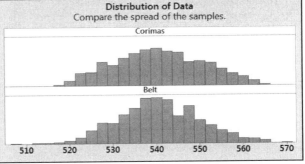

On the top right, we have our sample statistics. We see that both feeders are operating at almost the same mean level of 540. The average level of StDev for Belt is lower than that for the Corimas but remember there is insufficient evidence to say this difference was not created by anything other than chance.

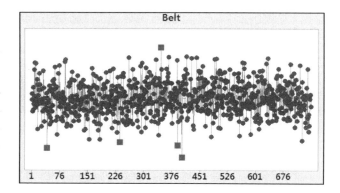

Please navigate to the Diagnostic Report.
At the top we see two basic control charts showing our sample data, I have only shown the one for the Belt feeder. This is because it contained some unusual data points. Looking at the 5 data points in question, they are not that far from the main body of data. I have 5 unusual data points in 750 which is 0.67%. As this is a very low percentage and the points are not that far out I am not going to take any action.

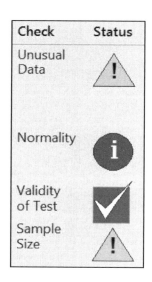

At the bottom of the Diagnostic Report, we get the analysis of Power. We are told that with our present sample with a requirement of detecting a difference of 10%, we had an 87.5% chance of detecting a difference if one existed. Our Power is above 80% but not quite 90%. The question is, are we satisfied that we had sufficient Power to detect a difference? My answer would be yes, 87.5% is a reasonably good Power level.

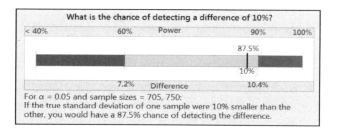

Please go to the Report Card. This gives us a summary of the validity of our test. We are told
1) There were unusual data points that might make our test results unreliable. However, we discounted them.
2) Normality of our data was not an issue due to our sample size.
3) Due to our sample size being greater than 20 the P-value should be valid for the test.
4) Finally, we are warned that our sample size was not sufficient to obtain a Power of 90%. We would have needed 789 samples in each group to achieve a Power of 90%.

There are two additional tests in the 'Compare two samples with each other' group, but we will not cover these two tests in this section. We will include similar tests in the next section, 'Compare more than two samples'. The reason for not including these in this section is that test set-up and interpretation is virtually identical between the two sections.

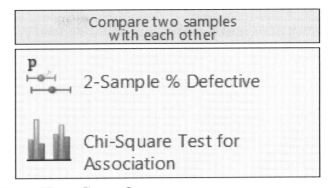

Tests Capable of Comparing More Than Two Samples
7.9   Chi-Square % Defective

Chi-Sqaure %Defective (for more than 2 groups)	
Function	Tests whether the populations of more than 2 defect rates are significantly different from each other.
Sample Size	The sample size must be sufficient to give a reasonable Power when trying to detect the difference that is meaningful to the user. There must be at least 5 observed defects in each group and Minitab will state whether the expected number of defectives in each group was sufficient.
Data type & Format	Counts of attribute data.
Considerations	The sample must be representative of the process. Each item tested must have the same chance of being defective as any other item. i.e. if it is known that one operator produces products with a lower defect rate then products should not be mixed when analysing. Samples must be randomly selected.

Example 7.9.1 Distributors

Kaley works for Nile, a major online retailer. She has been tasked to investigate how their third party distribution companies are performing in terms of delivery times. Nile processes all orders within 2 days so that they are ready for pick-up at local warehouses within 2 days. The distributors then have a further 2 days to deliver the orders to customers. Any delivery which is completed outside of the 4 day deadline is deemed to be a miss or defective. All four of the distributors operate out of all the warehouses, and Kaley takes all of the data for March, which is known to be a representative month. When asked Kaley says that a difference of 3% would be a significant difference for her investigation. Help Kaley do an initial investigation to establish if any of the distributors are operating significantly differently to any of the others.
The data is recorded in spreadsheet 08 Hypothesis Testing.xlsx in the worksheet 'Distributors'.

1.   Open the file and transfer the data into a new Minitab project file. We have 3 columns of data, Distributors, Late and Total.

2.   Click *Assistant<<Hypothesis Tests.*

3. Click on the **Chi-Square % Defective** box within the **Compare more than two samples** group.

4. The test menu opens. We are going to name the item that we are testing as 'Deliveries.'

5. Type in the X variable name as 'Distributors.'

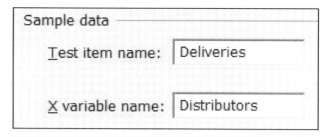

6. As we have 4 companies, we need to set 'Number of distinct X values' to '4'.

7. In the middle of the menu, we enter all our data by selecting the column names from the drop down menus. From the first drop down menu, select 'Distributors' to auto-populate the data. For the Total Number tested drop-down select 'Total' and finally for the Number of Defectives drop-down select 'Late.' Alternatively, type all the data in by hand if that pleases you.

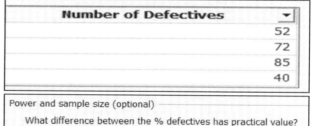

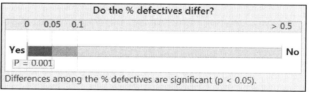

8. Kaley told us that she wants to be able to detect a difference of 3%, so we will enter '3' for 'Difference.'

9. Click OK to run the test. On this occasion, we have a 4 page report that is produced within the Output Pane.

Please navigate to the Summary Report.
In the top left corner, we are told that the % defectives differ. This means that at least one of the populations is different from the others.
We have to go to the % Defectives Comparison chart to find out which groups are different. We are told that 'Red intervals that do not overlap differ.' For Kaley, this means that SEL differs from Fence. We cannot say that SEL differs from Khanage or Walks and we cannot say that Fence differs from Walks or Khanage.

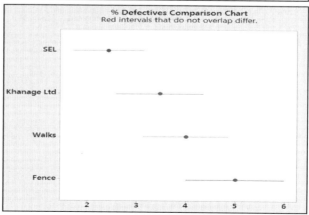

In the top left we see the Grouping Information table, and that helps clarify which groups differ. These tables are invaluable when there are many groups that differ significantly. The table confirms that the only distributors that differ are SEL and Fence.

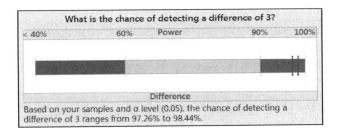

#	Distributors	Differs from
	Which % defectives differ?	
1	SEL	4
2	Khanage Ltd	
3	Walks	
4	Fence	1

In the Diagnostic Report, we see the number of Observed and Expected items for successful and failed deliveries. Below the table, we are told that the expected number of items in each group should be 1.5 to ensure the validity of the test.

	Number of Defective and Nondefective Items			
	Defective		Nondefective	
Distributors	Observed	Expected	Observed	Expected
Khanage Ltd	52	56.2	1448	1444
Walks	72	67.4	1728	1733
Fence	85	63.7	1615	1636
SEL	40	61.8	1610	1588

- To ensure validity of the test, the expected number of defectives and nondefectives should be at least 1.5.
- To ensure validity of the comparison intervals, the observed number of defectives and nondefectives should be at least 5.

To ensure the validity of the comparison intervals, the observed number of items should be at least 5 in each group.

In the Power Report, we are given a Confidence Interval for our power which is 97.26% to 98.44% for detecting a difference of 3.

We are also given a table of Powers that can be achieved with different sample sizes and the Confidence Intervals for each group. Those tables are not shown here.

What is the chance of detecting a difference of 3?

< 40%	60%	Power	90%	100%

Difference

Based on your samples and α level (0.05), the chance of detecting a difference of 3 ranges from 97.26% to 98.44%.

Finally, in the Report Card, we are told our test and intervals were valid, as also shown in the Diagnostic Report. And our sample size was sufficient to detect a difference.

This information tells Kaley that there is a performance difference between SEL and Fence, which could be investigated and used to improve SELs performance.

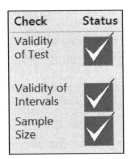

Check	Status
Validity of Test	✓
Validity of Intervals	✓
Sample Size	✓

7.10   Chi-Square Test for Association

Chi-Square Test for Association	
Function	Tests whether values of categorised components of different items are likely to have differing populations, where there are three or more category's for each item.
Sample Size	Minitab will state whether the expected number of items in each category was sufficient to ensure validity of the results.
Data type & Format	Counts of categorical data.
Considerations	Data must be collected randomly for each item. If the data is measured it must be allocated to only one category. There is no Power assessment for this test.

A number of the hypothesis tests associated with categorical data have similar-sounding names and functions. To avoid confusion, let's review the purpose of this test and the Chi-Square Goodness of fit test. The Goodness of fit test worked on a single item such as the grade boundaries in a single department and compared the calculated percentages to a target value. The test for association works for more than one item and assesses whether the populations of categories within those items contain differing percentages.

Example 7.10.1 Grades

Mahwish is checking the results of a local school across a number of broadly defined departments. She wants to check if the percentages of Pass, Fails, and Distinctions are the same across the departments of Humanities, Science, Technical and Languages. She obtains data that gives counts of categorical data from the department heads. Help Mahwish analyse the data to establish if any of the categories are likely to have differing populations.

The data is recorded in spreadsheet 07 Hypothesis Testing.xlsx in the worksheet 'Grades.'

1.   Open the file and transfer the data into a new Minitab project file.
2.   Click *Assistant<<Hypothesis Tests*
3.   Click on the ***Chi-Square Test for Association*** box within the **Compare more than two samples** group.

4.   The test menu opens, and we are asked, 'How will you enter your data?'. As we are efficient, we will get Minitab to pick up the data from the worksheet window by selecting 'Get from current worksheet.'

How will you enter your data?   Get from current worksheet ▼

5.   We then need to tell Minitab that our 'Outcomes are columns' as the data for our categories, Distinction, Pass, and Fail, are listed in columns.

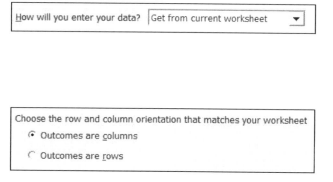

Choose the row and column orientation that matches your worksheet
  ⊙ Outcomes are columns
  ○ Outcomes are rows

6. Minitab asks us the 'Y name'. 'Y' refers to the response, which is the variable we are measuring as we change our inputs. Inputs are typically called 'X.' Our response is 'Grade' so we enter that against 'Y name.' We have 3 categories or outcomes of grade.

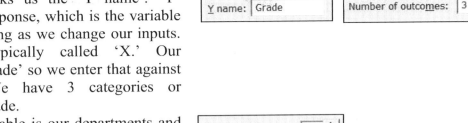

7. The X variable is our departments and we have 4 of those. Enter '4' for Number of X values.

8. Minitab will draw the empty table for us. We then need to select the appropriate column headings for Minitab to input the data.

9. Once you have entered the column headings and the data has been automatically populated, click OK to run the test.

Subject	Distinction	Pass	Fail
Technical	700	3960	280
Humanities	500	2880	160
Languages	960	4240	500
Science	720	3500	120

Please navigate to the Summary Report.
In the top left corner, we get the answer to the Investigation statement. The percentage profiles differ. This means that at least one pair of our category breakdowns differ.

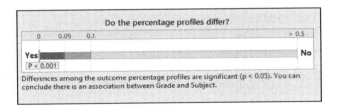

In the Percentage Profiles chart, we are shown how the percentages of the outcomes vary between the departments and we are shown the average levels at the top.

We see that each department had a similar profile, with the number of passes being the highest outcome in each category. The fail grade was less than 10% in each department and there was an average of 15% distinctions in each department.

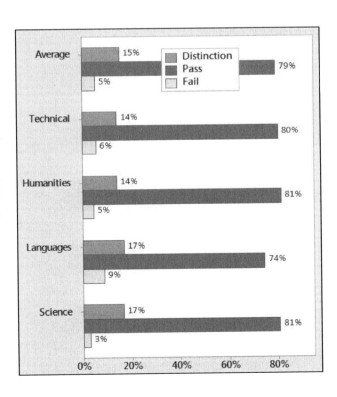

%Difference between observed and expected counts is a graph showing exactly what the title explains. Each bar shows the %difference between the observed and expected difference. For example, Science-Fails has a value close to -50%; this means that the observed fails were close to 50% less than expected. Conversely, Languages had almost 50% more observed fails than expected. These values appear to be high so I can make an educated guess and assume that they are categories that differ. The next most significant difference is Humanities-Fails which are at -21%. Without having a separate P-value, I can't say if Humanities-Fails is statistically significant.

I apologise if I am pointing out the obvious, the term 'Observed' means the value from the sample data, whereas, 'Expected' is calculated for each combination of Grade Vs Subject.

On the Diagnostic Report, we are given the actual breakdown of Observed and Expected values in a table. It can be seen that even though the percentage difference between Science and Language Fails was high, the real difference value was not that high.

Below the table, we are told that the expected value in each category must be at least 1 for this test for the P-value to be valid. We have met this condition.

In the Report Card, we are told that our results were valid as we had sufficient values in each of the expected count categories.

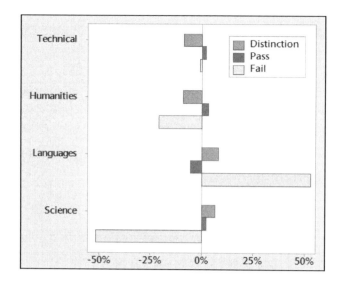

	Technical		Humanities		Languages		Science	
	Obs	Exp	Obs	Exp	Obs	Exp	Obs	Exp
Distinction	700	768	500	550	960	886	720	675
Pass	3960	3889	2880	2787	4240	4487	3500	3417
Fail	280	283	160	203	500	326	120	248
Total	4940		3540		5700		4340	

Expected counts should be at least 1 to ensure the validity of the p-value for the test.

Check	Status
Validity of Test	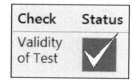

This concludes the chapter on Hypothesis Testing. You should repeat the examples until you can complete them without looking at the book. Once you can do that, try the exercises. Model answers for the exercises are available at www.rmksixsigma.com.

7.11 Hypothesis Testing Exercises

Detailed answers to all of the exercises are available from www.rmksixsigma.com
Exercise 7.11.1 PSS
Establish the sample size that you would need for a 1 sample t test where you had a Power of 90% under the following conditions
1) A one-way test where you are interested only if the alternate is greater than the null hypothesis
2) You are interested in being able to detect a difference of 3
3) The historical StDev has been 5.

Exercise 7.11.2 PSS
Establish the Power that you achieve with a 2 sample t test under the following conditions
1) A two-way test where you are only considering if the alternate is different to the null hypothesis
2) You have a sample size of 60 in each group.
3) You are interested in being able to detect a difference of 1
4) The historical StDev has been 3.
Before running the procedure try and estimate the power value that would be achieved and then compare your guess to the answer.

Exercise 7.11.3 Conduct a 1 Sample t
Analyse the data in File 07Hypothesis Testing.xlsx worksheet Pressure and answer the questions shown below. The data was collected randomly and is recorded in time order.
1)   Is the sample data within Column Pressure likely to have come from a population where the mean was different to 77?
2)   What is the confidence interval for the mean of the population?
3)   Have the requirements of the test that you have used been met?
4)   What was the Power of the test when you want to detect a difference of 2?
5)   Are there any issues associated with this level of Power ?
6)   Does the Report Card generate any warnings?

Exercise 7.11.4 Conduct a 1 Sample StDev
Analyse the data in File 07Hypothesis Testing.xlsx worksheet Pressure and answer the questions shown below. The data was collected randomly and is recorded in time order.
1)   Is the sample data within Column Pressure likely to have come from a population where the StDev was different to 5?
2)   What is the confidence interval for the StDev of the population?
3)   Have the requirements of the test that you have used been met?
4)   What was the Power of the test when you want to detect a difference of 1?
5)   Are there any issues associated with this level of Power ?
6)   Does the Report Card generate any warnings?

Exercise 7.11.5 Conduct a 2 sample t

Analyse the data in File 07Hypothesis Testing.xlsx worksheet Temperature and answer the questions shown below. The data was collected randomly and is recorded in time order.

1) Is the sample data in columns TempA and TempB likely to have come from different populations?
2) If the populations are different, which population mean is greater?
3) Have the requirements of the test that you have used been met?
4) What was the Power of the test when you want to detect a difference of 5?
5) Are there any issues associated with this level of Power ?
6) Does the Report Card generate any warnings?

Exercise 7.11.6 Conduct a 2 sample t

Analyse the data in File 07Hypothesis Testing.xlsx worksheet Frequency and answer the questions shown below. The data was collected randomly and is recorded in time order.

1) Is the sample data in columns Freq_A and Freq_B likely to have come from different populations?
2) If the populations are different, which population mean is greater?
3) Have the requirements of the test that you have used been met?
4) What was the Power of the test when you want to detect a difference of 3?
5) Are there any issues associated with this level of Power ?
6) Does the Report Card generate any warnings?

Exercise 7.11.7 Conduct a 2 sample t

Let's go back to Worksheet Temperature and delete the data in Temp B from where the shift in mean occurred, that is row 61 onwards. Then answer the questions shown below. The data was collected randomly and is recorded in time order.

1) Is the sample data in columns TempA and TempB likely to have come from populations with differing means?
2) If the populations are different, which population mean is greater?
3) Have the requirements of the test that you have used been met?
4) What was the Power of the test when you want to detect a difference of 5?
5) Are there any issues associated with this level of Power ?
6) Does the Report Card generate any warnings?

Exercise 7.11.8 Conduct a 2 sample StDev

Let's go back to Worksheet Temperature and delete the data in Temp B from where the shift in mean occurred, that is row 61 onwards, if you have not done that for the previous example. Then answer the questions shown below. The data was collected randomly and is recorded in time order.

1) Is the sample data in columns TempA and TempB likely to have come from populations with differing StDevs?
2) If the populations are different, which population StDev is greater?
3) Have the requirements of the test that you have used been met?
4) What was the Power of the test when you want to detect a difference of 25%?
5) Are there any issues associated with this level of Power ?
6) Does the Report Card generate any warnings?

Exercise 7.11.9 Conduct a 2 sample StDev

Analyse the data in File 07Hypothesis Testing.xlsx worksheet Frequency and answer the questions shown below. The data was collected randomly and is recorded in time order.

1) Is the sample data in columns Freq_A and Freq_B likely to have come from populations with differing StDevs?
2) If the populations are different, which population StDev is greater?
3) Have the requirements of the test that you have used been met?
4) What was the Power of the test when you want to detect a difference of 25%?
5) Are there any issues associated with this level of Power ?
6) Does the Report Card generate any warnings?

Example 7.11.10 Conduct a chi-sq % defective 2 groups.

Analyse the data in File 08Hypothesis Testing.xlsx worksheet Ex 7.11.7 and answer the questions shown below.

A questionaire is sent to a large number of companies. In one of the questions the companies are asked to select which sector their business would come under. This is then compared with the national average.

1) Are any of the population sectors different from the target samples?
2) Which population sectors are different from their target samples?
3) Have the requirements of the test that you have used been met?
4) Does the Report Card generate any warnings?

8 ANOVA

8.1 Introduction to ANOVA

The problem is that ANOVA stands for Analysis of Variance. However, it's easier to call this chapter ANOVA because it is an all-encompassing title for everything that we are going to be covering. You might remember that I left out two techniques from the Assistant's Hypothesis Testing menu. We are going to be covering 'One-Way ANOVA' and the 'Standard Deviations Test' using the Assistant in this section.

We are then going to be leaving the Assistant for a short amount of time, and we are going to be looking at the ANOVA General Linear Model (GLM). This will be an introduction to the GLM for Green Belts and in the Black Belt Edition, we can take a more in-depth look at the GLM. I did consider leaving out the GLM procedure from the Green Belt Edition but it is such a useful tool I did not want Green Belts to be without it.

Note that all the data for this chapter is in Excel file 08 ANOVA.xlsx which can be downloaded from WWW.rmksixsigma.com. The model answers for the exercises are also available from the same site.

8.2 The theory behind ANOVA

If we had two different materials, and we tested 50 samples of each for breaking strength, we might get the Individual Value Plot (IVP) shown. We could then calculate the mean strength of each material using the sample data. We have a continuous response variable which is strength and we have two different materials that we are testing. We could say that the property 'Material' has two levels, Material A and Material B.

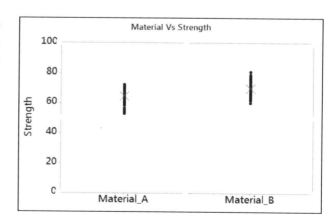

And as you have already completed chapters 6 & 7 I don't need to tell you that we would use the sample data to make a 95% confidence interval of the mean of the populations using a 2 sample T test for both materials. We would then compare the confidence intervals to say if one material was different from the other.

If we had more than two levels, we could still make the IVPs and then to assess if the levels were different we could use a number of 2 Sample T tests to establish which of the groups were different from each other. Luckily, Minitab is here to make our lives easy and has given us the One-Way ANOVA test.

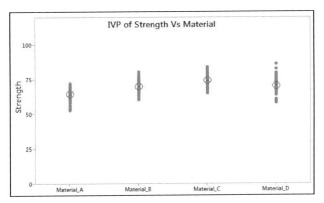

Let's go back to our example, we have 4 levels of material, and we have plotted the response variable for each level. Our Investigation Statement would be 'Does changing the material of construction have an effect on strength?'. Our null hypothesis is 'There is no difference in mean levels between any of the populations' and our alternate hypothesis is 'There is a difference in mean levels between at least one pair of populations'.

Basically, we want to know if any of our groups are different from each other in terms of mean strength.

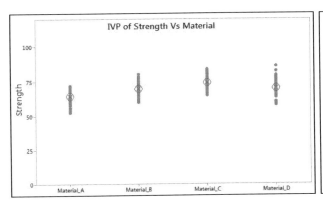
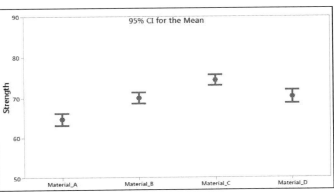

To establish if the levels of material are different, we could plot the 95% Confidence Interval (CI) for each level. We know that if the intervals don't overlap, then we have sufficient evidence to say that the groups are different. We can see that Material A & B are different, A & C are different, B & D are not different etc.

To explore how One-Way ANOVA works, let's ask ourselves what if the mean levels of each material were the same as in the diagram but there was more variability in the results. Look at the IVP and try to imagine that the variability in the groups is increasing but the mean levels are staying the same.

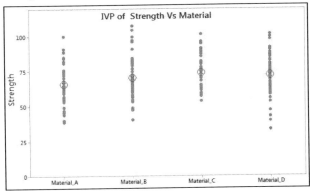
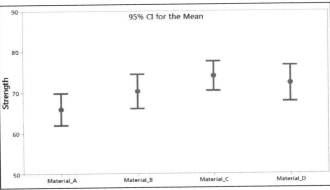

When the level of variability in the groups is increased, the confidence intervals begin to overlap and we cannot say that the groups are different. This means that in our example there are two factors which affect our ability to state whether we can say there is a difference between the groups, one is the difference in mean levels between the groups and the other is the variability within the groups.

The One-way ANOVA procedure calculates the between mean to within group variation ratio and calls it the F statistic.

$$\frac{Between\ Group\ Variation}{Within\ Group\ Variation} = F\ Statistic$$

Let's take it back to the Material versus Strength example and consider what is happening to the F-statistic when we change the Within Group Variation.

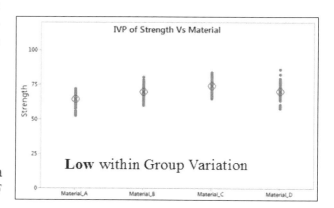

$$\frac{Between\ Group\ Variation}{Low\ Within\ Group\ Variation} = High\ F\ statistic$$

Just doing the calculation in relative terms with a low within group variation will result in a high F statistic.

And now if we can use our imagination again and increase the within group variation.

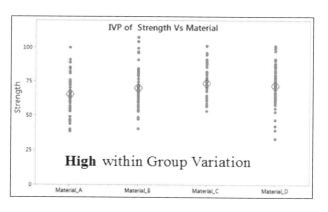

$$\frac{Between\ Group\ Variation}{High\ Within\ Group\ Variation} = Low\ F\ statistic$$

If you have a dynamic imagination and you have been imagining that the within group variation has been changing value, and the F Statistic has been changing value, you may be thinking 'okay, when will I have sufficient evidence that the value of my F-statistic will tell me that there is a difference between at least one pair of the groups?'

Minitab will calculate the F statistic and then compare that to the null distribution for this test, which happens to be called the F distribution. It will then generate a P-value, and the definition of the P-value is 'It is the probability of getting your sample results, including results that are more extreme, given that the null hypothesis is true'. If our P-value exceeds the limit we have set ourselves to say this event is beyond random chance, then we reject the null hypothesis.

The simple answer is that our P-value will tell us if we have sufficient evidence to reject or fail to reject the null hypothesis.

The above theory was discussed to give you a deeper understanding of the methods used for One-Way and GLM ANOVA methods used within the classic menus. The Assistant uses something called Welch's method which does not use the F-test. The advantage of Welch's method is that it does not require the groups to have equal variances.

Let's do some examples and see One-Way ANOVA in action.

8.3.   One Way ANOVA

One Way ANOVA test	
Function	Tests whether the population means of three or more levels of a single predictor differ given a sample of data from each population.
Sample Size	When there are up to 9 levels at least 15 data points are required at each level for normality, of the population that the sample is drawn from, not to be an issue. 20 samples are required when there are 10 or more levels. More samples may be required to obtain a reasonable power (<80%) depending on the minimum difference you wish to detect.
Data type & Format	The response data is randomly selected continuous data which should be time ordered from uni-modal distributions.
Considerations	The process must be stable. Unlike the classic method the method used within the Assistant does not require that the groups have equal variances.

Example 8.3.1 Material Breaking Strengths

Zee is checking the breaking strength of 5 different materials in a standardised test. Zee does around 25 tests on each of his samples and reports the breaking strengths in time order. Can you help Zee establish if any of the materials have different breaking strengths? Can the materials be categorised into groups? For the Power and sample size calculation Zee feels 4 is the minimum difference that he would wish to detect between groups.

We have Zee's sample data recorded in time order in spreadsheet 08 ANOVA.xlsx in the worksheet called 'Materials'.

Material_A	Material_B	Material_C	Material_D	Material_E
68.68	67.15	77.06	79.12	69.88
67.25	66	74.86	82.72	76.16
63.63	73.19	70.9	86.82	68.2
68.54	75.67	74.31	86.99	71.98
72.22	66.37	76.2	77.89	67.15
63.38	63.87	77.29	84.57	69.3

1.   Transfer the data into Minitab.
2.   Click *Assistant<<Hypothesis Tests*
3.   Click on the **One-Way ANOVA** box within the **Compare more than 2 Samples** group.
4.   The test menu opens. We have to tell Minitab how our data is arranged. The X data for the 5 levels is in 5 columns with the level title at the top of each column. This is traditionally called 'Unstacked Data'. Ensure 'Y data for each X value are in separate columns' is selected. The other

How are your data arranged in the worksheet?

Y data for each X value are in separate columns

Y data columns:

'Material_A'-'Material_E'

format is stacked data where there would be only two columns. The level title would be in one column and the response data in the other column.

5. Select the 5 columns of data, Material_A to Material_E as the Y data columns.

6. At the bottom of the menu, we tell Minitab the minimum difference between groups that has implications for us. Enter '4'.

7. Click OK to run the test.

The Assistant produces a 4 page report that is within the Output Pane. Scroll down to see all 4 pages and if necessary resize the Output Pane to be able to see a single full page of the report at a time. The 4 pages that are produced for a One-Way ANOVA Test are the Summary Report, Diagnostic Report, Power Report and the Report Card.

If you navigate away from this report, you can always click on the relevant One-Way ANOVA command, in the Navigator, to return to it.

Please navigate to the Summary Report.

In the top left corner we get the answer to our Investigation Statement 'Do the means differ?' and the answer is given as 'Yes'.

We see that we have a P-value of <0.001. As this is below our Significance level of 0.05, we have strong evidence to reject the null.

Below that we see the Means Comparison Chart. We are told that 'Red intervals that do not overlap differ'. This means that if an interval is red it is different to at least one other interval. In this case, it's not that much of a problem that they are all red as it is relatively easy to evaluate how you would split the groups using the comparison chart.

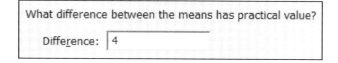

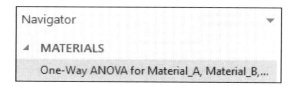

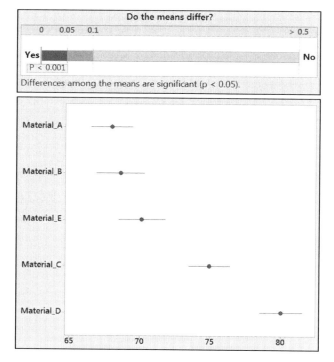

To help us understand the structure of the groups, we have the Grouping Information Table (GIT) on the top left. This tells us that A, B & E are different to C & D. Material C is in its own group as is material D.

		Which means differ?
#	Sample	Differs from
1	Material_A	4 5
2	Material_B	4 5
3	Material_E	4 5
4	Material_C	1 2 3 5
5	Material_D	1 2 3 4

To visualise the groups, I have put rings surrounding the materials that can be considered within the same group on the means comparison chart.

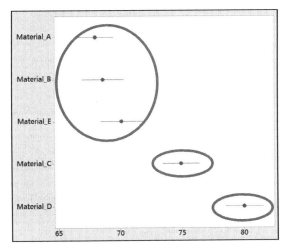

The Diagnostic Report contains histograms and SPC charts so that we can evaluate trends in time-ordered data, look for unusual data points and also look for bimodal distributions.

The SPC chart for Material C looks unusual, and I would personally make a note to check the results from Material C again. Minitab does not give us any warnings about the data.

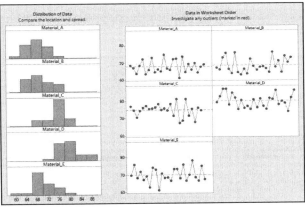

On the Power Report, we are told that we had a Power of somewhere between 73.98% to 85.66% in this test. This figure is slightly low but the test managed to detect a difference.

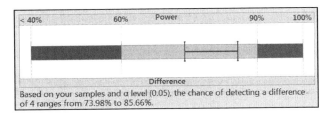

Finally, on the Report Card, we are given a summary on the validity of our test. We are told

1)   That there were no unusual data points that could make our test results unreliable.

2)   The sample size was sufficient to detect a difference between means.

3)   Normality was not an issue as we had a sample size of at least 15 within the groups.

4)

For information, we are told that the test within the Assistant does not require the data groups to have equal variances.

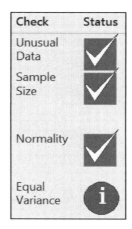

Check	Status
Unusual Data	✓
Sample Size	✓
Normality	✓
Equal Variance	i

8.4.   Standard Deviation Test

Standard Deviation test	
Function	Tests whether the population StDevs of three or more levels of a single predictor differ given a sample of data from each population.
Sample Size	20 samples are required in each group for non-normality not to be an issue.
Data type & Format	Randomly selected continuous data which should be time ordered from uni-modal distributions.
Considerations	The process must be stable. Power is not reported within this procedure.

Example 8.4.1 Material Breaking Strengths

Zee has established which of his materials belong in groups when it comes to the mean breaking strength. He then decides that he would like to know if any of the materials have different variances of breaking strengths. Help Zee evaluate his data and establish if any of the populations have differing variances?

We are using the same sample data recorded in the worksheet called 'Materials', as used in the previous example.

1.   Transfer the data into Minitab, if it is not there already.

2.   Click *Assistant<<Hypothesis Tests*

3.   Click on the *Standard Deviations Test* box within the **Compare more than 2 Samples** group.

4.   The test menu opens. We have to tell Minitab how our data is arranged. Ensure 'Y data for each X value are in separate columns' is selected.

How are your data arranged in the worksheet?

Y data for each X value are in separate columns

Y data columns:

'Material_A'-'Material_E'

5. Select the 5 columns of data, Material_A to Material_E.

6. This test does not provide a Power calculation, so we do not enter the difference we are interested in being able to detect.

7. Click OK to run the test.

The Assistant produces a 4 page report in the Output Pane. An additional command is added to the Navigator for this Standard Deviation Test.

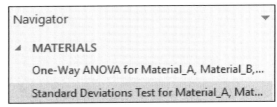

Please navigate to the Summary Report.
In the top left corner, we are told that our standard deviations do not differ. This means that we must accept our null hypothesis that there are no pairs of groups that have a differing standard deviation.

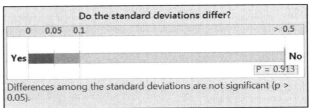

In the Standard Deviations Comparison Chart, we are told that 'Blue indicates no differences'.

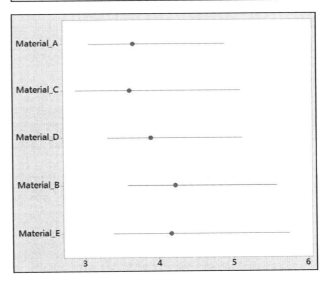

And the Grouping Information Table (GIT) tells us that no differences have been identified.

The Diagnostic Report is identical to that shown in the previous example. The graphs and charts do not display any unusual patterns or data points.

	Which standard deviations differ?	
#	Sample	Differs from
1	Material_A	
2	Material_C	
3	Material_D	None Identified
4	Material_B	
5	Material_E	

There is a table of data within the Descriptive Statistics Report that we may find useful. And the Report Card reports that there were no issues with our test that could lead to inaccuracies with the results. However, keep in mind we don't know the Power of this test.

Example 8.4.2 Khansini Space Probe

The Khansini probe recently gathered gravitational data on 10 of Saturn's moons. Firstly establish whether any of the moons are likely to have populations which have differing gravitational variances? Then establish if the moons can be grouped in terms of gravitational variance.

For the last part, establish whether any of the moons have different levels of mean gravity and whether they can be grouped in terms of their gravitational means. The minimum difference between groups that has implications for us is 0.3.

We will be using the sample data recorded in the worksheet called 'Saturn'. This data is recorded in time order.

1.   Transfer the data into Minitab.
2.   Click *Assistant<<Hypothesis Tests*
3.   Click on the *Standard Deviations Test* box within the **Compare more than 2 Samples** group.
4.   The test menu opens. We have to tell Minitab how our data is arranged. Ensure 'Y data for each X value are in separate columns' is selected.
5.   Select the 10 columns of gravitational data from columns Rhea to Albiorix.
6.   Click OK to run the test.

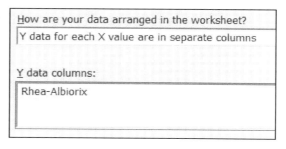

On the top left corner of the Summary Report, we are told that our standard deviations differ. This means that we must accept the alternate hypothesis that there is at least one pair of groups that have a differing standard deviation. We can examine which moons are different on the remainder of the Summary Report.

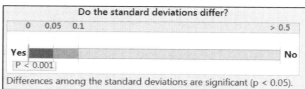

The best way to look at the group structure is to use the Grouping Information Table to establish the groups and then display the different groups on the Comparison Chart.

Sitting in the middle, we have Kiviuq and Skathi. I have called them A on the Comparison Chart. We cannot say that either of them differs from any of the other moons.

Then we have Hyperion; it only differs from Albiorix, Titan and Pheobe. On the Comparison Chart, we would say that B differs from E.

Paaliaq cannot be said to differ from Hyperion, Kiviuq or Sakthi, but it does differ from everything else. On the Comparison Chart C differs from D & E.

Sometimes we get caught in a paradox if we start making inferences e.g. If D& E don't differ why does B differ from E but not D. The way to think about it is to use pair-wise comparisons only. For example, we have sufficient evidence to say that B is different to E. We don't have adequate evidence to say that B is different to D. Similarly, we don't have sufficient evidence to say that D is different to E.

The Diagnostic Report does not highlight any unusual data. And the Report Card does not give us any warnings that our results may be inaccurate.

#	Sample	Which standard deviations differ? Differs from
1	Paaliaq	5 6 7 8 9 10
2	Hyperion	7 8 9
3	Kiviuq	
4	Skathi	
5	Rhea	1
6	Ijiraq	1
7	Albiorix	1 2
8	Titan	1 2
9	Phoebe	1 2
10	Iapetus	1

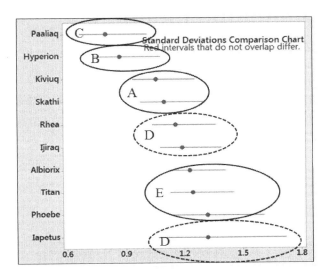

We will now use the One-Way ANOVA procedure to check if any of the planets have different mean levels of gravity.

7.   Click **Assistant<<Hypothesis Tests**

8.   Click on the **One-Way ANOVA** box within the **Compare more than 2 Samples** group.

9.   The test menu opens. We have to tell Minitab how our data is arranged. Ensure 'Y data for each X value are in separate columns' is selected.

10.   Select the 10 columns of gravitational data from columns Rhea to Albiorix.

How are your data arranged in the worksheet?

Y data for each X value are in separate columns

Y data columns:

Rhea-Albiorix

11. At the bottom of the menu, we tell Minitab the minimum difference between groups that has implications for us. Enter '0.3'.

12. Click OK to run the test.

Difference: | .3

Please navigate to the Summary Report.

On the top left of the Summary Report, we are told that the 'means differ' which tells us that at least two of the planets have differing population means of gravitational force.

Do the means differ?

| 0 | 0.05 | 0.1 | | > 0.5 |

Yes ▮▮▮ No
P < 0.001

Differences among the means are significant (p < 0.05).

The grouping for means are very different from standard deviations. Before we had Kiviuq and Skathi which could not be differentiated from any other group but this time we have Titan and Phoebe. I call this group A on the Means Comparison Chart.

		Which means differ?
#	**Sample**	**Differs from**
1	Paaliaq	2 5 6 7 8 9 10
2	Kiviuq	1 10
3	Titan	
4	Phoebe	
5	Skathi	1
6	Albiorix	1
7	Rhea	1
8	Ijiraq	1
9	Iapetus	1
10	Hyperion	1 2

Kiviuq is only different to both Paaliaq and Hyperion. Paaliaq is different from every other group apart from Group A. Group D is only different to C.

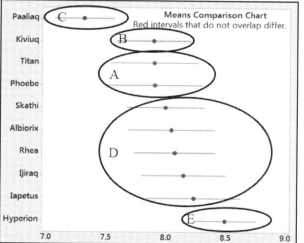

The Diagnostic Report does not show any unusual data points.

The Power Report shows that the Power that we had to actually spot a difference was very low. However, the test found a difference, so we don't need to worry about the low Power.

What is the chance of detecting a difference of 0.3?

| < 40% | 60% | Power | 90% | 100% |

Difference

Based on your samples and α level (0.05), the chance of detecting a difference of 0.3 ranges from 10.41% to 21.11%.

The Report Card gives us the all-clear.

This completes the section on One-way-ANOVA and the Standard Deviations Test. Both of which will prove to be very useful tools. In the next section is one of my favourite tools and it is called the ANOVA General Linear Model. Unfortunately, they have not put it into the Assistant yet so we have to learn it using the traditional menu's.

8.5 ANOVA General Linear Model

In the last section, we saw One-Way ANOVA in action. We noticed that if we had one predictor variable with fixed levels against a continuous response variable, we could use One Way ANOVA to establish if there was a difference in at least one pair of the levels. We also used the Grouping Information tables to group the levels of the predictor variables. The General Linear Model (GLM) gives us much more functionality and allows us to explore whether the difference between levels of multiple predictor variables are significant. The GLM can do much more but it only makes sense to look at the more common uses in this volume. As far as we are concerned, the GLM can do pretty much everything the Balanced ANOVA and Two Way ANOVA procedures can do.
Two guys who work in the same office as me, Mr Steve Griffiths and Mr Frank Gleeson, insisted that I put a zombie example into the book, you have them to thank for this example that I am going to use to explain GLM

In this example, we are going to be looking at the data gathered on a zombie survival horror game. The response is 'Survivability' as a percentage and this is defined as the number of gamers that manage to survive the first 10 levels of The Strolling Dead survival horror game. Let's say that I manage to keep all the variables that affect Survivability constant and only vary Skill Level and I get the results shown in the Individual Value Plot (IVP) shown. There are 9 results at each level of Skill Level. The chart appears to indicate that as you develop from Newb to Competent to Expert your chances of surviving the first 10 levels increases. I say 'appears' as we do not know if the populations are different or we see this variation due to random sampling. We need to conduct a One-Way ANOVA to confirm our hypothesis.

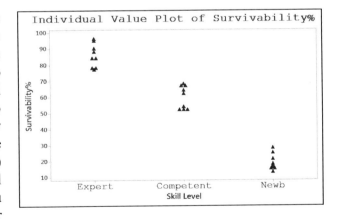

Again, if I keep all factors that could affect Survivability constant but this time change the players' weapon of choice, we will get the IVP shown. This time it appears going from knife to a sword to a gun will increase Survivability%. To know if the populations are really different, I would again use One-Way ANOVA.

Let's say that there are only two factors that affect Survivability in this game, and they are Skill Level and Weapon. I arrange play testing and I collect data for these factors together. The selection of data shown is every combination of the factors. As there are 3 levels of each factor we get 9 runs. However, when I arranged the play testing, I ran 3 repeats of every combination making 27 runs in total.

The reason for collecting the data for both factors together might be due to efficiency in terms of time, but there is a better reason and it is called 'Interaction'. We have seen that for each factor on its own, changing the level gives a reasonably straight line result in terms of Survivability. Yet there is a chance that when two factors work together, at a particular level, they produce a spark in the response variable giving an unexpected increase. This is called an Interaction and you can't find it when you are working with only one variable. Interactions can also work the other way and can cause a sharp decrease in the response. We will look at interaction plots and how to spot if interactions are significant a bit later.

Before we go into the GLM, we need to understand some of the terms that are used.

We have two factors that we think are predictors for Survivability; these are Skill Level and Weapon. We must decide if our factors are Fixed or Random because the calculation of effects is handled differently for both. This means our conclusions may be incorrect if we do not specify Fixed and Random Factors correctly when setting up the procedure.

A factor is Fixed when data has been collected from all the levels of interest in the study. The results obtained when using Fixed factors only apply to the levels within the study.

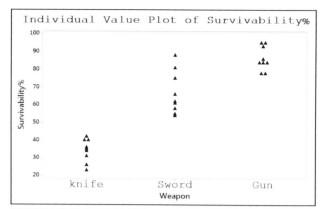

Weapon	Skill Level	Survivability%
knife	Expert	68
Sword	Expert	94
Gun	Expert	91
knife	Competent	52
Sword	Competent	61
Gun	Competent	82
knife	Newb	28
Sword	Newb	37
Gun	Newb	53

A factor is Random if there is a range of possible levels, but only a random sample of levels is included in the data. The results can then be applied to all possible levels, even those not included in the study.

We also need to know that having Fixed and Random factors will change what we are investigating with the GLM.

If you have Fixed factors, then you will be investigating how changes in the mean level of the factors will affect levels within the response.

However, if you have Random factors, they will tell you whether the variance within the factors is significant to variance within the response.

Now, let's go back to our zombie game and decide what type of factors we have. Weapon is a Fixed factor, there are other weapons in the game but we used data from the 3 that interested us. Also, we know that the results of the GLM will only apply to knife, sword and gun. For similar reasons Skill Level is also a Fixed factor.

Now let's pretend we had 'Player Age' as a factor and we randomly selected levels of 19, 26 & 42 to use in the study. We have not included other player ages, but we will want to apply what we have learnt to ages that have not been included, like say 30. This means that Player Age would be a Random factor. Also, if we used Player Age as a Random Factor, then we would find out whether the variation in player age was significant to the variation in Survivability when we ran the GLM. Minitab advises that if you have at least one Random Factor in your study, you use the Mixed Effects Model rather than the General Linear Model. The Mixed Effects Model is covered in the Black Belt Edition.

You also get Covariates within a GLM, but in order to keep things simple while you get to grips with GLM, we are only going to consider Fixed factors. Use of the GLM with Covariates is covered in the Black Belt Edition.

There's a couple of other bits of terminology that are worth learning at this time. The design of GLM that we have employed is called a 'Crossed' design; the other option is 'Nested'. These terms are much easier to explain in diagrams. A Crossed design is where all combinations of factors have at least one experimental run. Not all combinations of factors are run in a Nested design.

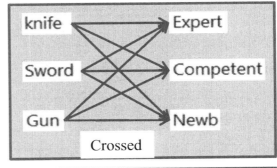

Crossed

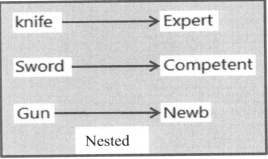

Nested

Take a look at the diagrams, and you can see how easily the terms are explained in a diagram.

In practice, the nested design is rarely used, but it is experimental conditions that dictate whether you use a crossed or nested design.

With respect to the whole design rather than factors, another couple of terms that are worth learning are 'Balanced' and 'Unbalanced'. A balanced design contains the same number of runs for each combination of terms. In the Zombie Game example, we have 3 runs for every combination of factors. Therefore, our design is balanced.

To validate our model, we must check something called 'Residuals'. In order to explain how we generate the Residuals and explain what we check I will use the Zombie Game example

Weapon	Skill Level	Survivability%
knife	Expert	68
Sword	Expert	94
Gun	Expert	91
knife	Competent	52
Sword	Competent	61
Gun	Competent	82
knife	Newb	28
Sword	Newb	37
Gun	Newb	53

Finally, there are several Graphs which provide helpful analysis before we go into the GLM. We will learn how to generate these and how we interpret them using the example. The graphs are

    1) Main Effects Plot
    2) Interaction Plot
    3) Multi-Vari Chart

The Main Effects Plot will show us the isolated effects of the factors and their levels. But it won't tell us if they are significant.
The Interaction Plot will show us if interactions are present but won't tell us if they are significant.
The Multi-Vari Chart delivers the data so we can see both main effects and interactions, but again we don't know if anything is significant.
And as a review, 'significant' means beyond what we would expect to see just from chance.

8.6 General Linear Model Examples

General Linear Model	
Function	It is used to build a model of significant terms that have an effect on a response variable.
Sample Size	There is no Power and Sample size procedure associated with the GLM. However, there must be sufficient data across the factors for Minitab to solve the necessary simultaneous equations.
Data type & Format	The response must be a continuous variable. Factors can use categorical, discrete numeric or continuous data, although continuous factors are not covered here. Factors for the GLM should only be Fixed Factors. Minitab recommends the Mixed Effects Model when there is at least one Random Factor.
Considerations	The design can be Crossed or Nested, Balanced or Unbalanced. I recommend graphical examination of the data prior to analysis. The model is validated using Residuals.

Example 8.6.1 The Strolling Dead

A software house wants to examine the Survivability of the first 10 levels of their new survival horror game, The Strolling Dead. They recognise that two factors are essential to model, Skill Level of Player and the Weapon used. They have collected the data and want you to firstly present conclusions from the Main Effects & Interaction Plots and also a Multi-Vari Chart. They then want you to use the GLM procedure to tell them which factors and interactions are significant to the response, Survivability.

The first part of the question requires us to produce the Main Effects plot and then interaction plots. We will start with the Main Effects plot, which shows us how the mean for each level of the factor varies. So that our plots look the same, we are first going to set the order of appearance of the categorical levels on the X-axis. We covered how to do this in chapter 4 section 8.

1. Transfer all the data from Worksheet 'Zombie' into a new Minitab Project file.
2. Place the active cursor in the Weapon column, C1, anywhere you wish.
3. Right-click and select **Column Properties<<Value Order.**
4. Using the radio buttons at the top of the menu select 'Order of occurrence in worksheet'.
5. Click OK.
6. Repeat steps 2 to 5 for the Skill Level column, C2.
7. Click **Stat<<ANOVA<<Main Effects Plot**
8. The graph menu opens. Under Response, enter 'Survivability%' and under Factors enter 'Weapon' and 'Skill Level'.
9. Click OK to produce the Main Effects Plot.

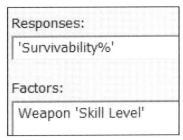

The Main Effects plot is useful as it isolates what each of the factors is doing to Survivability%. Within the plot each factor has its own panel. The data points represent the mean value for each level of the factors. The Y-axis represents our continuous response, Survivability%. You will notice that the Y-axis scale is common to both factors. As the 3 data points for Skill Level have a greater range on the Y-axis they are having a greater effect on the response.

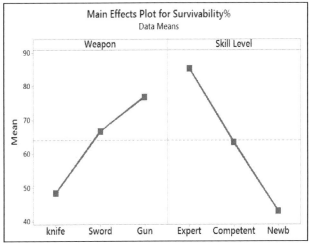

The dashed horizontal line represents the 'Observed Mean' or the mean of all the Survivability% data. For the GLM settings we will be using, we will be looking for levels that are significantly different from the Observed Mean.

We could also say that in terms of the factor 'Weapon' the level 'Sword' is not very different from the observed mean.

And we could make similar conclusions about the factor 'Skill Level'. We see the 'Competent' level is right on the Observed mean.

There could be levels of both Skill level & Weapon that are different to the Observed Mean, but as we have no P-values, we cannot say that theses levels are significant.

In summary, looking at the main effects plot, my conclusions would be
1) There are levels of both Skill level & Weapon that are close to the Observed Mean and different to it.

2) Changes in Skill Level appear to have a slightly greater effect on the response.

We will now produce the Interactions plot. This tells us if any combination of our factors or levels combines to produce a spark to change the response more (or less) than we otherwise would have expected.

10. Click *Stat<<ANOVA<<Interaction Plot*

11. The graph menu opens. Under Response, enter 'Survivability%' and under Factors enter 'Weapon' and 'Skill Level'. The order that we enter the factors does not really matter. Also, we don't need to see the full interaction matrix.

12. Click OK to produce the Interactions Plot.

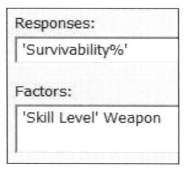

Interpretation of the Interactions Plot is straightforward. If the lines are parallel, then there will probably not be any interactions present. If the lines are not parallel, then there is probably an interaction present. The lines do not necessarily have to cross.

My interpretation of this plot would be that there may well be statistically significant interactions present. The interaction is between Sword and Expert. With the data presented here, if you are at Expert level, your Survivability% is almost as high as if you had a gun. This is not true of the other two skill levels.

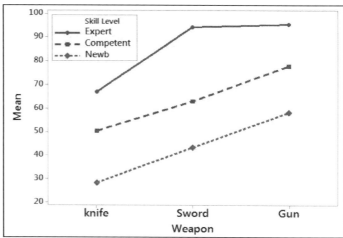

Finally, we have the Multi-Vari Chart. I think of this one as a cross between the Main Effects Plot and Interaction Chart. Drawing and interpretation of Multi-Vari charts is a skill in itself, and we will develop it more in the next example.

13. Click **Stat<<Quality Tools<<Multi-Vari Chart.**

14. The graph menu opens. Under Response enter 'Survivability%' and enter 'Skill Level' as the first Factor and enter 'Weapon' as the second. It does not really matter when there are two factors.

15. Click on the **Options** button and add the display for 'Means for Factor 1'. Click OK to produce the Multi-Vari Chart.

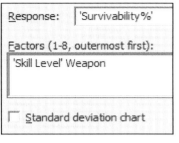

The Multi-Vari chart has been updated recently. There is more separation of the factors within panes, and so it has become easier to interpret, in my opinion.

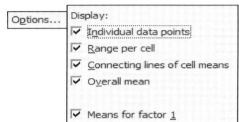

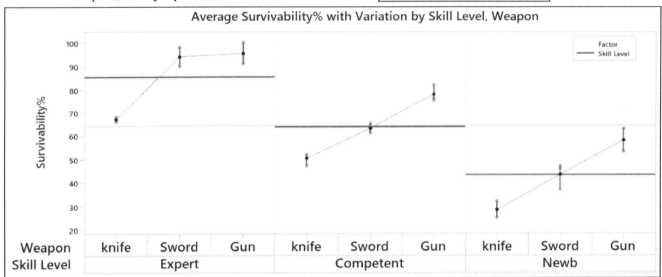

Using the new Multi-Vari Chart, it is easy to see the change in Skill Level across the panes and the change in Weapon within the panes.

Using the Options menu, we added the red lines which show the average response value for each level of Factor 1, Skill level.

And thanks to these red lines the Sword*Expert interaction can be spotted relatively easily, I still don't know if it is significant but I know to look out for it within the results of the GLM.

We have now produced the required graphs and have attempted to interpret how the factors interact and how they affect the response. We think both the factors are significant and there may be an interaction present. Significant means that the response of at least one of the levels is different from the observed mean.

We can only find out if our guesses are correct and statistically significant by conducting the ANOVA GLM procedure. We then need to validate the results by checking residuals.

16. Click **Stat<<ANOVA<<General Linear Model<<Fit General Linear Model**

17. The GLM menu opens. Under Response enter 'Survivability%' and under Factors enter 'Weapon' and 'Skill Level'.

18. To enter the Interaction, click the **Model** button. The Model menu will open. In the top left, you will see our factors. Hold down the **Ctrl** key and click on the factors to highlight them both. If you did this correctly the **Add** button in the top right will become enabled. Left-click on the **Add** button to include the interaction term into the model.

Note: that interactions are listed as Factor1*Factor2 for a 2 way interaction. Higher-order interactions are possible when there are more than 2 factors in the study.

19. Click OK and OK again to execute the procedure.

Responses:
'Survivability%'

Factors:
'Skill Level' Weapon

Factors and covariates:
'Skill Level'
Weapon

Factors and covariates:
'Skill Level'
Weapon

Terms in the model:
'Skill Level'
Weapon
'Skill Level'*Weapon

Please navigate to the Output Pane for this Command.

The Factor Coding means that we are comparing levels to the observed mean; other Coding methods are demonstrated in the Black Belt Edition.

Under the **Factor Information** section, we are given vital attributes of our two factors.

Under the **Analysis of Variance** section, you will find the terms that we wish to model along with their P-value. We can answer the questions posed within this example using the information given here.

For our Fixed Factors, a P-value below our significance level tells us that the response of at least one of the levels is different to the observed mean.

Factor Information

Factor	Type	Levels	Values
Skill Level	Fixed	3	Expert, Competent, Newb
Weapon	Fixed	3	knife, Sword, Gun

Analysis of Variance

Source	DF	Adj SS	Adj MS	F-Value	P-Value
Skill Level	2	8024.9	4012.44	274.27	0.000
Weapon	2	3736.9	1868.44	127.72	0.000
Skill Level*Weapon	4	239.6	59.89	4.09	0.016
Error	18	263.3	14.63		
Total	26	12264.7			

For our Interaction term, a P-value below our significance level tells us that combinations of certain factors have different effects.

We now know that there will be some difference in Survivability% between the different levels within Weapon. The same can be said for Skill Level.

We also know that the interaction is significant, so if we want to calculate Survivability%, we will have to account for the interaction as well as the separate factors.

Under **Model Summary,** we are told how well our model fits the data. There are four metrics here.

Model Summary			
S	R-sq	R-sq(adj)	R-sq(pred)
3.82487	97.85%	96.90%	95.17%

Think of S as a measure of error between the fitted line and your data. The lower the S, the better.

R-sq is the amount of variation in the response explained by the predictors. The issue is that for larger models, the more terms you add the better value you will get. Although, this may appear to be a fair compromise you may be encouraged to add non-significant terms into your model, which is not a good thing.

R-sq(adj) is similar to R-sq, but it is **adjusted** for the number of predictors in the model. This encourages you not to keep adding non-significant terms.

R-sq(pred) gives us a measure of how well our model will fit new data points. As it is a measure of prediction for new points and it is useful for comparing different models.

Under **Coefficients,** we are given more details regarding the levels within our Factors. The first thing that we need to look at is our VIF or Value Inflation Factors. They should be less than 5. They are a measure of stability in our model. If they are above 5 we need to start over as our model will not be stable. You can think of the VIFs as a measure of the health of the simultaneous equations used in forming the model.

You will have noticed that not all the levels for each factor are shown, there is one missing for each. For the next part of the explanation it would be helpful to have the full table.

Coefficients					
Term	Coef	SE Coef	T-Value	P-Value	VIF
Constant	64.111	0.736	87.10	0.000	
Skill Level					
Expert	21.33	1.04	20.49	0.000	1.33
Competent	-0.44	1.04	-0.43	0.674	1.33
Weapon					
knife	-15.56	1.04	-14.94	0.000	1.33
Sword	2.67	1.04	2.56	0.020	1.33
Skill Level*Weapon					
Expert knife	-2.89	1.47	-1.96	0.065	1.78
Expert Sword	5.89	1.47	4.00	0.001	1.78
Competent knife	2.22	1.47	1.51	0.149	1.78
Competent Sword	-3.33	1.47	-2.26	0.036	1.78

Full set of coefficients ▼

20. Press Ctrl+E, for Edit Last or Click *Stat<<ANOVA<<General Linear Model<< Fit General Linear Model* to open the GLM root menu.

21. Click on the *Results* button.

22. Then select 'Full set of coefficients' from the drop-down menu next to coefficients.

23. Then Click OK until the test is executed. Then find the Full Coefficients. I'm not showing the full table on this occasion.

Coefficients					
Term	Coef	SE Coef	T-Value	P-Value	VIF
Constant	64.111	0.736	87.10	0.000	
Skill Level					
Expert	21.33	1.04	20.49	0.000	1.33
Competent	-0.44	1.04	-0.43	0.674	1.33
Newb	-20.89	1.04	-20.07	0.000	*
Weapon					
knife	-15.56	1.04	-14.94	0.000	1.33
Sword	2.67	1.04	2.56	0.020	1.33
Gun	12.89	1.04	12.38	0.000	*
Skill Level*Weapon					
Expert knife	-2.89	1.47	-1.96	0.065	1.78

The P-values for the levels of the factors now tell us if the level was significant compared to the observed mean. If you think back, or even look back, at the main effects plot, you will recall that the Competent level was dead on the observed mean level. The P-value, like the Main Effects plot, is telling us that this level of the factor is not significant compared to the observed mean.

After Coefficients, we arrive at the **Regression Equation**. In this example, we have been lucky and we have not needed to reduce or change our model and this means that we can use the regression equation to predict values of survivability. However, please bear in mind that we have not validated our model by checking Residuals at this point. I have changed the layout of the regression equation to improve clarity. Let's say we want to calculate Survivability% for an Expert using a Sword. Any algebraic term containing the level Sword or Expert would become a 1, and everything else would be zero. The same applies to the interaction terms but the only term to be non-zero would be Sword*Expert (1x1=1) every other combination would be zero, for example, Sword*Newb (1*0=0). The equation for an Expert using a Sword becomes Survivability%=64.111+2.67+21.33+5.89 = 94.001% .

If you go to your Multi-vari chart and click on the point corresponding to an Expert using a sword you will see that the actual mean of the data was 94%, which is excellent considering I didn't set it up. The actual error of our regression equation will be higher than this as indicated by our R-sq(pred)=95.17%.

Survivability% = 64.111

- 15.56 Weapon_knife

+ 2.67 Weapon_Sword

+ 12.89 Weapon_Gun

+ 21.33 Skill Level_Expert

- 0.44 Skill Level_Competent

- 20.89 Skill Level_Newb

- 2.89 Weapon*Skill Level_knife Expert

+ 2.22 Weapon*Skill Level_knife Competent

+ 0.67 Weapon*Skill Level_knife Newb

+ 5.89 Weapon*Skill Level_Sword Expert

- 3.33 Weapon*Skill Level_Sword Competent

- 2.56 Weapon*Skill Level_Sword Newb

- 3.00 Weapon*Skill Level_Gun Expert

+ 1.11 Weapon*Skill Level_Gun Competent

+ 1.89 Weapon*Skill Level_Gun Newb

Fits and Diagnostics for Unusual Observations

Obs	Survivability%	Fit	Resid	Std Resid
8	37.00	43.33	-6.33	-2.03 R

Finally, we are told that one of our points was deemed to be unusual. Observation 8 had a value of 37 and the prediction equation thought it should have been 43.33. We may want to refer back to our data collection and check if something unusual occurred. However, on this occasion, there is only one unusual point and it is not too far out so no action is required.

Did you notice that '**Actual Value - Fit = Resid**'? 'Resid' is short for Residual, and this is important as we use Residuals to validate our model.

In this section, we are going to find out how to form the full set of Residuals and the four graphs of the Residuals that we need to examine to validate our model.

24. Press Ctrl+E, for Edit Last or Click *Stat<<ANOVA<<General Linear Model <<Fit General Linear Model* to open the GLM root menu.

25. Click on the *Graphs* button.

26. Under Residual Plots click the radio button for 'Four in One'. This will generate our Residual Four in One plot, which is something you will use quite often as you advance in Minitab. Click OK to step back to the GLM root menu.

27. Click on the *Storage* button.

28. Select the tick boxes for 'Fits' and 'Residuals'. This action will calculate the Fits and store them in the current Worksheet. Remember 'Fits' means the data points as calculated by the Regression Equation. It will also store the Residuals in the same place where **Actual Value-Fit = Residual.**

29. Click OK and OK again to execute the procedure.

Please go to the Data Pane. You will see that Minitab has stored our Fits and Residuals in Column C4 & C5, respectively. The Fits repeat every 9 points as they are based on the repeating combination of the levels of the Factors. The Residuals should not repeat in the same way because the values of the response don't repeat.

Please navigate to the Residuals Four-in-One Plot. As the name suggests, the Four-in-One Plot is a graph made up of 4 subplots of Residuals. In our example, we had 27 separate data points which each generate a residual, even though some of the residuals share the same value. The 27 data points are then plotted on the four plots. To validate our GLM the residuals must comply with the following rules

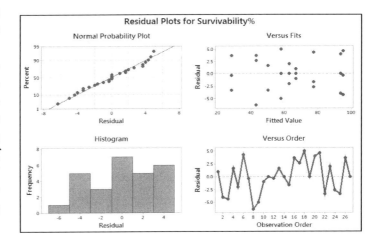

Residuals plots

○ Individual plots

☐ Histogram of residuals

☐ Normal probability plot of residuals

☐ Residuals versus fits

☐ Residuals versus order

● Four in one

☑ **Fits**

☑ **Residuals**

✦	C1-T	C2-T	C3	C4	C5
	Weapon	Skill Level	Survivability%	FITS	Res
1	knife	Expert	68	67.0000	1.00000
2	Sword	Expert	90	94.0000	-4.00000
3	Gun	Expert	91	95.3333	-4.33333
4	knife	Competent	52	50.3333	1.66667
5	Sword	Competent	61	63.0000	-2.00000
6	Gun	Competent	82	77.6667	4.33333
7	knife	Newb	28	28.3333	-0.33333
8	Sword	Newb	37	43.3333	-6.33333
9	Gun	Newb	53	58.0000	-5.00000

- They must be close to being normally distributed
- They must not be extremely skewed.
- They must show roughly equal variance.
- If the variables have been recorded in time order, they must not show any patterns.

We will now breakdown the Four-in-One plot and have a look at each of the subplots in turn and check if our model complies. When we look at the Normal Probability Plot, we want our Residuals to be close to being normally distributed. They pass that test. When checking residuals, we should not be as strict as we are when we are checking primary data for normality. If we can cover the points with a fat pencil, then that is good enough

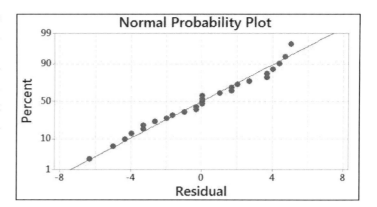

In the Histogram of Residuals, we want to see that the Residuals are not severely skewed. We can see a slightly skewed distribution but it is nothing to worry about.

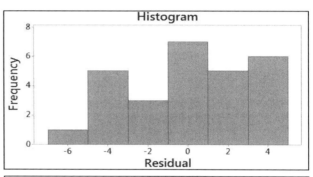

In the Versus Fits plot, we are looking for patterns and we are looking to see that residuals are equally spaced around the zero line. The Assistant within its Regression routines gives us some useful pointers on spotting patterns and what they mean.

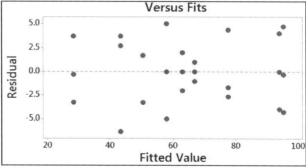

Clusters may indicate that a term is missing from the model, Strong curvature may indicate a higher-order term is missing.
Unequal variation would indicate a poorly fitting model.
Our Versus Fits plot does not show any issues.

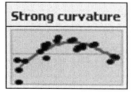

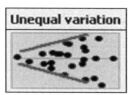

The Versus order plot is only applicable if the data was recorded in the order that it was taken but not if any kind of sorting has taken place. In this plot, we want to see a random pattern. If we were to see patterns such as two high points then two low points this would indicate a missing factor.

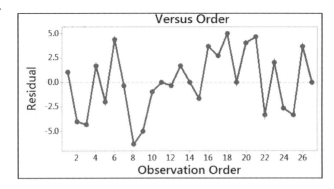

Example 8.6.2 Shift Pattern

Jules is doing a human factors study at his factory. He wants to find out if the percentage defect rate changes with factors relating to tiredness and where in the factory the teams are working. The factory works Monday to Friday and there are three shifts during each working day. The factory teams work a pattern where the Nightshift will move to Afternoons in their second week and then Mornings in their third week. In this way, each team will go around the pattern every three weeks. Jules collects 3 weeks worth of data so that each team has had a chance to work every shift. Jules does not want to cause ill-feeling between the shifts so he does not enter a factor for shift code.

The factors he takes into consideration are

Shift- This can be Morning, Afternoon or Night

Area- Preparation, Production or Packaging

Day- Monday, Tuesday, Wednesday, Thursday or Friday.

Before Jules conducts Analysis of Variance help him by creating a Multi-Vari Chart. Examine the chart, can you make any conclusions as to which factors may be significant to the defect rate?

Once you produced the Multi-Vari chart carry out a test to determine if any of the Factors and Interactions are significant? If the factors are significant, then establish which level of the factors are different from the observed mean. Can you make recommendations to say where Jules' improvement activities should be focused

Worksheet: Shift Pattern

Initially, we are going to look at the data using a Multi-Vari Chart.

1. Transfer all the data from Worksheet 'Shift Pattern' into a new Minitab Project file.

2. To produce the Multi-Vary Chart, click **Stat<<Quality Tools<< Multi-Vari Chart.**

3. Select Defect Rate % as the response. Select the factors in the order shown.

4. Click OK to produce the chart.

Day	Shift	Area	Defect Rate %
Monday	Morning	Prep	2.335
Monday	Morning	Prod	2.488
Monday	Morning	Pack	2.254
Monday	Afternoon	Prep	2.229
Monday	Afternoon	Prod	2.480
Monday	Afternoon	Pack	2.235

Response:	'Defect Rate %'

Factors (1-8, outermost first):

Day Shift Area

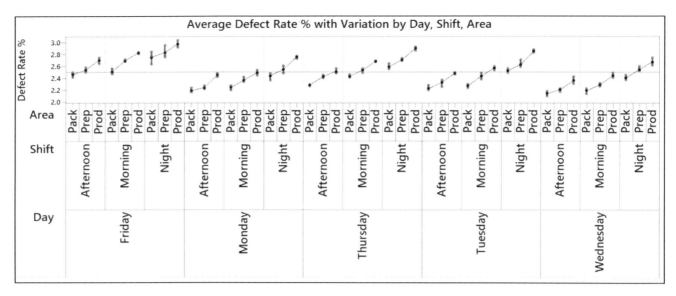

We could start to make conclusions about our data. However, we would be less likely to make mistakes if our data was ordered correctly. At present, the data is displayed in alphabetical order, which is the default for Minitab. However, we would prefer 'Day' to be shown in day-order. Also, we want 'Shift' to be ordered as Morning, Afternoon & Night and the flow through the factory is Preparation, Production and then Packaging.

We will correct the order of the data first and then look at the chart again.

5.   Navigate to the Data Pane and move the active cursor anywhere into column C1, which contains the 'Day' data.

6.   Right-click and select **Column Properties**<< **Value Order.** Note, it is the action of placing the active cursor that sets the value order for a particular column.

7.   The default is Alphabetical order, but we want to change this. Click on the radio button for 'Order of occurrence in worksheet'.

8.   Then click OK.

9.   Repeat this for the remaining factors but not the response column.

Note, we could also have used the option for 'User Specified Order' and made use of the predefined lists for 'Day'.

10. Produce the chart again by clicking **Stat**<<**Quality Tools**<< **Multi-Vari Chart.** Also, add the 'means for factor 1' via the options button. Then click OK.

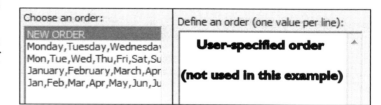

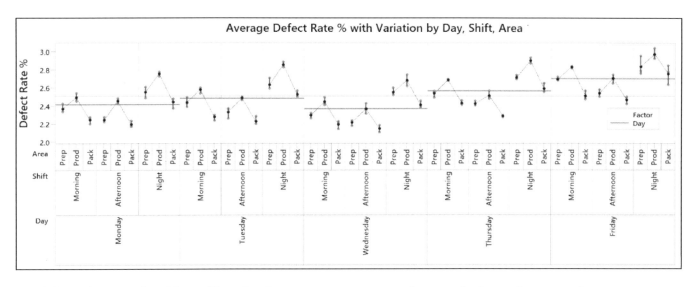

With less chance of making silly mistakes, we can start to make conclusions about our data.
- The defect rate is highest on a Friday and then Thursday. It is probably lowest on a Wednesday.
- The night shift in any particular area has the highest defect rate.
- The Production area has the highest defect rate then Preparation.

We will now use the GLM to establish which factors are significant and check if there are any interactions present

11. Click **Stat<<ANOVA<<General Linear Model<<Fit General Linear Model** to open the GLM root menu.

12. Under Response, enter 'Defect Rate %' and under Factors enter 'Day', 'Shift' and 'Area'.

13. Click on the **Model** button. Hold down the Ctrl key and highlight all three factors.

14. From the drop down menu for 'Interactions through order' select '3'. Then click on the **Add** button.

15. When you click the **Add** button the terms in the model will change as shown. We now have our factors in the model, two-way interactions and the single three-way interaction in the model.

16. Click OK and OK again to execute the model.

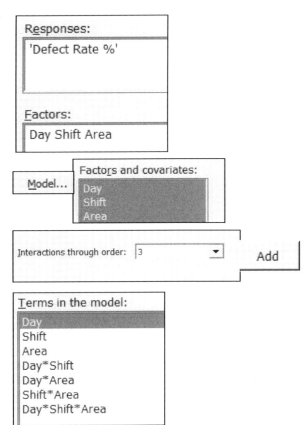

17. Go to the Output Pane for this command and find the Analysis of Variance table to establish which of the factors and interactions are significant. We see that none of the interactions are significant but the three main Factors are significant. We should modify our model to only include significant terms.

Analysis of Variance

Source	DF	Adj SS	Adj MS	F-Value	P-Value
Day	4	1.88095	0.47024	209.62	0.000
Shift	2	2.19759	1.09880	489.80	0.000
Area	2	1.65003	0.82502	367.76	0.000
Day*Shift	8	0.02636	0.00329	1.47	0.180
Day*Area	8	0.01015	0.00127	0.57	0.803
Shift*Area	4	0.01588	0.00397	1.77	0.142
Day*Shift*Area	16	0.03070	0.00192	0.86	0.621
Error	90	0.20190	0.00224		
Total	134	6.01357			

18. Click **Stat<<ANOVA <<General Linear Model <<Fit General Linear Model** to open the GLM root menu or press Ctrl+E.

19. Click on the **Model** button to go to the Model menu.

20. Click on the **Default** button The terms in the model should be reduced to the default terms.

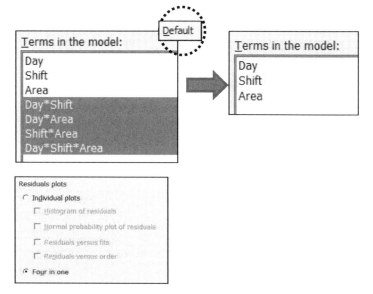

21. Click OK to return to the main GLM menu and then click on the **Graphs** button. Select the radio button for the four-in-one Residual plots. As we know we will not be modifying the model any further we should produce the residual plots at this point.

22. Click OK and OK again to execute the procedure.

23. In the Output Pane find the Analysis of Variance table. We see that only the main factors remain in the model as significant terms. We also have a Lack-of-Fit test appearing for our model. The null hypothesis for this test is that our data fits our model. With a P-value of 0.444, we do not have sufficient evidence to reject this model.

24. The model summary indicates that we have a good model with a large amount of the variation explained and the model can be used for making future predictions.

Analysis of Variance

Source	DF	Adj SS	Adj MS	F-Value	P-Value
Day	4	1.88095	0.47024	207.90	0.000
Shift	2	2.19759	1.09880	485.80	0.000
Area	2	1.65003	0.82502	364.76	0.000
Error	126	0.28499	0.00226		
Lack-of-Fit	36	0.08309	0.00231	1.03	0.444
Pure Error	90	0.20190	0.00224		
Total	134	6.01357			

Model Summary

S	R-sq	R-sq(adj)	R-sq(pred)
0.0475587	95.26%	94.96%	94.56%

25. We also need to check the table of Coefficients and ensure that the VIFs are below 5. It may be tempting to ignore this step but remember VIFs are a measure of the health of the simultaneous equations used to form the model.

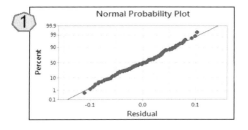

Coefficients					
Term	Coef	SE Coef	T-Value	P-Value	VIF
Constant	2.50503	0.00409	612.00	0.000	
Day					
Monday	-0.09044	0.00819	-11.05	0.000	1.60
Tuesday	-0.02262	0.00819	-2.76	0.007	1.60
Wednesday	-0.14030	0.00819	-17.14	0.000	1.60
Thursday	0.05889	0.00819	7.19	0.000	1.60
Shift					
Morning	-0.03863	0.00579	-6.67	0.000	1.33
Afternoon	-0.13332	0.00579	-23.03	0.000	1.33
Area					
Prep	-0.01547	0.00579	-2.67	0.009	1.33
Prod	0.14247	0.00579	24.61	0.000	1.33

The Lack-of-Fit test told us that our model fitted our data well, but we also need to check the residuals to validate the model before we proceed with the rest of the problem.

Navigate to the Residuals Four-in-One plot.
1- Residuals are normally distributed and will pass the 'fat pencil' test.
2- Histogram of residuals is not severely skewed.
3- Residuals are reasonably equidistant about the zero line. They don't show signs of clustering or forming a cone.
4- If the data was recorded in time order the residuals should look random and they do.

Our residuals fit the above criteria so we can be confident that we have a good model.

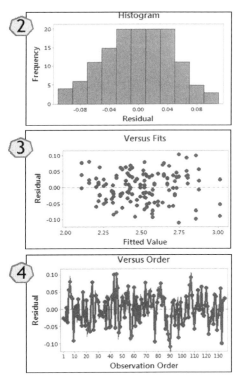

For the next part of the question, we have been asked if any of the levels differ from each other. Although not part of the solution I have produced the Main Effects plot showing the individual factor effects on the response. For Day, can Monday and Tuesday or Monday and Wednesday be considered to be part of the same group or are they in separate groups. With One-Way ANOVA, we would have asked Minitab to conduct pair-wise comparisons and produce a Grouping Information Table for us. The GLM can do something similar.

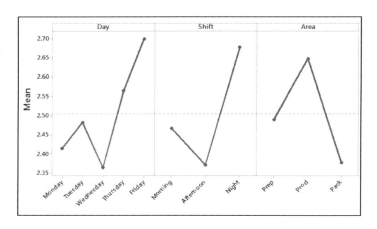

26. Click *Stat<<ANOVA <<General Linear Model <<Comparisons.*

27. Ensure the correct response column is selected, and the 'Type of Comparison' is set to **Pairwise**. We have the option of selecting the type of comparison method we are going to use; we will stick with the default Tukey method.

28. In order to select the factors that we will be comparing tick on each of the factors.

29. Click OK and locate the Grouping Information Tables (GITs) in the Output Pane.

| Response: | Defect Rate % |
| Type of comparison: | Pairwise |

Method

☑ Tukey   ☐ Bonferroni

☐ Fisher   ☐ Sidak

Choose terms for comparisons:

☑ Day
☑ Shift
☑ Area

It's pretty clear that the GITs are telling us that the levels of all of the factors should be treated individually. The GITs have also ordered the levels starting with the worst, in terms of defect rate%, at the top.

The last part of the question was to make recommendations for improvement. My advice would be to look at the Production area and establish why they are causing the most defects. I would also link tiredness into causes of defects as they are occurring towards the end of the week and mostly on night-shift. We might want an education program on how to manage night-shifts and a changing shift pattern for the shift personnel.

Day	N	Mean	Grouping			
Friday	27	2.69950	A			
Thursday	27	2.56392		B		
Tuesday	27	2.48241			C	
Monday	27	2.41459				D
Wednesday	27	2.36473					E

Means that do not share a letter are significantly different.

Shift	N	Mean	Grouping		
Night	45	2.67698	A		
Morning	45	2.46640		B	
Afternoon	45	2.37171			C

Area	N	Mean	Grouping		
Prod	45	2.64750	A		
Prep	45	2.48956		B	
Pack	45	2.37803			C

That wraps up the Green Belt level chapter on ANOVA. I wanted the GLM section to be an introduction into using the more complex classic menu's, and that becomes a lead into the more sophisticated techniques used in the Black Belt Edition. The Black Belt Edition covers alternate coding and shows how random factors and covariates are handled in ANOVA.

8.7 ANOVA Exercises

Exercise 8.7.1 One Way ANOVA

Evelee golf balls monitors the golf ball weights produced by its 5 moulding machines. From capability tests they know that they are well below the max weight of 45.93 grams. They have hired you as a consultant and want to know if any of the moulding machines are producing golf balls at different mean weights. They feel that smallest difference that they would want to be able to detect between machines is 0.05g.

Analyse the data in File 08 ANOVA.xlsx worksheet Ex 8.5.1 and answer the questions shown below. The data was collected randomly and is recorded in time order.

1)   Is there a difference in populations between the golf ball weights produced by any of the moulding machines?

2)   Can the machines be grouped ?

3)   Have the requirements of the test that you have used been met?

4)   What was the Power of the test when you want to detect a difference of 0.05?

5)   Are there any issues associated with this level of Power ?

6)   Does the Report Card generate any warnings?

Exercise 8.7.2 Conduct a StDev Test

This time at Evelee golf balls someone has the bright idea that it might also be a good idea to find out if any of the moulding machines are producing golf balls at different standard deviations.

Analyse the data in File 08 ANOVA.xlsx worksheet Ex 8.7.1 and answer the questions shown below. The data was collected randomly and is recorded in time order.

1)   Is there a difference in populations between the golf ball weights standard deviations produced by any of the moulding machines?

2)   Can the machines be grouped ?

3)   Have the requirements of the test that you have used been met?

4)   Does the Report Card generate any warnings?

Exercise 8.7.3 Use the ANOVA GLM

Compo has got a new toy. It's an injection molding machine for making phone cases. Compo loads the machine with plastic granules and then sets the temperature and pressure and the molding machine forms the phone cases.

As Compo is prone to dropping things he wants to ensure the strength of the cases is maximised. He sets up an experiment where he varies three factors, the grade of the plastic granules, temperature of the heater and the pressure used for the extrusion. In this experiment **Strength** is the response and the factors are called **Temp**, **Press** and **Material**. The levels for Temp and Press are set using a dial which has fixed settings. This makes all the factors fixed. In the experiments Temp has 3 levels; 100, 110 &115 degc. Press has 3 levels; 7, 10 and 13 psi and there are two types of plastic granules called A & B. Analyse the data in File 08 ANOVA.xlsx worksheet Ex 8.7.3 and answer the questions shown below. The data was collected randomly and is recorded in time order.

1) Form the Main Effects Plot and Interactions plot. Can you guess which factors and interactions are significant?
2) Which Factors and Interactions are significant when you use the ANOVA GLM ?
3) What is the Regression Equation for this model? And how much of the variation in Strength does it account for?
4) What settings would maximise the strength of the phone cases?
5) DO the VIFs indicate any problems with the model?
6) Do the residuals and Lack-of-Fit Test indicate any issues with your model ?

Exercise 8.7.4 Use the ANOVA GLM

A multi-media service provider wants to analyse some of their sales data. They have data on property size across 3 regions in a city. They want to know if sales are affected by property size and city region. Are there differences within the property size bands and sales? Also are there differences within the city regions and sales?

Analyse the data in File 08 ANOVA.xlsx worksheet Ex 8.7.4 and answer the questions shown above and additionally those shown below. The data was collected randomly and is recorded in time order.

In this procedure are Fixed Factor s are **Prop_size** and **Region.** The response is **Sales.**

1) Form the Main Effects Plot and Interactions plot. Can you guess which factors and interactions are significant?
2) Which Factors and Interactions are significant when you use the ANOVA GLM ?
3) How much of the variation in Sales does the model account for?
4) Which Property Size and Region will generate the highest Sales?
5) DO the VIFs indicate any problems with the model?
6) Do the residuals indicate any issues with your model ?

9 CONTROL CHARTS

9.1 Introduction to Control Charts

Control charts are one of the most straightforward tools that you will come across and yet they are an essential part of our Minitab tool kit. It's often the case that the simplest tools are very useful when used correctly. Control charts help us to decide whether our process is operating in a stable and predictable manner or whether forces are acting on the process which will generate undesirable outcomes. A single control chart monitors a single variable that we wish to track. We enter time ordered and independent data into the chart. Control limits are calculated and if our data goes beyond the control limits our process is unstable or out of control. If it remains within the control lines, we say that it is stable or in control.

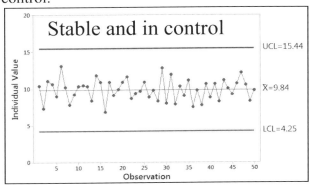

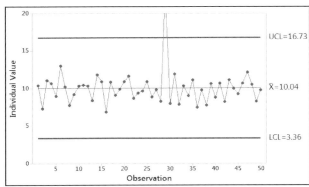

If our process lives within the control limits, we say it is only exhibiting the natural random variation that we expect. However, you might argue 'isn't all variation due to something ?' and if you said that you would be right because it is a bit subjective. If we are within our specification limits for the process and the customer is happy, we may not wish to find causes for these variations which are within the control limits.

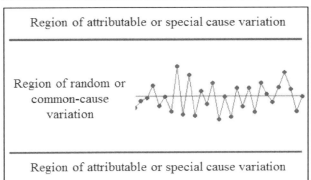

If our process continually crosses into the region of attributable variation, we now say that something has been influencing the measured variable. For example

You weigh yourself every morning and record the weights on a control chart. You get a single out of control result that is low. It was because you accidentally held onto the towel rail while measuring your weight.

You take a sample from the product line and test it for weight and record the results on a control chart. The weight is low and after investigating you find that one of the feeders had become jammed.

You produce a control chart showing your fuel efficiency to work every morning. You find that on a particular day, the fuel efficiency was worse and out of the control limits. It was the day you listened to the rock radio station instead of classical.

Process Capability is going to be the next module that we look at, but I wanted to stress the link with control charts at this point. As a rule of thumb, we should not display specification limits on a control chart as it often confuses people. However, I will break the rule to make a point. This chapter assumes that our control limits are always going to be inside our specification limits. A specification limit is a limit that an internal or external customer cares about. This is because the parameter being measured will result in defects when it goes beyond the specification limit.

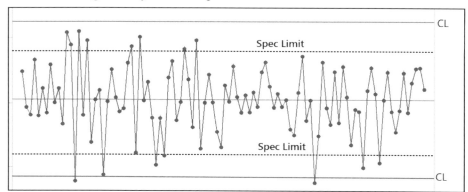

When you initially examine a process, if you find that the control limits are outside of the specification limits, then you have significant problems with process capability and you need to address those immediately using the appropriate tools such as a DMAIC project.
If you find that the control limits are well within the specification limits, you can continue to use control charts to monitor/improve your process.

9.2 When should we use Control Charts

There are several broadly defined occasions when we should use control charts and these are 1) When we want to know if our process is in control or not, 2) When our process is out of control or 3) When our process is already in control and we are using control charts for monitoring.
For item 1) If you are conducting a DMAIC project, you will want to establish if your process is stable late in the Measure phase. This is because even if the goal of your project is not to bring stability to the system if your system is out of control, you will need to remove special cause variation before you proceed with the project.
If you worked through the book sequentially, you would have already used control charts to determine whether your data was being influenced by special causes. Do you remember the Diagnostic Reports when you were conducting hypothesis testing? The Assistant uses control charts to point out special

cause variation in your data. If any out-of-control points were found it would tell you in the Report Card that 'unusual data can have a strong influence on the results, you should try to identify the cause of its unusual nature'.

For item 2) If the process is out-of-control, we will want to find out what is affecting our process and then apply ERIC to it and remove the parameter that is influencing the process. (ERIC = Eliminate, Reduce, Isolate, Control with a hierarchical preference).

For item 3) If the process is in control, then we want to monitor it and ensure that nothing happens to our process/system. We will have already reduced our process variability so that our control limits are within our customers' specification limits for the process. If an uncontrolled factor upsets our process, and we get a result outside of the control limits, we can then take action. Hopefully, this will still be before we make the out-of-specification product.

9.3 False Alarms

False alarms are out of control points that are generated when the process is behaving as it should. For example, when Dr Walter A. Shewart first invented control charts, he used 3 StDevs from the mean to set the control limits.

(We still use similar default values for control limits even now. The calculations can be reviewed within the Help<<Methods and Formulas menu of Minitab. As this book lets Minitab do the calculations, we will not be discussing the exact method of calculating the control limits.)

If you have a perfectly normal distribution and set the control limits at 3 StDevs then 99.73% of the points will be within the control limits; we know this from our early review of the normal distribution in Chapter 5. This works out to 1 in 370 points on average will be in the region of special cause variation. However, these are false alarms and are generated as probable events that are at the extremes of the distribution.

If we do get an out-of-control point, then we need to investigate if it was caused by an attributable factor or by being a legitimate point that was at the extremes of our distribution. As this takes time, we need to ensure we don't get too many false alarms as people will quickly lose faith in the system. If you are using the traditional drop-down menu's to produce the control charts then you can increase the number of tests for special causes, going beyond 3 StDev's is not the only way to detect an attributable influence on your process. Also, when we start moving away from a normally distributed process, we will get more false alarms.

We can protect ourselves from false alarms by using subgrouping and by reducing the number of tests we use to detect special cause variation. We will take our first look at subgrouping in the next section.

9.4 Subgrouping

Have you ever seen those TV programs where they show you how a fast-moving consumer good is made? Where items like aerosol cans are flying down a conveyor in single file. And there is an operator at the side of the line and she takes four cans out of the moving line and then she would weigh each one to check for fill level. The operator is taking a subgroup from the main line. The reason for taking the subgroup is two-fold 1) It gives our control chart protection against false alarms and 2) It helps us to understand common cause and special cause variation that the process is experiencing.

A subgroup is a group of items that have been made under/exposed to similar conditions. They don't have to be consecutive items, but they usually are. The sample should be taken over a relatively short time frame. We then set a longer time frame between subgroups samples.

We select a short time frame to sample the sub-group as we do not wish to capture any special cause variation within the subgroup. We want to be able to say that the subgroup variation is only made up of the random process variation. We also want to be able to say that the special cause variation will occur between subgroups.

9.5 Subgroup Size and Sampling Frequency

If we could sample everything we would not need to use sub-groups; our control charts would just consist of all the data plotted as individuals. However, we usually can't sample everything due to cost, time or the sheer number of samples available.

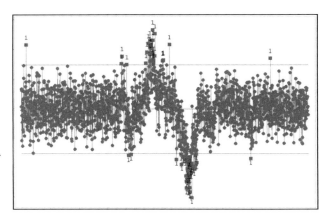

This first control chart shows 2000 data points which represent 2000 sequential items from a production line. We see two types of special cause variation. There are individual points that are out of control, and there are shifts of the mean which cause out of control points. Let's take a look at how the control chart looks if I choose my subgroup size as 5 and decide that I will resample after 95 parts. So I am sampling the first five out of every 100.

This is an Xbar R Chart with my sampling regime of taking 5 parts as my sample and then leaving the next 95 parts. The bottom half of the chart represents the range within each subgroup, and the top half is the mean within each subgroup. The chart does pretty well at picking up the shifts in mean but not the single points where we get an instantaneous out of control point.

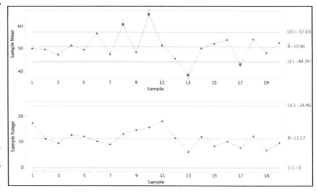

Adding more sampling points will improve our resolution. With the additional samples we may or may not hit one of the single out of control points and capture some special cause variation within the subgroups. This is not a problem but it is a problem if we are systematically capturing special cause variation in the subgroup.

When thinking about your subgroup size and sampling frequency think about the following
   1) How many samples can I analyse?
   2) Will I continue to systematically capture special cause variation within my sub-group?
   3) What type of unusual behaviour am I trying to capture?
Over what period will a shift in mean take place? This is probably the most important.

9.6 Detection Rules for Special Cause variation

You would be forgiven if you thought there was only one rule for detecting special causes. Within Minitab, there are 8 rules for detecting special cause variation that can be used within the traditional drop-down menus. Each of these 8 tests is designed to alert us to a particular event occurring in our data. If the test activates, it is deemed to be more likely to be due to an attributable cause rather than randomness.

Even though we are going to be focusing on using the Assistant, which only uses a couple of the rules, it's worth knowing what can be applied if required.

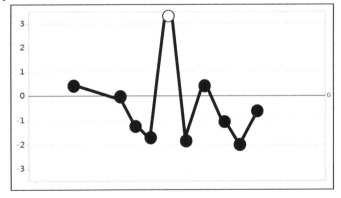

Perform selected tests for special causes	K
☑ 1 point > K standard deviations from center line	3
☐ K points in a row on same side of center line	9
☐ K points in a row, all increasing or all decreasing	6
☐ K points in a row, alternating up and down	14
☐ K out of K+1 points > 2 standard deviations from center line (same side)	2
☐ K out of K+1 points > 1 standard deviation from center line (same side)	4
☐ K points in a row within 1 standard deviation of center line (either side)	15
☐ K points in a row > 1 standard deviation from center line (either side)	8

To access this option, select the Chart options button, for example, 'I-MR Options', at the root menu for any of the continuous data control charts and then click on the 'Tests' tab. Not only can the rules be switched on or off from this menu it is also possible to modify how they are applied. For example, if we wanted the particular chart to apply rule 2 but only look for 5 points on the same side of the centre line we would simply change the value of 'K' to '5' for test 2 instead of '9'. We would also ensure that the test was switched on.

Remember, the more tests we have switched on, the more chance there is of generating false alarms but we also have more chance of detecting attributable special causes.

Let's graphically have a look at Minitab's detection rules with the default 'K' values. The graph that we will be displaying has been constructed and not all data points are shown. The Y-axis, is in units of StDev from the mean.

Test 1, 1 point more than 3 StDevs from the center line.

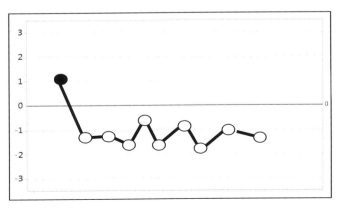

Test 2, 9 points in a row, all on the same side of the center line. Test 2 is very useful in that it detects for shifts in the mean of the process. One point that can be a bit confusing is that for certain tests involving sequences of points Minitab will only report the last point that is out of control. This stops the chart from getting too messy. For example, if you produce a chart with test 2 activated and 9 points in a row meet the condition for special cause variation Minitab will only report the last point as having failed test 2.

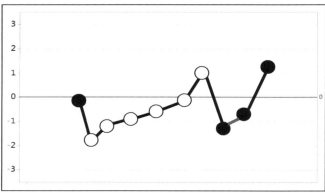

Test 3, 6 points in a row all increasing or all decreasing

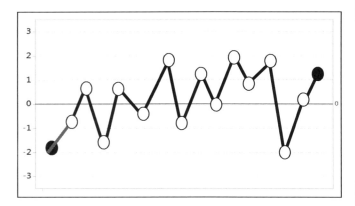

Test 4, 14 points in a row alternating up and down.

Test 5, 2 of 3 points more than 2 StDevs from the centre line on the same side.

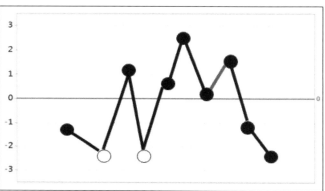

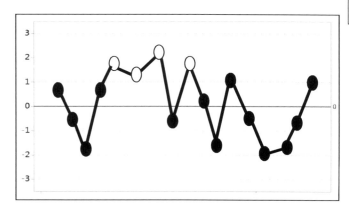

Test 6, 4 of 5 points more than 1 StDev from the centre line on the same side.

Test 7, 15 points in a row within 1 StDev of the centre line, either side.

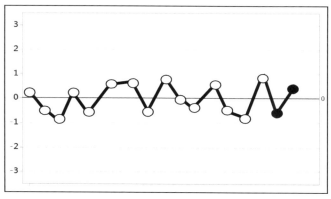

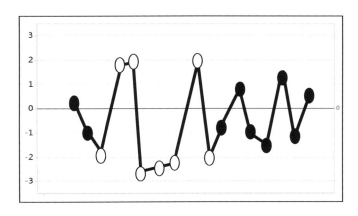

Test 8, 8 points in a row more than 1 StDev from centre line, either side.

9.7 Control Chart Selection for Continuous Data

Control chart selection can be very easy or reasonably hard depending on how deep you want to start. If you are beginning absolutely from the start of the process where you only have raw data, then you need to think about your subgroup size and sampling frequency and answer the following questions.

1) What are my analysis limitations? How many samples can I take and how often can I analyse? Usually, we can only sample a small fraction of the population. If it is at all possible, we want to be analysing subgroups. Having individual data points is a fall-back position.
2) Will I continue to systematically capture special cause variation within my sub-group? You want to set your sampling frequency and subgroup size so you don't get any special cause variation within the subgroups.
3) What type of unusual behaviour am I trying to capture? Ask yourself if tests 1, 2 and 7 are sufficient or whether you want to check for one of the other 5 special causes within Minitab. If you do, then you should not use the Assistant.

Once you have answered the above questions, it is straightforward to select the appropriate chart. If data was not collected in subgroups, then we use the I-MR chart. If the data was collected in subgroups, we select the appropriate chart depending upon the size of the subgroup.

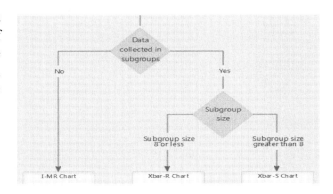

9.8 I-MR Chart

I-MR Chart using the Assistant	
Function	Tests whether a process is stable (in control). This chart is used when the only option is to take a single sample, meaning sampling in subgroups not possible.
Sample Size	The Assistant gives the choice of whether existing control limits are applied or whether control limits are estimated from the data. The recommendation is to have at least 100 data points when estimating control limits from the data.
Data type & Format	Continuous data which is captured at regular intervals is required. Ensure the data is captured frequently enough to capture process shifts but not so frequently that it overwhelms the process.
Considerations	The I-MR chart consists of two halves. At the top is a plot of the Individual (I) data within control limits which are estimated using the average Moving Range (MR) which is displayed on the bottom half of the chart. The points on the MR chart are the difference (or range) between successive data points. If Minitab detects a high degree of non-normality within the data it may recommend a transformation of the data. At Green Belt level you should seek advice from a Black Belt if this occurs. The Assistant will apply tests 1,2 on the I chart to detect special causes and test 1 only on the MR chart.

Example 9.8.1 Stock Accuracy Results

A company conducts a stock count every week at all of its store locations. The overall stock accuracy is recorded as a key performance indicator. Cooks has been asked to evaluate the stability of stock management at Store1 using a control chart. Due to the time taken to conduct a stock count, it is not possible to take samples with subgroups so an I-MR chart must be used. All data for this chapter is in '9 Control Charts.xlsx' and the data for this example is in the worksheet called 'I-MR'.

The reason for not trying to collect data within subgroups is the time and resources taken to complete the stock count. It would mean too much time and resource allocation for the company to conduct multiple stock counts.

	Store1	Store2
1	67.80	76.3
2	88.00	77.4
3	75.00	88.1
4	78.80	83.0
5	76.00	91.7

1. Transfer both columns of data into Minitab.
2. Click **Assistant<<Control Charts**
3. Click on the **I-MR Chart** box, which is used for continuous data which does not have subgroups.

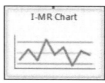

I-MR Chart

4. The test menu opens. Initially, we are only going to examine data from Store1, so enter that as the Data Column. As we don't have historical control limits, we will use Minitab to calculate control limits from the data by making the appropriate selection from the drop down list. As soon as we do that Minitab conducts a check on the data and will give us a warning if the data is unstable. We are given the option of excluding that data from calculations even though it will still be displayed on the chart.

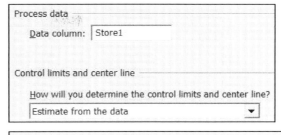

5. Click OK to produce the charts.

Minitab does not do it in this example, but it would be at this point that Minitab might offer us the option of transforming the data. This only happens if a transformation would reduce the number of out-of-control points. As a Green Belt, I would advise that you seek advice from a Black Belt at this point as a transformation may not be beneficial in practice.

This command generates a 3 page report in the Output Pane; please navigate to the Summary Report.

In the top left corner, we are told that the process mean is not stable as 4.9% of the points on the Individuals chart are out of control, which is 5 points out of 102. There are no P-values associated with this statement.

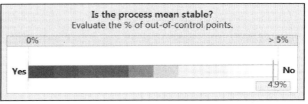

At the bottom of the Summary Report, we get to see the full I-MR Control Chart, shown below. The X-axis has the Observation number which is common to both halves of the chart. The left hand Y-axis are scaled to show the Individual values and Moving ranges respectively. The right-hand side shows the control limit values and the average moving range, MR bar. This is denoted as 'MR' with a line on top of it. MR bar is used to calculate the control limits for the individuals chart. The average MR or MR bar is an estimate of StDev used in I-MR charts. We can see which points are out-of-control as they are red squares but we don't know why they are out-of-control until we refer to the Stability Report.

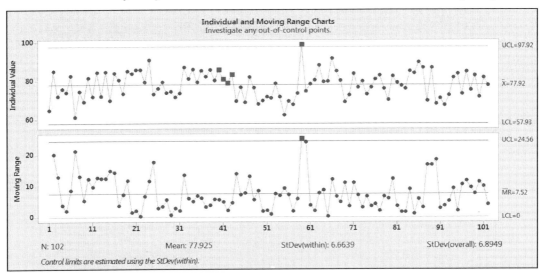

The Stability Report tells us that Observation 59 failed as it was outside the control limits, Test 1, on both the I & MR charts. Observations 40-43 failed Test 2 on the I-Chart. Test 2 tells us if 9 points in a row were on either side of the centre line, it is looking for shifts in the process. Remember, Minitab is only reporting the last point in the row of 9 each time. This means it's actually 12 points in a row that were on the same side of the centre line.

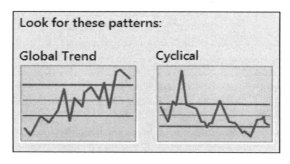

I think it is worth remembering that on the left-hand side of the Stability Report are examples of unusual trends. I would recommend that it is worth familiarising yourself with the patterns shown and making it a habit to check the control chart for these trends.

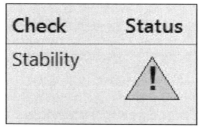

Finally, on the Report Card, we are given a summary of the findings and some general information. For this control chart, we are given a warning regarding stability. In particular, we are told that as one point was out of control on the MR chart, it may affect the control limits that were calculated using the average MR on the I chart.

Exercise 9.8.2 Stock Accuracy Results

The company states that certain best practices in stock management have been used at Store2. The company invites Cooks to produce an I-MR chart of the Store2 stock accuracy results and check for stability. They also ask for pertinent differences in the Stock Accuracy results between the two stores.
Help Cooks produce and I-MR chart for Store2 and check for Stability. To check for differences between the stores also use the Before/After control Chart menu within the Assistant.
All data for this chapter is in '9 Control Charts.xlsx', and the data for this example is in the worksheet called 'I-MR'.

On the Summary Report for the I-MR chart for Store 2, we are told that there are no out-of-control points. Using values shown on the I-MR chart, we could compare the values for mean level and average moving range; however, the Before/After Control charts better display the differences.

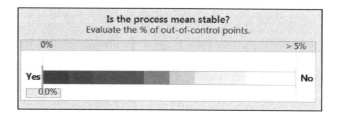

On the Summary Report for the Before/After comparison, we are shown the hypothesis test for a reduction in StDev and mean. There is a difference between the two stores. This can be seen in the side-by-side control charts for the two stores. Therefore, stock management practices used in Store2 have resulted in a higher stock accuracy score and lower variance in the stock accuracy.

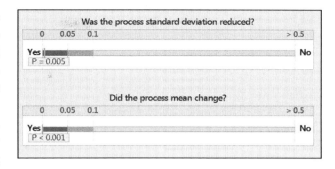

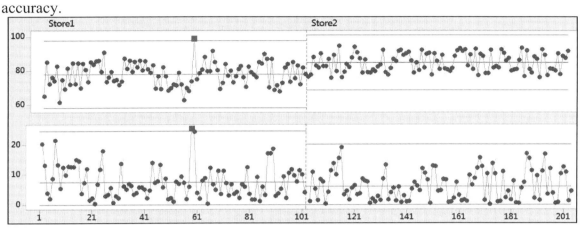

9.9 Xbar-R Chart

Xbar-R Chart using the Assistant	
Function	Tests whether a process is stable (in control). This chart is used when the data has been collected in subgroups with sizes of between 2 and 8.
Sample Size	The Assistant gives the choice of whether existing control limits are applied or whether control limits are estimated from the data. The recommendation is to have at least 100 data points when estimating control limits from the data.
Data type & Format	Continuous data where the subgroup samples are captured at regular intervals is required. Ensure the data is captured frequently enough to capture process shifts but not so frequently that it overwhelms the process.
Considerations	The Xbar-R chart consists of two halves. The top is a plot of the average value of each subgroup. The bottom plot is the range within each subgroup. The control limits of the Xbar chart are calculated using the average range value. Therefore, always look at the range chart first as a high average range value may make it appear that you are in control on the Xbar chart. You can get a high average range value if you trap special cause variation within your subgroups. The Assistant will apply tests 1,2 on the Xbar chart to detect special causes, with test 7 also being applied if the control limits are estimated from the data. The Assistant will only apply test 1 on the R chart. There isn't a significant increase in the false alarm rate for non-normal data when using charts with subgroups. Once control limits for the process have been established they should be used when producing additional charts for that process. However, if a process change occurs then new control limits should be calculated.

Example 9.9.1 Cup Cakes

Mahwish's cup cakes are coming out of the continuous oven at 300 cakes per hour. Every hour four cakes are check weighed. Using an Xbar-R chart check that the cupcake weights are in control. The data for this example is in the worksheet called 'XbarR'.

1.   Transfer the data into Minitab. There are five columns of data in 50 rows. Each row represents a subgroup sample taken every hour.

	Cake1	Cake2	Cake3	Cake4	Cake5
1	120.52	123.12	120.93	122.54	118.47
2	120.32	120.33	121.69	118.57	120.62
3	119.51	117.93	122.06	116.20	116.75
4	123.89	121.25	125.14	123.35	119.46
5	119.94	119.11	119.32	118.69	116.88
6	122.61	121.20	120.97	118.56	119.96
7	119.53	118.23	121.14	116.39	115.83
8	116.25	121.06	118.58	118.26	115.62
9	119.98	116.56	121.78	118.71	120.03

2.   Click *Assistant<<Control Charts*
3.   Click on the **Xbar-R Chart** box, which is used for continuous data which has a subgroup size of 8 or less.

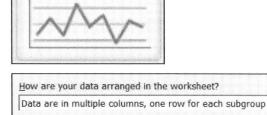

4.   The test menu opens. Minitab asks us how our subgroups are arranged so in the drop-down menu we have to tell it that the 'Data is in multiple columns with one row for each subgroup'.
5.   Select columns Cake1 to Cake5 as the Data Columns. As we don't have historical control limits, we will use Minitab to calculate control limits from the data by making the appropriate selection from the drop down list. As soon as we do that we are given notification that one of the points on the chart is out-of-control and we get the option of omitting it from the chart.

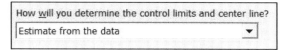

How are your data arranged in the worksheet?

Data are in multiple columns, one row for each subgroup

Data columns:

Cake1-Cake5

How will you determine the control limits and center line?

Estimate from the data

6.   Click OK to produce a 3 page report in the Output Pane

Please navigate to the Summary Report.
In the top left corner, we are told that the process mean is stable. The Xbar portion of the chart displays the mean of each subgroup, which is stable.

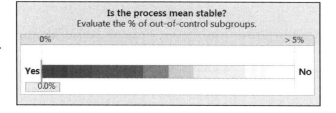

Is the process mean stable?
Evaluate the % of out-of-control subgroups.

At the bottom of the Summary Report, we get to see the full Xbar-R Control Chart. We see that we have a single out-of-control point on the R chart and we are told on the Stability Report that it fails test 1 (the only test that the R chart uses). The average range value for the chart is 4.87. If I hover over the out-of-control point with my mouse, I am told that the range for sample 20 is 14.81. We need to investigate this data point as it may have an impact on the control limits for the Xbar chart.

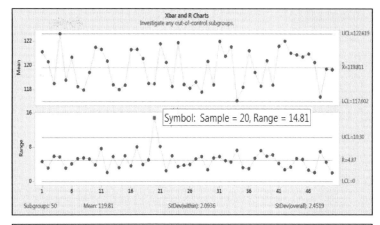

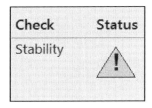

Finally, on the Report Card, we get a warning regarding stability. It states that although the process mean is stable the process variation (R chart) is not. And because the average range is used to calculate the control limits in the Xbar chart, we should not validate the Xbar chart as being stable until we have investigated the out of control point.

Chart	Test	Out-of-Control Subgroups
R	Test 1: Outside control limits	20

Check	Status
Stability	⚠

We will go back to the source data and check the subgroup for data point 20. The range is made up of the difference of the highest point and lowest point, Range=125.81-111=14.81.

Let's pretend that we investigated the operator's paperwork and found that there was a typo. 111 should have been 121.

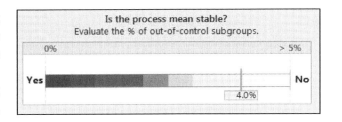

19	119.48	117.68	121.10	118.02	116.17
20	118.62	125.81	116.95	119.95	111.00
21	119.69	125.04	120.43	125.04	117.81

19	119.48	117.68	121.10	118.02	116.17
20	118.62	125.81	116.95	119.95	121.00
21	119.69	125.04	120.43	125.04	117.81

7. Correct the data and run the Assistant with the new data. When using the Assistant, we cannot use the 'Update Graph' facilities.

On this occasion, the new Summary Report indicates that the process mean is not stable.

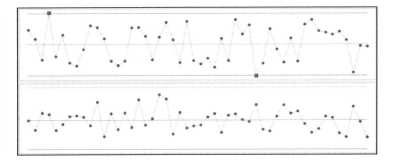

When we look at the Control Charts, we see that two points are out-of-control on the Xbar chart and the R chart is now in control. Our correction has resulted in a new average range value of 4.75 and when this is used to calculate the new control limits for the Xbar chart it was enough to make two of the points fail Test1 on the Xbar chart.

Finally, on the Report Card, we are told that the process variation (shown on the R chart) was stable but the process mean was not stable.

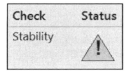

Check	Status
Stability	⚠

9.10 Xbar-S Chart

There are no differences between using Assistant procedures for the Xbar-R or Xbar-S apart from the recommended subgroup size. As it is more useful for Green Belts to experience the classic menus for producing control charts, this example has been written to show the features of control charts using the traditional menu's.

Xbar-S Chart using the classic menu's	
Function	Tests whether a process is stable (in control). This chart is used when the data has been collected in subgroups with sizes of 9 and over.
Sample Size	The recommendation within the Assistant is to have at least 100 data points when estimating control limits from the data. There is no reason why this should be different for the classic method where the only option is to calculate control limits from the data.
Data type & Format	Continuous data where the subgroup samples are captured at regular intervals is required. Ensure the data is captured frequently enough to capture process shifts but not so frequently that it overwhelms the system.
Considerations	The Xbar-S chart consists of two halves. The top is a plot of the average value of each subgroup. The bottom plot is the StDev within each subgroup. The control limits of the Xbar chart are calculated using the average StDev value or Sbar. Therefore, always look at the Stdev chart first as a high average StDev value may make it appear that you are in control on the Xbar chart. You can get a high Sbar value if you trap special cause variation within your subgroups. There isn't a significant increase in the false alarm rate for non-normal data when using charts with subgroups.

Example 9.10.1 Wafer Biscuit Breaking Strengths

Snappy wafer biscuits use the snap of their wafer biscuits as a Unique Selling Point for their product. They ask Raeesa to establish if the snap strength of their wafer biscuits is in control, there are two types of biscuit, A & B. Initially, help Raeesa produce a control chart of Type A and assess stability.
The data for this example is in the worksheet called 'XbarS'.

1. Transfer the data into a new Minitab project worksheet. There are 11 columns of data in 132 rows. Column C1, 'Type' primarily tells us the wafer biscuit type that is being produced, for now, we are only interested in Type A. 'Time' tells us the time that the subgroup sample was taken we then have 9 columns of data where each row contains subgroup data of the breaking strength.

2. Click *Stat<<Control Charts <<Variable Charts for Subgroups*

<<Xbar-S. The root menu for the Xbar-S Chart opens.

3. Minitab asks us how our subgroups are arranged. In the drop-down menu, we have to tell it that 'Observations for a subgroup are in one row of columns'.

4. Select columns Strength1 to Strenght9 as the Data Columns.

5. Click on the **Scale** button that is present on the root menu.

6. Under X Scale, click on the radio button for Stamp. This gives us the option of using our own index for the data points. We can display up to three columns.

7. Enter 'Time' and 'Type' as labels to be used for the Index.

8. Click OK & OK again to produce the charts.

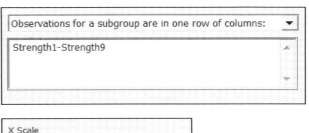

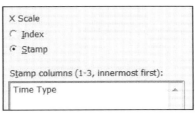

We can see patterns in both charts straight away. Type A and Type B wafers appear to have a differing mean level of strength, although the within-group variation seems to be at the same level. However, the biscuits made during start-up and change-over are again at differing levels of mean and variation. As we need to check the stability of Type A wafers, we need to eliminate the rest of the data from the chart. Note that this will break the rule of having regular time intervals between samples. However, we do have sacrificial change-over samples that should remove special variation between runs of Type A and Type B. We need to check that this hypothesis holds true when the chart for Type A is produced.

9. Press Ctrl+E or click on the Edit Last icon to return to the Xbar-S chart root menu.

10. Click on the **Scale** button and remove Type as a Stamp Column. As we know, all of the data will be for Type A, we can save some space on the X-axis.

11. Click OK to return to the root menu.

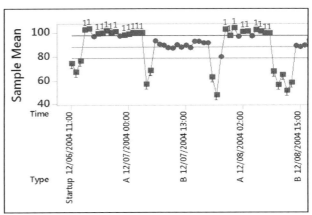

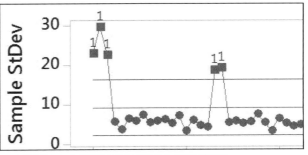

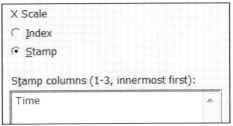

12. Click on the **Data Options** button. Within this menu, we can set the data that is either going to be included in the chart or excluded from the chart by using the radio buttons at the top. We will leave the setting on 'Include'.

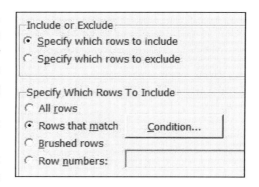

13. To tell the menu which rows we want to include, we have a number of options. Select the radio button for 'Rows that match' and then click on the **Condition** button.

14. There are many ways to set the condition, including logic operators such as AND & OR. All we need to do is specify the following condition TYPE="A", which means include any row of the specified data when the Type is A.

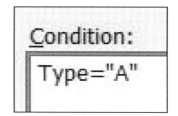

15. Click OK three times to produce the chart.

With data from Type B, Changeovers and Start-ups removed from the chart, it looks much more like a control chart should. There were 4 runs of Type A wafer and it is not clear from the chart where the runs intersect so we can say we have not made an error by not collecting data at regular intervals.

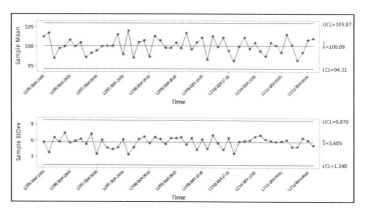

Can Raeesa conclude that the process is stable? Well by default, the classic menu will only use Test 1 for special causes. In order to be thorough, we should check for the presence of other types of special cause variation.

16. Press Ctrl+E or click on the Edit Last icon to return to the Xbar-S chart root menu.

17. Click on the **Xbar-S Options** button.

18. Click onto the **Tests** tab.

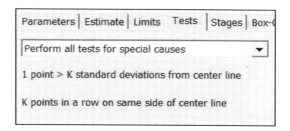

19. The drop-down menu can be used to set whether no tests, all tests or selected tests are conducted. Please choose the option to 'Perform all tests...'.

20. Click OK and OK again to produce the Xbar-S chart again.

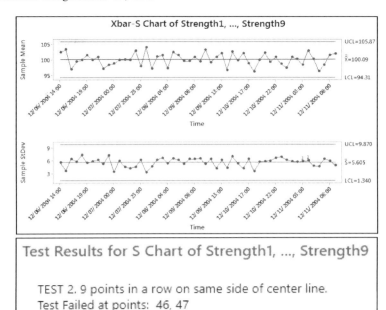

We see that two points on the S chart have failed Test2. The Session Window tells us that points 46 and 47 have failed because 9 points in a row were on the same side of the centre line.

Test Results for S Chart of Strength1, ..., Strength9

TEST 2. 9 points in a row on same side of center line.
Test Failed at points: 46, 47

Exercise 9.10.2

Help Raeesa check whether Type B wafer biscuits strengths are also stable by producing an Xbar-S chart. Use all the Tests for special causes.

The Xbar-S chart for Type B wafer biscuits is in control even when all of the tests for special causes are applied.

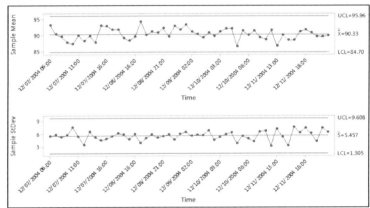

9.11 Control Charts for Attribute Data

We are going to be looking at two of the main control charts for counts of attribute data. These are the P & U charts, and if those don't work, we will switch to the Laney P' and U' charts, which were introduced by David B. Laney.

A P Chart only considers the number of fails or defectives within a subgroup. Subgroup sizes can vary, but the items within the subgroup can only be graded as pass or fail, it does not matter if they have multiple faults.

Pass   Fail   Fail   Fail   Fail   Pass   Fail

Within this subgroup of 7, we have 5 Fails

For the U chart, we count the total number of defects within the subgroup and report that against the subgroup size

| 0 defects | 1 defects | 2 defects | 1 defect | 1 defect | 0 defects | 2 defects |

If we were using a U chart with multiple categories of defects, we would report 7 defects against a subgroup size of 7.

P & U Charts for Attribute Data using the Assistant	
Function	Tests whether the defect count within a sample is stable (in control).
Sample Size	The Assistant gives the choice of whether existing control limits are applied to data or whether control limits are estimated from the data. The subgroup size can be unequal. Average proportion of defective items (denoted by Pbar on the P chart) multiplied by the subgroup size must be 0.5 for each subgroup when estimating control limits from the data. Otherwise, the control limits may not be estimated correctly.
Data type & Format	Both charts use counts of defects within a sample that can either have a set or variable size. The difference is that items counted on the P chart can only be given a single defect classification or a pass. A single item on the U chart can have multiple defects.
Considerations	There are well known issues with P & U charts which led David B. Laney to develop the Laney P' & U' charts. If Minitab suggests using the Laney charts then say yes and trust that Minitab knows best. The issues occur when there is more variation across the data than random sampling would suggest. This results in narrower control limits leading to more false alarms. This is called overdispersion. There is also a reverse of this condition called underdispersion. P & U charts only use tests 1 & 2 within the Assistant.

Example 9.11.1 Party Balloons

Party Balloons Ltd want to know if their balloon manufacturing process is stable. They ask you to produce a control chart of their data using their existing control limits. Naturally, you ask what kind of data do they have, and they reply that they test 200 balloons every day and each balloon is rated as a pass or a fail. Their historical lower control limit is 0.01 and the upper is 0.13. The usual mean defect rate is 0.07. The data for this example is in the worksheet called 'Balloons'.

1. The data into Minitab. There is a single column of data that has 150 rows.
2. Click *Assistant<<Control Charts*

3. Click on the **P Chart** box, which is used for attribute data where one item can only contribute to 1 defect in the count of defects.

4. The test menu opens. Our count of defective items within the subgroup is in the column called Defects, so select that column.

5. The subgroup size is always constant, so all we need to do is select the appropriate radio button and tell Minitab that the subgroup size is 200.

6. We will be entering the historical control limits so tell Minitab that we will 'Use known values'. Enter the values as stated.

7. Click OK to produce a 3 page report in the Output Pane.

Please navigate to the Summary Report.

On the top left of the Summary Report, we are told that we have 1.3% out-of-control subgroups. In the adjacent Comments box, we are told that the proportion of defectives may not be stable as this exceeds the expected level of 0.7%. Hence, we are in an intermediate area of being possibly unstable.

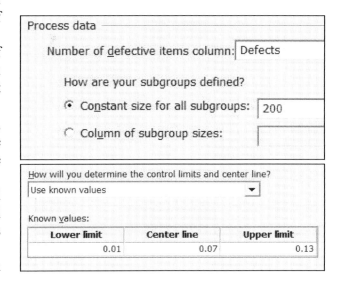

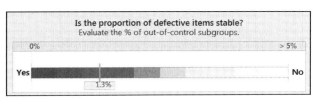

Still, on the Summary Report, we see the P chart that has been produced. Reading this in conjunction with the Stability Report we find out that points 23 & 39 have failed Test 1. The P Chart has some useful summary information at the bottom. We find that 2166 of the 30,000 balloons tested were defective, which makes 7.22%.

It is interesting to note how many tests it takes to produce a control chart with attribute data rather than continuous data. I would advise that if given attribute data you should be looking for a way to convert it into continuous data. The report card provides us with a warning that the process may not be stable as 1.3% of the subgroups are out of control.

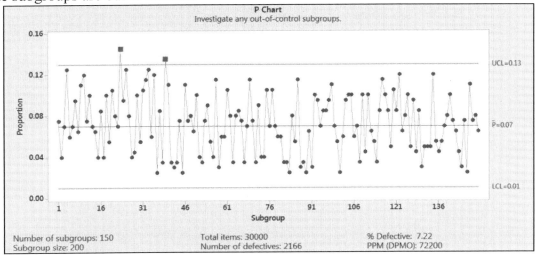

Example 9.11.2   Crazy Coffee

Coffee is big business when it can be sold as a high-quality niche product. However, the higher the cost the fussier the customer. Crazy Coffee treats its customer complaints as defects and they have categorised the complaints into several types. You have been asked to analyse their data and assess whether the complaints about the store are in control. The data for this example is in the worksheet called 'Coffee'.

1. Transfer the data into Minitab. There are two columns of data that have 100 rows.
2. Click *Assistant<<Control Charts*
3. Click on the *U Chart* box, which is used for attribute data where one item can contribute multiple defects to the count of defects.
4. The test menu opens. Our count of defective items within the subgroup is in the column called Complaints, so select that column.
5. The subgroup size is not constant, so we need to tell Minitab that the subgroup count is in the column called Sales. Do this by selecting the appropriate radio button and selecting the Sales column.
6. We want Minitab to Estimate control limits from the data so select that from the drop down menu when prompted. As soon as you do that Minitab will list the out-of-control points and give you the option to omit the out-of-control points.
7. Click OK to execute the procedure.

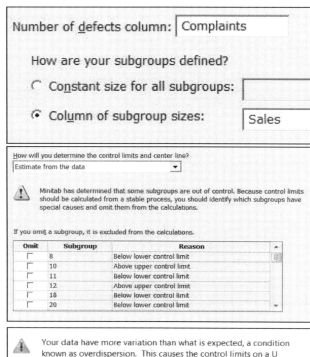

8. Minitab detected overdispersion in the data and suggests you use the Laney U' chart instead. Click the 'Yes' button to use the Laney U' chart.

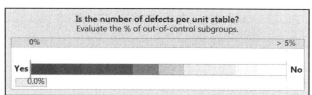

Please navigate to the Summary Report.
On the top left of the Summary Report, we are told that we have 0% out-of-control subgroups. This means that although there are complaints, the process of producing complaints is stable.

Still, on the Summary Report, we see the Laney U' chart that has been produced. Notice that none of the points are out of control and that due to the varying subgroups size the upper control limit is also varying. The Laney U' Chart has some useful summary information at the bottom. We find that there were 2395 complaints in 20,919 Sales. A single sale may have generated more than one complaint.

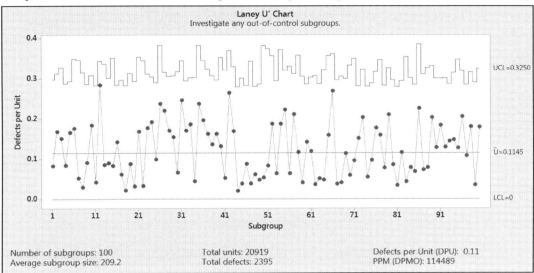

The Diagnostic Report gives us a chart showing the level of variation that is acceptable for the standard P & U charts and the equivalent Laney chart.

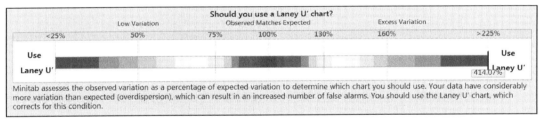

Also on the Diagnostic Report, we are shown the U chart we would have had against the Laney U' chart. We can see that we would have had many out-of-control points on the U chart which would have led us to a very different conclusion about the stability of the process. The Summary Report gives us the all-clear.

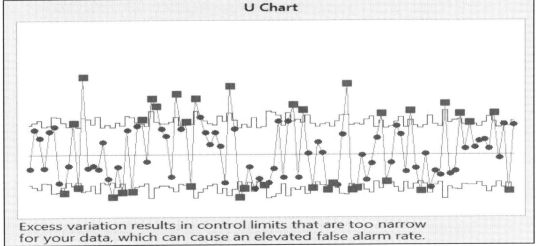

9.12 Control Chart Exercise

Exercise 9.12.1 Control Charts

Data is taken from a process in time order. Check for stability using the appropriate control chart. First use the Assistant and estimate control limits from the data. Once you have done that use the classic menu and test the data for all the available tests for special causes.

Analyse the data in File 09 Control Charts.xlsx worksheet Ex 9.12.1 and answer the questions shown below.

1) Is the process stable?
2) When using the Assistant on which chart are the stability issues?
3) When you use the classic menus and use all the tests for special causes are any additional test activated?

10 PROCESS CAPABILITY

10.1   Simple Process Yield Metrics

Process Capability tells you how well your process meets the customer requirements, and it's that simple. In the Measure phase, you would carry out an initial process capability study and then after you have gone through the Improve phase, you could show your achievements and do a final process capability and compare.

Process Capability is a specific methodology for measuring your process defects in Six Sigma. You may also be aware of other measures, such as process yield or Defects per Million Opportunities (DPMO).

10.1.1. Yield and DPMO example

Please calculate the yield and DPMO of a process where you have made a total of 625 parts, of which 49 are defective.

$$\text{The Process Yield} = \frac{Good\ parts\ produced}{Total\ parts\ produced} \times 100\% = \frac{625-49}{625} \times 100\% = 92.16\%$$

$$\text{DPMO} = Defect\ Rate \times 1,000,000 = \frac{Defective\ parts\ produced}{Total\ parts\ produced} \times 1,000,000$$

$$= \frac{49}{625} \times 1,000,000 = 78,400 ppm$$

92.16% may sound okay as a yield figure, but it means that if you produce 1 million parts with that yield 78,400 parts will be defective out of that million.

Another term that you might hear is Rolling Yield. This is where the yield of a number of sub-processes is combined by multiplying the individual yields together. For example, a process has three sub-processes with yields Y_A, Y_B & Y_C; the rolling yield would be $Y_A \times Y_B \times Y_C$.

10.2 Introduction to Process Capability

We are now going to focus on Process Capability and try to understand what the calculations mean in practical terms. Six Sigma is all about the customer and we call our customer requirements the Voice of the Customer (VOC). We call our process output the Voice of the Process (VOP). We should have in the

Define phase determined which parameter we would be monitoring to establish our VOP. And also during the Define phase, we would have looked at the needs of our customer and established the VOC. We select VOC and VOP to have the same units so that Process capability, P_p, is a dimensionless number.

$$\text{Process capability} = P_p = \frac{VOC}{VOP}$$

We are going to call process capability, P_p. You may have seen it called C_p in other texts but I believe that leads to an incorrect understanding of process capability when using Minitab, so I am going to teach it correctly from the start. Let's go through a worked example and see how we calculate process capability. To help our understanding, we are going to limit ourselves to normally distributed data or distributions where the underlying data is normally distributed in the Green Belt Edition. We will have a more detailed discussion about that statement later in the module.

I am going to develop the explanation of process capability calculations using an example of filling a bag with peanuts. This example will continue through the next couple of sections.

When you buy a 200g packet of peanuts, the machine that filled the bag of peanuts works to a specification. The lower specification limit (LSL) is 200g, you should never have less than 200g nett weight of peanuts in your bag. But to save on cost, the machine also has an upper specification limit (USL) of 220g. VOC is described as 220-200=20g or USL-LSL. This is also called the tolerance width or just tolerance. It is the difference/distance between the USL and LSL.

10.3 Basic Process Capability

The VOP is the width of the distribution delivered by the filling machine. Let's say that we have measured the net weight from 200 samples. This is useful as bag weight also has the same units, grams, as the spec limits meaning that the units will cancel each other out when we calculate the P_p.

Here is a histogram of our 200 data points. The curve of best fit for its normal distribution is also shown. If you remember back to the core statistics section, we said that one of the characteristics of a normal distribution is that 99.73% of the data is within 3 StDevs of the mean.

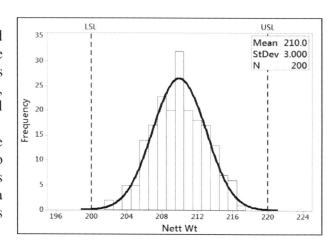

Or we could say that our process delivers 99.73% of its's population in 6 Stdevs (3 from each side of the mean). This means that VOP is the StDev delivered by the process multiplied by 6. When the distribution is not normally distributed, it gets much harder to calculate the VOP. The Green Belt edition of this book only considers normally distributed processes but the Black Belt Edition covers distributions where the underlying distribution is not normally distributed.

Let's have a look at our process capability equation and substitute our data from the peanut filling machine.

$$\text{Process capability} = P_p = \frac{VOC}{VOP} = \frac{USL-LSL}{6StDevs} = \frac{USL-LSL}{6\sigma} = \frac{220-200}{6\,x\,3} = \frac{20}{18} = 1.111$$

10.4 Z scores

I like to think of process capability as a ratio of widths; it is the width of the spec limits divided by the width of the process delivery.

$$\text{Process capability} = P_p = \frac{VOC}{VOP}$$

A higher value of process capability is better as this means that the process width is small and easily fits within the specification limits. It's good to have a safety margin. If VOC and VOP are equal, then P_p =1, your process fits precisely within your spec limits and you have no room for error. But if we are hyper-technical that is not true because if VOC=VOP=6σ, then only 99.73% of the process is within the specification limits and 0.27% will still be rejects.

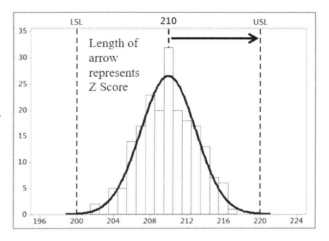

While we are thinking of widths, we can also determine the distance from our mean to the USL (or LSL). If we think of this distance in units of StDev, we can also get a measure of the capability of our process. This number is expressed in units of StDevs and is called the Z score.

$$Z = \frac{USL - Xbar}{\sigma} = \frac{220 - 210}{3} = 3.333$$

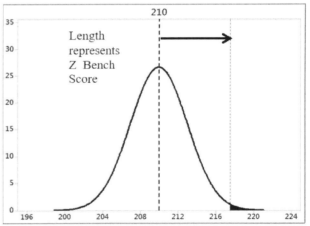

Again, the higher the Z score, the more capable the process. There is also another metric called the Z Bench score. This is the distance in units of StDev from the mean to a line that marks all process defects as drawn under the normal curve. All process defects means collecting the defects under both tails and then adding them together.

Let's say that we have done an improvement project on the peanut filling machine and we have reduced the fill weight StDev from 3 to 1.667, a good improvement. What's our process capability now?

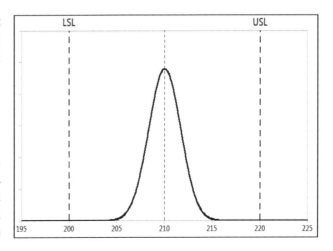

$$\text{Process capability} = P_p = \frac{VOC}{VOP} = \frac{220 - 200}{6 \, x \, 1.667} = \frac{20}{10} = 2$$

Our Z score would be 6 as the mean is six StDev's away from either spec limit. This is now a Six Sigma process and this is where the name for Six Sigma originates. It's the aspirational target of having a process where the mean is 6 sigma's away from the nearest specification limit. You may have heard that a Six Sigma process only produces 3.4 defects per million opportunity and has a Yield of 99.99966%.

There are tables available that will tell you what your DPMO or Yield% will be for a particular process capability or Z score.

Process Capability	Z score or Sigma Level	DPMO	Yield%
0.333	1	691462	31
0.667	2	308538	69
1	3	66807	93.3
1.333	4	6210	99.38
1.667	5	233	99.977
2	6	3.4	99.99966

10.5 Sigma Shift

If you look at the table again and look at the Yield% for a Z score of 3 you might get a little confused. The Yield% stated in the table is 93.3% but I have previously said that 99.73% of all data under a normal curve lies within 3 StDev's of the mean. Is 93.3% a mistake in the table? Personally, I don't like the Sigma shift concept but it is not a mistake. What is happening is that a 1.5σ shift is applied to the defects to account for the long term deterioration of process capability. If you see the DPMO of a 6σ process reported as 3.4, you will now know that a 1.5σ shift has been applied to that data. The actual number of defects generated by a 6σ process, in the short term, is actually only 0.002 DPMO.

Like it or not, this reporting convention exists, and it does install a safety margin that becomes more important at lower Z scores. The problem is that it is applied to most tables but not all.

10.6 Off-Centre Distributions

It may feel like a long time ago but I am going to go back to the peanuts where we had a 200 sample distribution and spec limits of 200 to 220g for the fill weight. When we calculated our original P_p, it came out at 1.111. What if a clumsy person accidentally knocked into the controls of the filling machine and it started to put more peanuts into each bag. Let's say that the mean increased to 215g. If the mean has moved then the whole distribution will also move but in my story, the width of the distribution stays the same. Looking at the plot, we can see that many of the bags would be out of specification. Let's work out the process capability for this distribution.

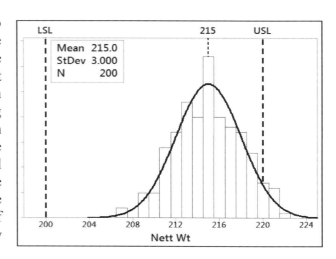

$$\text{Process capability} = P_p = \frac{USL - LSL}{6\sigma} = \frac{220 - 200}{6 \times 3} = \frac{20}{18} = 1.111$$

As this is the same capability value as before we can conclude that an off-centre mean does not affect this type of process capability calculation. We need a modified calculation that can cope with means that are not centred. The calculation that we use is based on the distance from the mean, Xbar, to the nearest specification limit divided by half the process width. It looks like

$$\text{Process capability} = P_{pk} = \frac{Xbar - LSL}{3\sigma} \text{ or } \frac{USL - Xbar}{3\sigma} \text{ , whichever is lower.}$$

Notice that the new symbol is P_{pk}. Our new process capability becomes

$$\text{Process capability} = P_{pk} = \frac{USL - Xbar}{3\sigma} = \frac{220 - 215}{3 \, x \, 3} = 0.556.$$

If you see both P_{pk} and P_p in a capability report and their values are similar, you will know that the distribution is at the centre of the spec limits. Otherwise, P_{pk} will always be lower than P_p.

10.7 Overall and Within Capability.

In section 9.4, we said a subgroup was a group of items that are made under similar conditions and that the subgroup was captured in a short space of time. We subgroup to reduce the amount of analysis we have to do and it can protect us from non-normal distributions. We also said that our subgroup should only contain short term random variation and not special cause variation. We saw that an IMR chart was used when subgrouping was not possible and Xbar R & S were used when it was possible. Process capability also uses subgroups when possible but rather than employ different tools it gives you different metrics.

Overall process capability is P_{pk}, but we are given another measure of capability for just the short term random variation seen within subgroups. This is Within Process Capability or C_{pk}.

If you remember we said that the Voice of the Process, VOP, was 6σ. The VOP for C_{pk} is calculated using six times the StDev within the subgroups, $6\sigma_{within}$. As $6\sigma_{within}$ will be less than $6\sigma_{Overall}$, this means that C_{pk} will be greater than P_{pk}. This is even true when there isn't any special cause variation due to the way within StDev is calculated.

All I need is a good C_{pk}.

The critical point is that if special cause variation is present C_{pk} will be greater than P_{pk}. But the C_{pk} value is aspirational as it can only be achieved if you work hard to remove all the special cause variation. Now you know the secret that a good C_{pk} value does not always indicate a capable process. Therefore, if you have a supplier telling you that there C_{pk} is 2.0 always ask what is the value of the overall capability as it may be worse.

10.8 Normality.

Earlier in this module, I said that 'we are going to limit ourselves to normally distributed data or distributions where the underlying data is normally distributed'. You might have thought that was an odd way to phrase the sentence and that there might be something more to that statement. If you did, you would be right. Give yourself a pat on the back! When conducting a process capability study, you can expect to perform or see the results of a normality test. If the results show that the data is normally distributed you can proceed without any issues. However, if the results show the distribution is not normal then things get a bit sticky.

Take a look at Distribution1, which is made up of 200 data points. We see that the fitted normal curve matches the data pretty well. And when it is tested for normality, a P value of 0.68 is returned with the Anderson-Darling test which indicates that the data probably came from a normally distributed population. We would not have a problem using the capability tools for normal data described within this module for this data.

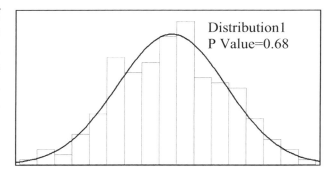

Now take a look at Distribution2, which is also made up of 200 data points. The fitted normal curve does not match the data. The data returns a P-value of less than 0.005 indicating that the data probably does not come from a normally distributed population. With a bit more experience or with help from a Black Belt, you could try transforming the data or applying a different distribution to the data. This is covered in the Black Belt Edition of this book.

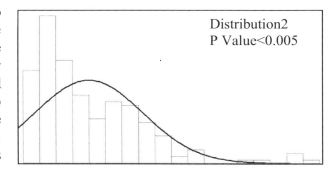

Distribution2 can be fitted with a Gamma distribution, and the VOP part of the capability calculation can be modified to cope with a Gamma distribution. The point for Green Belts is that the shape of the histogram is clearly not meant to be aligned with a normal distribution.

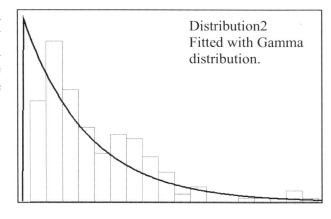

Finally, we get to the sticky bit I mentioned earlier. Distribution3 is made up of 200 data points again. It is fitted with a normal curve which matches the data pretty well. The Anderson-Darling test for normality returns a P-value of 0.02 and as you know this indicates that the data probably does not come from a normally distributed population.

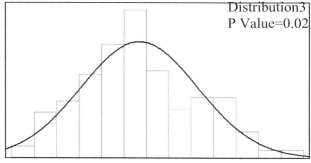

This bit is sticky as it relies on guesswork, however, the risk of making a mistake is reduced by experience and combining our knowledge of SPC. The guess that must be made is whether the underlying distribution is normal and is being affected by special cause variation or whether the underlying distribution is of a different type. If your judgement and SPC indicate the problem is due to special cause variation then you can use the tools described in this chapter in order to calculate capability metrics. But remember, due to the random nature of special cause variation, any metrics calculated when special cause variation is present should not be used for predicting future trends. They should only be used to describe the sample data set.

However, if you feel it is another distribution or the data requires transforming, please read the Black Belt Edition or ask a suitably experienced and qualified Black Belt for help.

10.9 Summary of Process Capability

1. Process capability is described as the Voice of the Customer, VOC, divided by the Voice of the Process, VOP.

$$\text{Process capability} = P_p = \frac{VOC}{VOP} = \frac{USL - LSL}{6StDevs}$$

VOP is taken to be six StDevs. VOC is the tolerance.

2. An overall capability of 2 describes a Six Sigma process. The specification limits will be six StDevs away from the mean.

3. We can use lookup tables to find the Yield% or DPMO for some capability levels. However, we need to be aware of the 1.5 sigma shift that is applied to represent the deterioration of capability over time.

4. P_p is helpful as a learning tool but it is not very good when the process is not centred. We, therefore, start to use P_{pk}, which looks at the distance of the mean to the nearest specification limit.

5. P_{pk} is used to represent overall capability. C_{pk} represents within capability; the calculation is based on the within subgroup StDev. If special cause variation is present C_{pk} is aspirational.

6. The methods and examples shown in the Green Belt Edition are for continuous data related to situations where the underlying distribution is normally distributed.

10.10 Process Capability for Continuous Data

Process Capability for Continuous Data within the Assistant	
Function	Reports the capability of a process which uses continuous data. Process capability is used to understand how well the process can meet the customer requirements. Minitab offers the Complete analysis or the Snapshot analysis within the Assistant.
Sample Size	The recommendation is to have at least 100 data points in order to ensure all sources of variation are captured.
Data type & Format	Time ordered continuous data captured in sub groups is preferred. However, if that is not possible individual data captured over a long period is also suitable. If only individual data over a short period is available use the Snapshot analysis. Also use this if the data is not in time order.
Considerations	The data should be normally distributed or close to being normal. The Assistant may offer to transform your data under certain conditions but that is not covered in this edition.

Example 10.10.1 Yellow Dot Squash Ball

The World Squash Federation has strict specifications for the equipment used in the game of squash. The single yellow dot ball must have a diameter between 39.5mm and 40.5mm. Brauer Squash Balls Ltd empties one of its boxes and checks the diameter of 100 squash balls. Use their data on diameter to conduct a capability assessment of their manufacturing process.

All data for this chapter is in '10 Process Capability.xlsx' and the data for this example is in the worksheet called 'Ball Diameter'.

As a box of squash balls have been emptied and then measured, we have no way of knowing if they were made in time order. Additionally, because we don't know anything about the time they were made, we cannot produce sub-groups. It is for these reasons that we must use the Snapshot Analysis for Process Capability.

1.   Transfer the data from the spreadsheet into Minitab.

2.   Click *Assistant<<Capability Analysis*

3.   Click on the *Capability Analysis* box, which is used for continuous data.

4.   The test menu opens. To start with we need to select whether we want to do the Complete or Snapshot analysis using the radio buttons. Select 'Snapshot'. When Snapshot is selected, any menu options used for the input of subgroups disappear.

5.   Under Process Data, use the drop-down selector to tell Minitab that 'Data are in one column'. Select 'Diameter' as the single column of data.

6.   Enter the specification limits of '39.5' and '40.5'. As it is sensible to have the process in the centre of the specification limits we can check whether our process has a mean of 40. Enter the target for the mean as '40'.

7.   Click OK to execute the procedure and generate the Report Card and Summary Report within the Output Pane.

In the top left corner of the Summary Report, we are shown the histogram of our process data with fitted Normal curve, the specification limits and target for the process mean. We can see that our squash ball distribution is closer to the USL than the LSL. None of the balls that were checked are out of specification.

Type of analysis

  ○ Complete

  ⦿ Snapshot (only use with individual data that are not in time order)

Process data

How are your data arranged in the worksheet?

Data are in one column

Column: Diameter

Specification limits (at least 1 required)

Lower spec: 39.5

Upper spec: 40.5

Mean test (optional)

Enter the target value for the process mean.

Target: 40

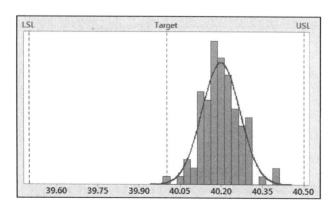

Below the Capability Plot, we have the Normality plot for our process data. With a P-Value of 0.856, we can say that our sample data probably did come from a normally distributed population. This is a critical step in the analysis as it is the fitted curve that lets us predict the shape of the population.

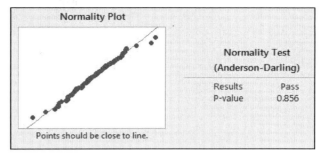

On the right, underneath the Customer Requirements section, we have the Process Characterization which delivers our capability data. As we used the Snapshot analysis, with no option for subgrouping, all the capability metrics are for Overall Capability.

We are told that the sample mean is 40.199 and that the mean is off-target. If you think back to the 1 sample t Test, this means that the population of ball diameters is not likely to have a mean diameter of 40.

Process Characterization	
Total N	100
Mean	40.199
Mean off target	Yes
P-value	0.000
Standard deviation	0.069176
Capability statistics	
Pp	2.41
Ppk	1.45
Z.Bench	4.35
% Out of spec (observed)	0.00
% Out of spec (expected)	0.00
PPM (DPMO) (observed)	0
PPM (DPMO) (expected)	7

Our process has a simple capability, P_P, of 2.41. As this value is above 1 we know that the process width fits within the spec limits. As the overall capability, P_{pk} is significantly less than P_p we can establish that the process is not centred. Also, as P_{pk} is greater than 1 we know that the process is not breaching the closest spec limit.

We are then given data on %defects and PPM (parts-per-million) or DPMO defects. Expected and observed relates to the fitted curve and the actual sample, respectively.

The conclusions from this analysis would be that the process is performing well against the spec limits. However, if it were centred, it would be quoted as being a Six Sigma process.

The report card tells us that our data was normally distributed; therefore, this analysis was appropriate. The amount of data we had was sufficient for establishing normality and giving accurate results. Finally, we are given information on the selection of the Snapshot analysis.

Process Characterization	
Total N	100
Mean	40.199
Mean off target	Yes
P-value	0.000
Standard deviation	0.069176
Capability statistics	
Pp	2.41
Ppk	1.45
Z.Bench	4.35
% Out of spec (observed)	0.00
% Out of spec (expected)	0.00
PPM (DPMO) (observed)	0
PPM (DPMO) (expected)	7

Check	Status
Normality	✓
Amount of Data	✓
Complete Analysis vs Snapshot	ⓘ

Example 10.10.2 More Squash Balls

Brauer Squash Balls Ltd want to qualify a secondary supplier, Parky Squash Balls limited. Parky Squash Balls claim that none of their squash balls will be out-of-spec on weight. The weight specification on squash balls for the WSF is 23g to 25g. Parky Squash balls send data from their production line on ball weights using a subgroup size of 3. Use their data on ball weight to conduct a capability assessment of their manufacturing process.

All data for this chapter is in '10 Process Capability.xlsx' and the data for this example is in the worksheet called 'Ball Weight'.

1. Transfer the data from the spreadsheet into Minitab. There are two columns of data. The 'Weight' column contains the continuous data of ball weight and the 'Group' column is an index of the subgroup number.

2. Click *Assistant<<Capability Analysis*

3. Click on the *Capability Analysis* box, which is used for continuous data.

4. The test menu opens. As we have data in subgroups, we can use the Complete Analysis. Select the radio button for the 'Complete' analysis.

5. Under Process Data, use the drop-down selector to tell Minitab that 'Data are in one column'. Select 'Weight' as the single column of data. We could use the radio button for a subgroup with a constant size or we can tell Minitab which column the subgroup IDs are in. I have opted for the latter.

6. Enter the specification limits of '23' and '25'. As it is sensible to have the process in the centre of the specification limits we can check whether our process has a mean of '24'.

7. Click OK to execute the procedure and generate a 4 page report within the Output Pane.

Let's start with the Summary Report, which is mainly based on the overall capability. The only exception is the bar display which tells us how capable the process is in terms of Z Bench score. Here we get the Z actual (overall score) and the Z potential score. Although, there should be no out-of-spec ball weights the score is less than 3. We are also told that the process mean is different to 24.

Process data

How are your data arranged in the worksheet?

Data are in one column

Column: Weight

How are your subgroups defined?

○ Constant size for all subgroups:

● Column of subgroup IDs: Group

Specification limits (at least 1 required)

Lower spec: 23

Upper spec: 25

Mean test (optional)

Enter the target value for the process mean.

Target: 24

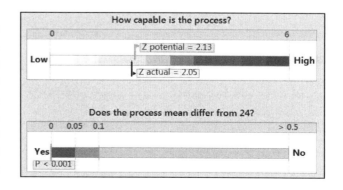

On the bottom left of the Summary Report, we have the Overall Capability Plot. We see the sample data as a histogram together with the fitted Normal curve using the Overall StDev. It is clear that the mean is to the right of the target and is closer to the USL than the LSL.

On the right, underneath the Customer Requirements section, we have the Process Characterization, which delivers our capability data. We have a simple capability, P_P, of 0.99. This value is very close to 1 which means that the process width is just shy of fitting within the specification limits. As the overall capability, P_{pk} is 0.68 we can establish that the process is not centred and should be making defective parts.

When we are given data on %defects we are told that there should be 2.01% defective parts. This should be setting off alarm bells. The capability study states that there should be 2.01% defects, but Parky Squash balls state that none of their balls will be out-of-spec. Let's look at the rest of the data before we make any conclusions.

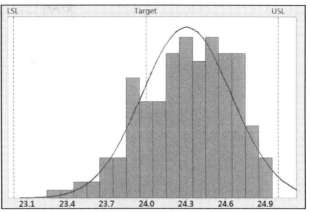

Process Characterization	
Mean	24.306
Standard deviation (overall)	0.33812
Actual (overall) capability	
Pp	0.99
Ppk	0.68
Z.Bench	2.05
% Out of spec	2.01
PPM (DPMO)	20097

Let's have a look at the SPC charts on the Diagnostic Report. We are presented with an Xbar R chart. From the chapter on control charts, we already know that that is the appropriate chart when you have a subgroup size of 3. We see that two points are out of control on the Xbar half of the chart. It does not tell me anywhere why these points are out of control but I deduce that it is because of Test 2 (9 points all in a row on either side of the centre line).

Below the Xbar R chart, we have the Normality plot for our process data. With a P-Value of 0.011, we can say that our data probably did not come from a normally distributed population. However, the fitted curve fits our sample data rather well; it's only the right-hand side of our sample data that is missing. We discussed Normality of our data in section 10.8. This is the

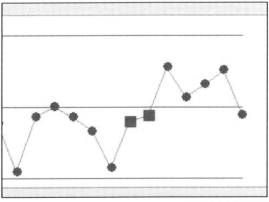

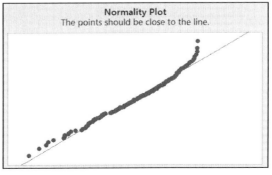

Normality Plot
The points should be close to the line.

occasion that we have to think about whether the underlying distribution is normal and is being affected by special cause variation or whether the underlying distribution is of a different type. We can only use the metrics in this study if we can conclude that the low P-Value for normality is due to special cause variation.

Again, just keep this in mind until we review all the data.

We then get to the Process Performance Report. This adds Within (or Potential) capability data to the information we have seen in the Summary Report already. Rather than go over the differences between the Actual and the Potential data, let's have a look at the Observed and Expected data. The Observed % Out-of-spec is 0%. As stated by the manufacturer you won't get a ball that is out-of-spec on weight. But the Expected % Out-of-spec is 2.01%. What this probably means is that the manufacturer is checking all the weights and removing those that are out-of-spec. Hence, the nice distribution with the right-hand side chopped off. This is also why the P-value for the Anderson Darling test was so low. This removal of the out-of-spec balls is a form of special cause variation.

The conclusion is that if you are buying from this manufacturer, you want them to continue with the 100% inspection. On the downside, it is probably their customers that are paying for the 2% of defects and the 100% inspection. I would steer well clear of this company.

What this example does show is a positive facet of capability studies. And that is you don't have to have all the data on a parameter to assess a process. You only have to have enough samples to be able to fit a distribution and check SPC charts.

Normality Test (Anderson-Darling)	
Results	Fail
P-value	0.011

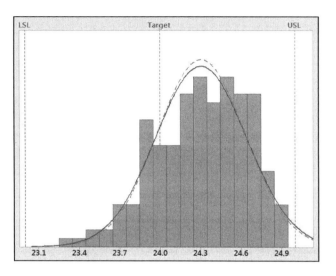

Capability Statistics	
Actual (overall)	
Pp	0.99
Ppk	0.68
Z.Bench	2.05
% Out of spec (observed)	0.00
% Out of spec (expected)	2.01
PPM (DPMO) (observed)	0
PPM (DPMO) (expected)	20097
Potential (within)	
Cp	1.02
Cpk	0.71
Z.Bench	2.13
% Out of spec (expected)	1.67
PPM (DPMO) (expected)	16672

10.11 Process Capability for Attribute Data

Process Capability for Attribute Data using the Assistant	
Function	Reports the capability of a process which uses attribute data to describe defective items. Unlike continuous data this capability is reported in defects per unit and % yield for Poisson Capability. And %Defects and DPMO for Binomial Capability. Much like the attribute data selection for control charts there are two types of capability to choose. Where the items being checked are only designated as pass or fail, no matter the number of defects, we use Binomial Capability. When an item can have more than 1 defect and we are counting the total defects of a subgroup we use Poisson Capability.
Sample Size	The recommendation is to have at least 100 data points in order to ensure all sources of variation are captured.
Data type & Format	Both capabilities use counts of defects within a sample that can either have a set or variable size. The difference is that items counted on the Binomial Capability can only be given a single defect classification or a pass. A single item on the Poisson Capability can have multiple defects.
Considerations	In order to establish whether the process is stable Binomial Capability will use the P chart and Poisson will use the U chart. If the charts are suffering from over or under dispersion Minitab will offer to convert them to the equivalent Laney chart. If this happens use the Laney chart. Usually, around 25 subgroups of data is sufficient to deliver accurate results. If required, Minitab will report the subgroup size that is required to deliver accurate results.

Example 10.11.1 Late Deliveries.

An online retailer wants to check the capability of its on-time delivery service. They collect data over 40 days on the number of dispatches that they make and whether the dispatch was late or not. They have an internal target of only having 3% of orders as late. Can you establish their capability and state whether the process is stable so that the actual figure can be used to make future predictions?
All data for this chapter is in '10 Process Capability.xlsx' and the data for this example is in the worksheet called 'Late Deliveries'.

1.   Transfer the data from the spreadsheet into Minitab. There are two columns of data. The 'Total Orders' column contains the number of orders shipped that day and the 'Late Order' contains the number of those orders that were late. In this example 'Late' is defective.

2.   Click *Assistant<<Capability Analysis.*

3. Click on the ***Binomial Capability Analysis*** box. We are using Binomial as the order only has two states; On-time or Late, with Late being considered defective.

4. The test menu opens. Enter 'Late Orders' as the column that contains the count of defective items. Select the Radio button for 'Column of subgroup sizes' then select 'Total Orders' as shown.

5. In this analysis, we don't compare the ratio of the VOP to the VOC. We conduct a test to check if the defect rate of the population is at a particular maximum level. We will enter 3%.

6. Click OK to execute the procedure and produce a 3 page report in the Output Pane.

Starting with the Summary Report, we see that on the top left, we have the results of the Hypothesis Test which asks is %defective at or below 3%. The answer is No so we must be above 3%.

The histogram on the bottom left shows our data against the 3% target, and it also shows the 95%CI of the defects. Therefore, we can say that the mean defect rate of the population is likely to be above 3%; we are later told that it is between 4.38 and 4.98.

On the top right of the Summary Report, we are given the Process Characterization data. We are told that 19,609 items were tested. You can see the immense amount of data collection that is required to drive Attribute Analysis and why you should always try and convert to continuous data collection systems wherever possible.

We are then given the Overall Capability data, and there isn't a great deal of it. We have a %defective of 4.57 which gives us a DPMO of 46,713. This is equivalent to a Z score of 1.68.

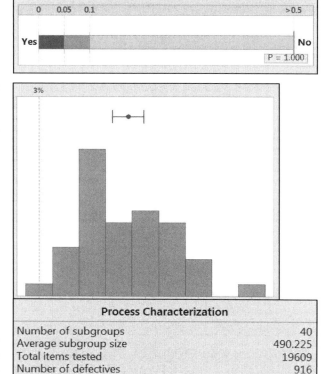

Process Characterization	
Number of subgroups	40
Average subgroup size	490.225
Total items tested	19609
Number of defectives	916

Process Capability (Overall)	
% Defective	4.67
95% CI	(4.38, 4.98)
PPM (DPMO)	46713
Process Z	1.68

On the Diagnostic Report, we have the P Chart. You will remember that the P Chart is the appropriate chart for attribute data that considers only the ratio of defective items to parts tested. Where a part can only have two designations, either as a defective or good part.

As we have a stable process we can use the capability data in the summary report to predict future performance.

The Cumulative % Defective chart shows how the accuracy of the estimate is improved by having more subgroups of data.

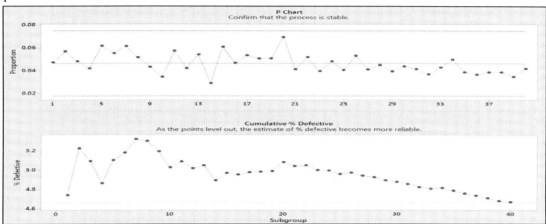

The Report Card, not shown here, confirms that we had a stable process and that we have a sufficient number of subgroups. The report card also makes the comment that if the 95% CI for the estimate of mean defects was too wide we could reduce the size of the CI by obtaining more data.

Example 10.11.2 Fish Distribution.

The EU Council Regulations fix the quotas that EU countries are allowed to fish in certain areas. They limit fish types, size and quota for a particular country. Several boats had their catches inspected within the IVb region over the last year. The total number of fish within the catch and the number of violations were recorded. Note, each fish could be subject to a number of violations. EU law states that the total number of violations for 100 fish should be no more than 4, which works out as 0.04 Defects per Unit (DPU). Please establish the capability of the fishing data collected and establish if it is capable.

Gadus morbua

All data for this chapter is in '10 Process Capability.xlsx' and the data for this example is in the worksheet called 'Poisson'.

1.   Transfer the data from the spreadsheet into Minitab. There are two columns of data. The 'Total catch' column contains the total number of fish within the catch and the 'Violations' column contains the total number of EU rules that were breached.

2.   Click *Assistant<<Capability Analysis*

3.   Click on the *Poisson Capability Analysis* box. We are using this as a single fish can have more than one violation.

4. The test menu opens. Enter **Violations** as the column that contains the count of defects. Select the Radio button for 'Column of subgroup sizes' then enter Total Catch as shown.

5. This analysis conducts a test to check if the defect rate of the population is at a particular maximum level. We will enter 0.04 defects per unit.

6. Click OK to execute the procedure.

7. Minitab detects Over-dispersion in our data which could result in the control limits of the U chart being too narrow. It is suggested that we use the Laney U chart instead. Click Yes to use the Laney U Chart.

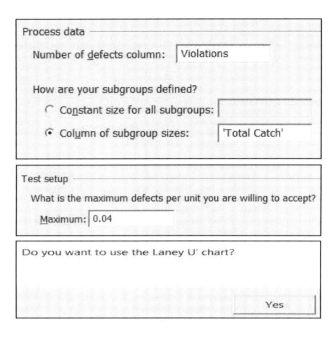

A 3 page report is produced in the Output Pane. Starting with the Summary Report, we see that on the top left, we have the results of the Hypothesis Test which asks is the DPU at or below 0.04. The answer is Yes.

The histogram on the bottom left shows our data against the 0.04 DPU target, and it also shows the 95%CI of the violations. We can see that the mean violation rate of the population is likely to be below 0.04 DPU; in fact, we are later told that it is between 0.0234 and 0.0307.

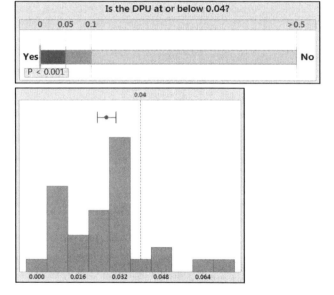

On the top right of the Summary Report, we are given the Process Characterization data. We are told that 8112 items were tested.

Process Characterization	
Number of subgroups	32
Average subgroup size	253.5
Total units tested	8112
Total defects	218

Below the Process Characterization data, we are given the Overall Capability data. The average DPU from the sample is 0.0269 and the Yield is 97.3%, where Yield is defined as the chance of producing a unit with no defects.

Process Capability (Overall)	
Defects per unit (DPU)	0.0269
95% CI	(0.0234, 0.0307)
Yield	97.3%

Yield is the chance of producing a unit with no defects.

On the Diagnostic Report, we have the Laney U Chart. We have a stable process so we can use the capability data in the summary report to predict future performance.

The Cumulative % Defective chart shows how the accuracy of the estimate is improved by having more subgroups of data, not shown here.

The Report Card, not shown here, confirms that we had a stable process and that we have a sufficient number of subgroups.

10.12 Process Capability Exercise

Exercise 10.12.1 Process Capability

Data is taken from a process in time order with a subgroup size of 7. Use the Assistant to calculate capability metrics using the Complete Analysis for continuous data. The LSL is 87, the USL is 97 and the target for the process mean is 92.

Analyse the data in File 10 Process Capability.xlsx worksheet Ex 10.12.1 and answer the questions shown below.
1) Is the process stable and is it normally distributed?
2) How capable is the process?
3) Is the process breaching either spec limit?
4) Is the process aligned between the spec limits?

Exercise 10.12.2 Before/After Process Capability

Unicorn Shampoo uses the Gobee 50 filling machine. The LSL is 200g and the lower spec limit is the legally binding limit. The company save money by keeping as close to the LSL as possible but also want to always be legally compliant. Therefore, they have an internal rule for filling machines that the mean delivery weight must be set so that it is 4 StDevs away from the LSL. For example, if the Gobee 50 had a StDev of 4g, the mean delivery weight would have to be set to 216g.

Unicorn Shampoo are offered the newer Gobee 200 machine and are told that they will be able to generate savings in fill weight by going to the new machine, as it will have a lower delivery StDev. You have been given the job of assessing the Gobee 200 against the existing Gobee 50.

Using the Before/After Capability Analysis within the Assistant and the data in File 10 Process Capability.xlsx worksheet Ex 10.12.2 and answer the questions shown below. The data contains two columns of delivery weights, one from each of the machines.
1) Is normal capability analysis applicable to both these filling machines?
2) Is the mean delivery of the Gobee 50 set at the correct level for it's current StDev?
3) Does the Gobee 200 have a lower delivery StDev than the older machine?
4) Based on the test data, what can the mean delivery weight of the Gobee 200 be set to?
5) Based on a cost of £0.003 per gram of Shampoo and a volume of 20million bottles per month, what will the saving be?

11 Evaluation of Measurement Systems

11.1   What is Measurement System Analysis (MSA)

The first thing to keep in mind is that Measure has a stage dedicated to it in DMAIC. Everything else you have been doing is a study within one of the DMAIC stages. The objective of the measure phase is to measure your current state and understand the gap to the required state. To start measuring, you must have a reliable measurement system. Understanding your measurement system is extremely important and yet it takes an experienced practitioner to give it the respect it deserves. On this occasion experienced means someone who has not done the Measure Analysis correctly in a past project and then regretted it.

Variance due to
measurement = 3g

Variance due to
Process = 5g

Total observed Variance = 8g

Var weigh scale **+ Var** process

Maximum acceptable level of Variance = 10g

Let's say that we had a process where we were filling bags of sand to sell. The process filled the bags, and we weighed them on a cheap set of scales. The bag filling process will have variation. The weigh-scale also has variation. This might appear harder to appreciate but if you weighed the same weight on it over and over again it would give slightly differing values, it is a cheap weigh-scale after all.

As we have used variances and not StDevs, we can add the variances together to show the total observed variance.

We can then compare our Total Observed variance with what we deem is acceptable.

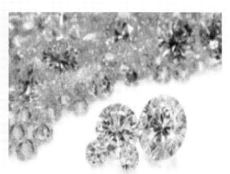

Variance due to measurement = 3g

Variance due to Process = 2g

Total observed Variance = 5g

Var weigh scale + Var process

Maximum acceptable level of Variance = 3g

Okay, now our process is not filling bags with sand anymore. We are filling them with small diamonds. Suddenly our maximum acceptable level of variance changes. It's obvious we don't want to give away more than we have to and our customers are susceptible to being short-changed.

We need to change our total observed variance. Do we tackle the measurement system or the process? Well if we don't try and understand the error generated by our measurement system we won't make an informed choice.

In simplistic terms, the MSA technique we are going to concentrate on looks at our measurement error and either compares it to our process variation or our customer tolerance. Depending on the value of the ratio, our measurement system will be graded as acceptable, marginal or unacceptable.

Although not covered here, if the measurement system must be improved, we need to understand the type of measurement error that caused the problem and then figure out how to eliminate it or reduce it.

11.2 Why MSA is fundamental to DMAIC

This section is here purely to say 1) Take MSA seriously, 2) Don't try and leave this step out and 3) Don't give in if you are being leveraged to ignore this step.

If the fact that the observable reading always contains measurement error has not been enough to satisfy doubters of MSA, you could still face the arguments shown below for not doing the MSA.

1) MSA can be time-consuming, both in the initial study and especially if improvements to the measurement system are required. Replacing a measurement system is going to be hugely time-consuming.

2) The measurement system you are assessing has been in use for some time without any issues being reported.

3) There does not appear to be any added value by conducting an MSA only a delay from the time it takes.

The response to these arguments are

1) Yes, it can be time-consuming but in the long run, it will save time and improve the process.

2) There has been error in every measurement system ever built. Even established measurement systems will add error to the observed measurement. You will never really find out how much until you assess the measurement system.

3) The value of this step is added through the successful completion of the project. Most legacy measurement systems will probably not be rated as adequate. Missing out the measurement step altogether usually leads to the project team backtracking to complete the measure phase later on.

11.3 When to Apply MSA

As soon as we have finished the Define phase on the DMAIC roadmap, we should know what is our key output variable. The first thing we do in the Measure phase is set up the MSA exercise on the systems that measure that key output variable. Once we have a reliable measurement system, we can then start to measure the process and assess where the gaps are and conduct SPC and Process Capability studies.

What about when we have completed the Analyse phase and we understand which key input variables affect the key output variable? Is it as essential to have robust measurement systems in place for the key input variables? The answer is yes, we should check that our key input variables are being reliably measured as well.

11.4 What We Cover

MSA is covered within the Assistant and within the traditional menu's and several tools can be used. We are going to be covering essential tools for Six Sigma Green Belts. These are the Gage R&R Study (Crossed) and the Attribute Agreement Analysis. To support the Gage R&R Crossed study we will also look at the Gage run Chart in the classic menu's. I don't cover how to produce the Gage R&R worksheets as this is straightforward.

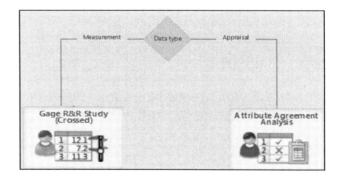

The Black Belt Edition covers Gage R&R Expanded, Type 1 Gage study and the Gage Linearity and Bias Study.

There are other types of project where the Key Output Variable may also depend on transactional systems where the tools mentioned above are not required. For instance, on a Stock Accuracy Project where the final metric depends on transactions as well as measurement systems. In this case, Process Mapping and Failure Modes and Effects Analysis (FMEA) can be used to reduce the measurement risk. As this is a Minitab book, this methodology won't be covered here but I wanted to make you aware there were still options outside of Minitab to improve transactional measurement systems.

11.5 Types of Measurement Error.

Two of the most important terms in MSA are Precision and Accuracy. I have always seen precision and accuracy taught by firing arrows at targets, so I thought I would try something different. Precision relates to the spread of the measurements and accuracy refers to how well the mean of the measurements aligns to the real value.

To provide an example based definition of Precision and Accuracy, I am going to take the opportunity of putting a picture of my kids into the book. It was taken around 2010. My youngest daughter, Raeesa, is at the front, then my son Humzah in the middle and then my oldest daughter Iqra at the back. Let's pretend that I give them each the task of measuring Iqra's height. They have to take 100 separate measurements. As fathers are very knowledgeable, I know that Iqra's real height is 165cm. Using the measurements provided by Iqra, Humzah and Raeesa I form the Normal distributions of their measurements and display them on the chart shown against the real height of 165cm.

Raeesa had a few problems measuring Iqra's height as she was a bit shorter and suffered a parallax error which made the mean of her measurements different to the real value. But her measurements did not have much variation. We can say that her measurements are not accurate but they are precise as accuracy relates to alignment with the mean and precision to the spread of measurements.

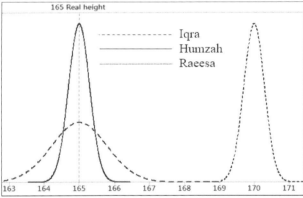

Next, we will look at Humzah's measurements. The mean of his measurements aligns with the real value and his measurements did not have much variation. We can say that Humzah's measurements are accurate and precise.

Finally, we will look at Iqra's measurements. The mean of her measurements aligns with the real value. However, as she had to measure her own height, her measurements did have a lot of variation. We can say that Iqra,s measurements are accurate but not precise.

There is another error type that usually does not get a significant mention and this is Resolution. Resolution for measurement systems is the smallest degree as to which a change can be detected. An example of a system with poor resolution would be measuring a 100m sprint race with a sundial. We usually eliminate resolution error when we design/purchase a measurement system. A good rule of thumb is that the measurement system should be able to resolve to $1/10^{th}$ of the tolerance width.

11.6 Accuracy Errors

Accuracy errors can be broken down into Bias, Linearity and Stability errors. Let's say that I have an ordinary pan weigh-scale and 10, 20, 30, 40 & 50 gram weights.

I put the weights one at a time and record real load versus the observed measurement from the weigh scale. If I had a bias error, I would find that the difference between the real load and the observed measurement was constant across the range of weights. The error that is the difference between the real and observed measurement is called the offset. For this weigh scale we have a positive offset of 4 grams. Even when there is no load on the weigh scale, it is still reading 4 grams. A bias error can have a positive or negative offset. Minitab can tell us if the bias error is statistically significant using the right analysis.

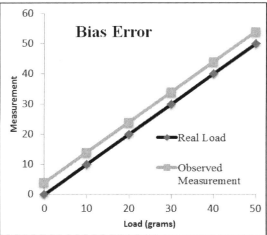

If my weigh scale had an offset that changed across the range of measurements, that would be called a Linearity Error. Minitab can tell us if the linearity error is statistically significant using the correct analysis.

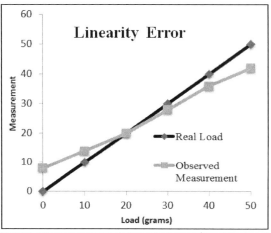

In the previous two cases, the x-axis on the graph was the range of the weights used. Stability Errors are different in that they manifest themselves over time. So let's say that I placed only the 30 gram weight on the weigh scale and took scale readings every 10 hours. A stability error would show itself as an increasing offset over time.

It is possible to have a measurement system that has all three types of accuracy errors.

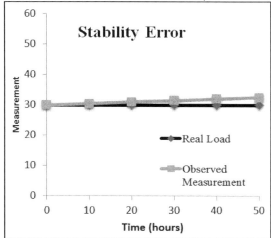

11.7 Precision Errors

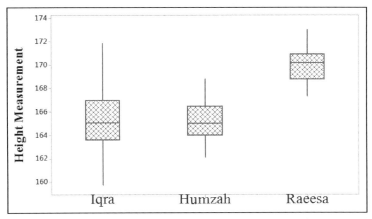

If you remember back to when we started this section, we used the narrative of my kids measuring Iqra's height. Let's go back to that example for the next section and have a look at what the boxplot of the data might have looked like.

Precision Errors break down into two components, and these are called Repeatability and Reproducibility. Repeatability is the measurement error produced when one person repeatedly measures the same thing. We can see that all three kids contribute to the total repeatability error. We can also see that Iqra has the highest repeatability error of the three, as her measurements have the greatest spread. Reproducibility is the measurement error that is obtained due to different people measuring the same thing. We have a reproducibility error because Raeesa is measuring differently to Iqra and Humzah.

Reproducibility can be further broken down into an Operator*Part error if the interaction is present, otherwise, it is all down to the difference in Operators/measurers. The Operator*Part interaction occurs when an operator is having trouble measuring a particular part.

11.8 A Breakdown of Measurement Errors

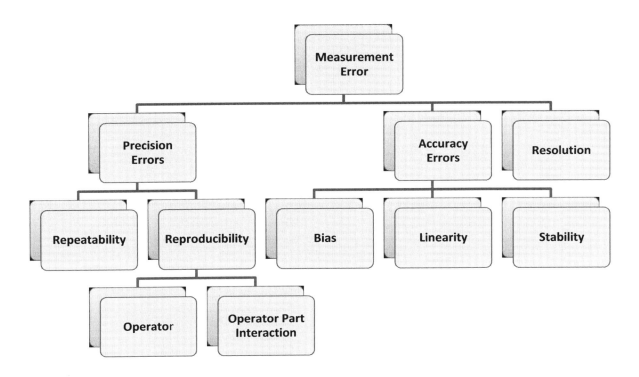

11.9 Gage R&R Introduction

A Gage R&R study will establish the Repeatability and Reproducibility of a measurement system. Repeatability is the measurement error when the same person measures the same thing repeatedly. Reproducibility is the measurement error when different people measure the same thing. Let's call the 'same thing' the part and the measurer an operator (an operator does not have to be a person; it can be a machine). Whether it's the same operator or different operators, you can appreciate that Gage R&R involves a lot of measuring the same part over and over.

Therefore, if your measurement system is measuring parts that are transient, you cannot perform a Gage R&R. This may not apply to everyone but I work in the Chemical Process Industry and we have lots of instrumentation measuring the process. We have a lot of instruments measuring parameters like flow, pressure and temperature of the continuous process. However, you would not be able to conduct a Gage R&R because the part is transient and you cannot perform repeat measurements. For example, if you had a process flowmeter that was measuring water delivery through a pump, you could ask an operator to take one measurement. However, you would not have a part where you could ask different operators to measure it or the same operator to take repeat measurements. The best approach for these types of measurement systems is sending them back to the manufacturer for calibration or to try and check one instrument against another.

Also, if you are measuring something that will change in a short time scale you also need to take care that your operators are not measuring a part that is changing

As a minimum, you need three columns of data to make your Gage R&R study work. You need a column identifying the Operators and Parts and the continuous data for the Measurement.

Formed in 1982, the Automotive Industry Action Group (AIAG) was a non-profit organisation that was originally created to form a framework for quality improvement in the automotive industry. It's membership and scope have increased considerably since then but in the early years, they suggested the framework for a Gage R&R Crossed should be as a minimum 3 operators, 2 repeats and 10 parts, which made 60 measurements in total. At that time, it was thought that 10 parts were sufficient to give an accurate measure of the part to part variation. However, in the development of the Assistant the research conducted by Minitab has found that 10 parts may not be sufficient to provide an accurate measure of the part to part variation. Minitab now recommends that the historic standard deviation is entered as a separate parameter. If that is done then 10 parts will be sufficient for the study. If a historical standard deviation is not available then you need to have more than 10 parts. The more the better, typically 15 to 35.

The parts used must be selected randomly and must be normal good parts produced by the process. The reason for this is that the amount of measurement error will be compared to the process variation. If we artificially increase the part to part variation by selecting out-of-specification parts then that will make our measurement system metric better than they deserve to be. However, this does not apply if we enter a historic standard deviation which is only taken from good parts.

Operator selection is also important. Operators should be randomly selected out of the group that actually conducts the measurements as a part of their role. Don't make yourself an operator if you are short of volunteers, unless the measurement is within your normal duties.

At the heart of the Gage R&R is a 2 way ANOVA where Parts and Operators are Random Factors. If we start to deliberately select them it will cause a problem with the mechanics of the ANOVA study.

Also, when asking the operators to measure the parts keep the part numbers hidden from the operators, this is called a blind study. And randomise the order the operators are measuring the parts. If this is not done operators tend to remember their previous measurements, especially if they had a problem with a particular part.

When using the Assistant for Gage R&R, you will be presented with one decision bar in the Summary Report that will tell you whether your measurement system is Acceptable, Marginal or Unacceptable. This decision is based on whether the ratio of measurement system variation to process variation is <10%, between 10% and 30% or >30%. This is called the %Study Variation. It's best to be aware that in older versions of Minitab, if a historical process variation value was entered then, %Study Variation would be called %Process Variation. This convention has now changed and the term '%Study Variation' is used regardless of whether a historical value is used or not..

If the measurement system is associated with a tolerance (specification limit) you should also enter it into the procedural menu's. This will generate another decision bar which will ask whether you can differentiate good parts from bad. This decision is based on whether the ratio of measurement system variation to tolerance is <10%, between 10% and 30% or >30%. It's the same numbers again so it is easy to remember. This metric is called %Tolerance.

With two decision bars, it is possible to get conflicts and then things get interesting. For example, if your %Study Variation is marginal, but your % Tolerance is unacceptable at 31%, what do you do? Would you improve the measurement system or would you try and change the process specifications to get a larger tolerance. Or what if the %Tolerance was <10% but the %Study Variation was unacceptable?

The key to the dilemma is to consider whether the MSA is being conducted to improve the process performance or whether it is to improve the recognition of defective parts. For process improvement, %Study Variation becomes the primary metric and for identification of defective parts, it is %Tolerance.

The standard gage structure is the crossed structure, as shown in the upper diagram. Each operator will measure each part more than once. This is because repeat measurements are required to calculate the repeatability term. Notice how the arrows cross each other, I like to think that is how this type of Gage R&R got its name.

It is possible to have measurement systems that are destructive. For example, fire resistance testing of safety devices, bursting disc failure or strength testing. To conduct repeat measurements for this type of testing, we need to be able to make a batch of parts that have identical properties. If we can make enough identical parts so that all the operators can measure every part the required number of times, then we can still use the Gage R&R Crossed.

However, if we can't make enough identical parts that every operator can measure them with the required repeats, then we can use the nested structure. Using this method parts are nested with a single operator. If identical parts cannot be manufactured then a Gage R&R study cannot be conducted.

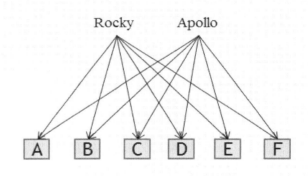

Crossed Structure without shown repeat measurements

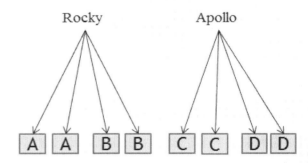

Nested Structure, shown with repeat measurements

We should now know enough Gage R&R terminology to go into the examples and exercises.

11.10 Gage R&R Crossed

Gage R&R Crossed	
Function	Determines whether a measurements system is suitable in terms of precision errors, reproducibility and repeatability.
Sample Size	The sample size is driven by the need to have as a minimum 3 operators checking 10 parts with a repeat reading. The minimum data requirements are dependant upon having a value for the historical process deviation which is entered into the procedural menu.
Data type & Format	Continuous measurement data is required.
Considerations	Gage R&R assumes that the gage is calibrated and ready to use. Try to employ a blind study with the order of the parts randomised. The parts should be randomly selected from a stable process and should be normal good parts. Parts should not be taken at the extremes of the process. Operators for the study should be randomly selected, the number of operators used affects the accuracy of the reproducibility value.

Example 11.10.1 Lithium Concentration in Drinking Water

Khan Smart Water claims to contain lithium in the ionic form which boosts intelligence. The team in the lab uses X-ray Fluorescence Spectrometry to verify the lithium concentration. To ensure they were working consistently, a Gage R&R crossed data collection exercise was conducted. The data collection involved 4 lab operators, 4 repeat measurements and 8 parts. By checking previous analytical data, it was found that the process StDev was 0.14 µg/ltr. Analyse the result of the Gage R&R and establish if the measurement system is acceptable. If it is not acceptable, make recommendations for improvement.

All data for this chapter is in '11 MSA.xlsx,' and the data for this example is in the worksheet called 'Water'.

The first thing we are going to do is look at all the data and get a feel for what the results are going to show. The Assistant is very visual when it presents results anyway, but I find the Gage Run Chart an excellent first tool for looking at the results of a Gage R&R Crossed study. It is accessed via the classic menus.

1. Transfer the data into Minitab. There are 3 columns of data.

2. Click *Stat<<Quality Tools<<Gage Study<<Gage Run Chart*

3. Enter the column headings as shown in the main menu. Note, I use column headings that are aligned to the appropriate menu selections to reduce human error.

Part numbers:	Part
Operators:	Operator
Measurement data:	Measurement

4. It is always useful to log some information about your study mainly when different iterations are used, and then it becomes difficult to distinguish the charts from the various studies. Click on the **Gage Info** button. Enter the relevant details.

5. Click OK & OK again to create the chart. View the chart within the Output Pane.

Gage name:	X-ray Fluorescence Spectrometry
Date of study:	14-June-2016
Reported by:	Bedford Team
Gage Tolerance:	
Miscellaneous:	25 micro g/ltr study

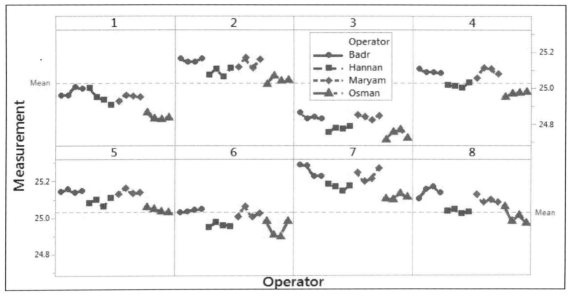

The number above each of the sub-charts indicates the part that was measured. Within each sub-chart are the 4 repeat measurements made by the 4 operators. To look for the range of the parts, look to the highest average measurements compared to the lowest. I estimate that part 7 has the highest concentration of lithium and part 3 has the lowest concentration. To look for repeatability issues, check how well the operators agree with themselves within the subplots. To check for reproducibility issues, check how well the operators agree with each other across the subplots. I estimate that I see more reproducibility than repeatability.

Having got a feel for what we expect, the results will show we can now produce the results of the full study and examine them.

6. Click **Assistant<< Measurement System Analysis**

7. Click on the **Gage R&R Study (Crossed)** box, which is used for continuous data.

8. The test menu opens. Enter the data columns into the menu, as shown. Using the appropriate column headings makes life much easier.

Measurement data	
Operators:	Operator
Parts:	Part
Measurements:	Measurement

9. In the Process Variation section, you can see that using the historical StDev is the default option. Enter 0.14 as the historical value of StDev. As we only had 8 parts we were in danger of not getting an accurate estimate of process variation had we not entered a historical value.

10. Click OK to execute the procedure and produce a 3 page report in the Output Pane.

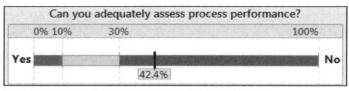

In the top left corner of the Summary Report, we have the decision bar which tells us that we cannot adequately assess process performance with this measurement system. Our Measurement System Variation is 42.4% of the process variation and we need to be less than 10% for our measurement system to be acceptable, between 10% and 30% for marginal.

Below the decision bar, we have the Variation by Source plot, which shows how the Total Gage Variation can be broken down. If you click on the bars, you can get the exact percentages. But hang on a minute! 38+17 does not equal 42! Unfortunately, that's how these metrics work as they are based on percentages of StDevs. As they are based on StDevs, they no longer make sense when added together. What we can say is that Reproducibility is greater than Repeatability.

On the top left of the Variation Report, we have the Operator by Part plot. This plot can show reproducibility issues and Operator*Part interactions. In this chart we have 4 series, one for each Operator, they show the average of the measurements by Operator for each part. In the diagram, the profiles for each operator are almost parallel with almost a constant bias between some of the operators. This indicates the operators are consistently getting different results.

If there were an operator part interaction, the lines would not be parallel and would probably cross. As our lines are parallel and not on top of each other, we have reproducibility errors. Incidentally, as we don't know the real measurement for any of

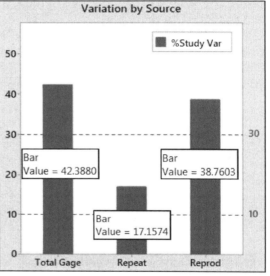

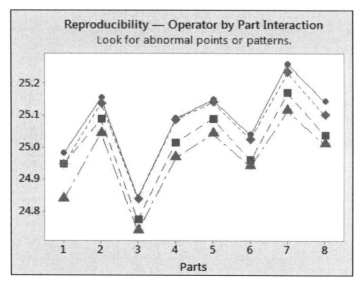

the parts we cannot say which operator is reading high or low compared to the real value.

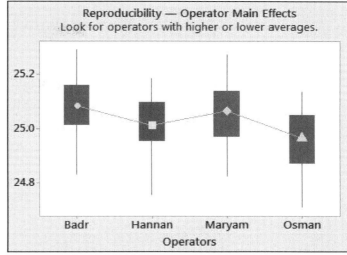

On the bottom left of the Variation Report, we have the Operator Main Effects plot. This shows the measurements taken by the operators for all parts in the form of a box plot. Badr and Maryam are taking measurements that are higher than those of Hannan and Osman. Again we don't know whose measurements are correct.

On the top right of the Variation Report, we have the Test-Retest Ranges, which can highlight repeatability issues. The chart on the left shows the Operator Ranges by Part. On average Badr had the lowest repeatability error and Osman had the highest. We also see that Hannan measured most of the parts reasonably well apart from one in which he had trouble. We can hover the mouse pointer over that part to find out that he had issues with part 1.

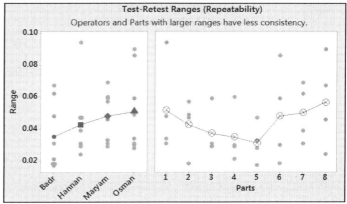

The chart on the right shows the Part measurement ranges by Operator. The part which had the greatest measurement range was part 8.

On the bottom right, we are given the breakdown of %Study Variation. At the bottom of the table, we are reminded that the &Study Variation was calculated from the historical StDev value.

Finally, we reach the Report Card, which gives information on the number of parts that should be used for the study and the process standard deviation. The Report Card is not shown here.

Source	StDev	%Study Variation
Total Gage	0.059	42.39
Repeatability	0.024	17.16
Reproducibility	0.054	38.76
Operator	0.054	38.76
Part-to-Part	0.127	90.57
Study Variation	0.140	100.00
Study Variation (StDev): historical standard deviation		

In conclusion, this measurement system would be rated as unacceptable. It suffered from both repeatability and reproducibility issues, but the reproducibility was by far the more significant issue. There is an almost constant bias between the operators, indicating that they are doing something consistently different in the measurement procedure.

Example 11.10.2 Improved Procedure for analysis of Lithium Concentration in Drinking Water

Following the poor results from the previous gage study, the lab team has reviewed its procedures and implemented standard working with visual standard operating procedures. The team has now conducted a data collection exercise for a Gage R&R Crossed using the improved procedures.

The number for process StDev remains at 0.14 µg/ltr. The team now also wants to introduce specification limits for lithium-ion concentration which are 24 to 26 µg/ltr. Analyse the result of the Gage R&R and establish if the measurement system is acceptable. If it is not acceptable, make recommendations for further improvement.

All data for this chapter is in '11 MSA.xlsx,' and the data for this example is in the worksheet called 'More Water.'

Let's start by looking at the Gage Run Chart again.

1. Transfer the data into Minitab. There are 3 columns of data.
2. Click **Stat<<Quality Tools<<Gage Study<<Gage Run Chart**
3. Enter the column headings as shown in the main menu.
4. Click on the **Gage Info** button and enter some useful information regarding the study.
5. Click OK & OK again to create the chart.

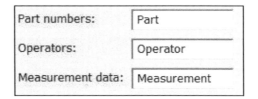

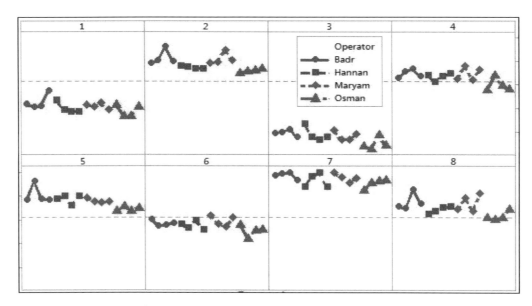

Navigate to the Gage Run Chart. The same parts were used for this study, so parts 3 and 7 still represent the range of the parts. By looking at the chart I would conclude that there appears to be a better agreement between the operators than in the previous study, which means Reproducibility should have improved. I don't think the repeatability of the operators has improved.

Let's run the full Gage R&R study and see if the Reproducibility has improved.

6. Click **Assistant<< Measurement System Analysis**

7. Click on the **Gage R&R Study (Crossed)** box, which is used for continuous data.

8. The test menu opens. Enter the data columns into the menu, as shown.

9. Enter 0.14 as the historical value of StDev.

10. On this occasion, we have the tolerance values for the process so we can check whether the measurement system can distinguish good parts from bad. Enter the tolerance as shown or enter a tolerance width of 2.

11. Click OK to execute the procedure and produce a 3 page report in the Output Pane.

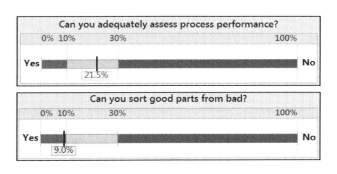

In the top left corner of the Summary Report, we now have two decision bars. The first is the same as before and asks us if we can adequately assess process performance with this measurement system. Our Measurement System Variation is 21.3%, which is a great improvement on the time before. However, this only grades our measurement system as marginal.

The other decision bar asks whether we can sort good parts from bad based on our tolerance/specification limits. As this value is 9%, our measurement system is actually graded as acceptable for sorting defective parts.

Below the decision bar, we have the Variation by Source plot which shows how the Total Gage Variation can be broken down in terms of both %Study Variation and %Tolerance. Remember both of these metrics are totally different and have different meanings. This chart tells us that reproducibility is now less than repeatability, which indicates that those improvements the team made really worked. The repeatability component of %Study Variation is now 15.88% which is a very small reduction on the previous study.

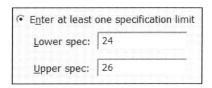

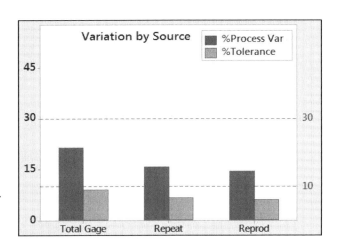

On the top left of the Variation Report the Operator by Part plot shows that we still have a very slight bias between the operators. We also see that again the tie lines are mostly parallel indicating that an operator part interaction is not present. An operator part interaction means that a particular operator is having problems with a particular part.

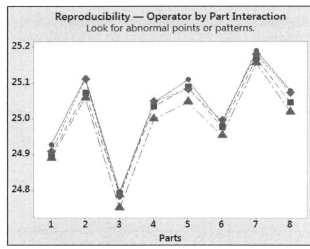

On the bottom left of the Variation Report, the Operator Main Effects shows that Badr and Maryam are still taking measurements that are higher than those of Hannan and Osman. The improvements made between the studies have made things better but perhaps there is still work to be done. Further improvements might make the %Study Variation acceptable as well.

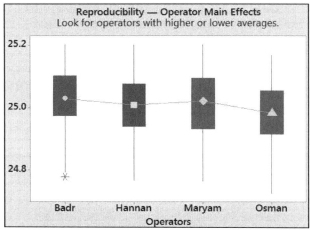

Let's go to the top right of the Variation Report, where we have the Test-Retest Ranges. From having the lowest repeatability error, Badr has now gone to having the highest. Previously, Hannan had issues measuring part 1, these problems have now disappeared.

The chart on the right shows the Part measurement ranges by Operator. The part which had the greatest measurement range is still part 8.

On the bottom right we are given the breakdown of %Study Variation and %Tolerance. One thing that I did not mention previously is that if there were an operator part interaction, its contribution to Total Gage variability would be shown here. As the operator part interaction is not significant, it is removed from the calculation.

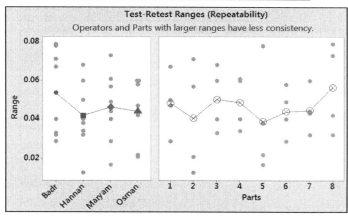

Source	StDev	%Study Variation	%Tolerance
Total Gage	0.030	21.46	9.01
Repeatability	0.022	15.88	6.67
Reproducibility	0.020	14.43	6.06
Operator	0.020	14.43	6.06
Part-to-Part	0.137	97.67	41.02
Study Variation	0.140	100.00	42.00

Study Variation (StDev): historical standard deviation
Tolerance (upper spec - lower spec): 2

The Operator by Part interaction was not statistically significant and was removed from the table.

Finally, we reach the Report Card, which gives information on the number of parts that should be used for the study and the process standard deviation. The Report Card is not shown here.

11.11 Attribute Agreement Analysis within the Assistant

Attribute Agreement Analysis in the Assistant	
Function	This analysis checks for consistency and accuracy across appraisers. The keyword is 'appraisal' and not measurement. This procedure rates systems of inspection for subjective ratings provided by appraisers.
Sample Size	The recommendation is to have at least 3 appraisers and have 2 repeats. The minimum number of parts required is not specified. However, to generate useful confidence intervals around 15-20 parts should be the starting point.
Data type & Format	The consistency of checks against a binary 'pass' or 'fail' is assessed in the method used by the assistant. The method used within the classic menu's can assess for classifications with more than two levels.
Considerations	Each appraiser should check the same number of items. Each part must be correctly appraised by a master appraiser. This appraisal is known as the 'Standard' for the part. Parts should be presented to the appraiser in a randomised order with part number not visible to the appraisers.

Example 11.11.1 Used Car 101 Point Reliability Check

Hurts Used Cars are very proud of the 101 point reliability check they carry out on their used cars prior to sale. They take it so seriously that they regularly test their engineers using Appraiser Agreement Analysis. They take 20 cars and have them assessed by their Chief Engineer. If they pass all 101 checks, they get a Pass designation but if they fail any check they get an overall fail designation. Four engineers have conducted the checks on the 20 cars and the data has been recorded. Analyse the data to check how well the four engineers agree with the Chief Engineer.

All data for this chapter is in '10 MSA.xlsx,' and the data for this example is in the worksheet called 'Cars.'

1. Transfer the data into Minitab. There are 4 columns of data.
2. Click **Assistant<<Measurement System Analysis**
3. Click on the **Attribute Agreement Analysis** box, which is used to assess appraisers.
4. The test menu opens. The Engineer column gives the name of our appraisers, so enter that against Appraisers. Our part descriptions, listed as numbers between 1 & 20, are listed in the Vehicle column, enter that against Test Items. The Eng Result column is the decision the engineers/appraisers made so that goes against Appraisal Results. Our known standard is in the column called Chief Engineer.

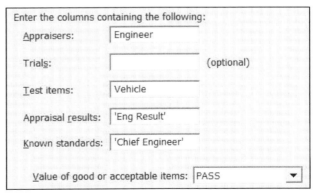

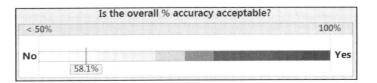

5. As we can use any words to express a 'good part' we have to tell Minitab what we are calling acceptable items, enter 'PASS' using the drop-down selector.

6. Click OK to execute the procedure.

The Assistant generates 4 pages report in the Output Pane, which is packed with information. We will cover some of the highlights.

At the top left of the Summary Report, we have our decision bar which asks is the overall% accuracy acceptable. There can be no guidance on what the correct score might be as it is specific to the appraisal system you are checking. For this appraisal, I would say that a 58.1% agreement is not acceptable.

Below the decision bar, we can see the scores for the appraisers. We see that they all scored into the sixties except for Miro, who scored an inferior 42.5% agreement.

On the top right of the Summary Report, we are given the Misclassification Rates. We can see the breakdown and see that 38.6% of the Passes were graded incorrectly as Fails, with 45.8% the other way. On 28.7% of occasions, the appraisers rated the same vehicle differently between their own repeat measurements. At least this indicates the parts were kept blind and the study was probably randomised.

Let's move on to the Accuracy Report to see if we can establish what is happening. On the top left, we see 95% confidence intervals for appraiser agreement with the standard. As Miro's 95%CI overlaps with the other engineers, we cannot say that he is appraising differently. This is a shame even though we had 20 parts; the 95%CIs are still fairly wide.

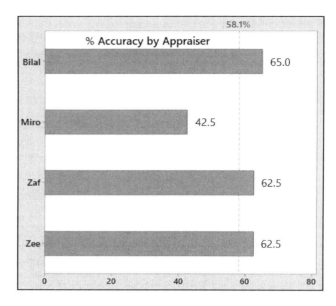

Misclassification Rates	
Overall error rate	41.9%
PASS rated FAIL	38.6%
FAIL rated PASS	45.8%
Mixed ratings (same item rated both ways)	28.7%

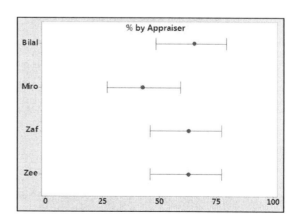

The other graph of interest, which is shown on the top left of the Accuracy Report, shows how well the Appraisers agreed when the Standard was a Pass. We see that on this occasion that Miro is grading more cars as Fails when they are Passes. In terms of Agreement this is actually a bad thing but for the customer, it is good as Miro is risk-averse. However, he will be sending more cars for repair than required by the Chief Engineer.

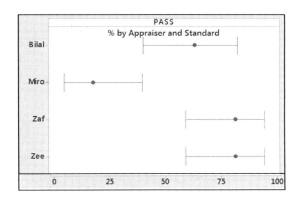

The other part of this graph looks at how well appraisers agreed when the standard was a fail. On that graph, which is not shown here, all 95%CIs overlap. Again, reducing the CIs with more samples might show something different.

Let's move onto the Misclassification Report and see what part of the story this reveals. On the top left and right, we can establish which parts were most often misclassified. I have shown the chart for Passes rated as Fails and we see that part 6 was most often misclassified. If one part stood out, it might be worth investigating the part and finding out if there was something obscure about the part.

At the bottom of the Misclassification Report, we have three charts detailing appraiser misclassification rates. On the %Pass rated Fail chart, we see that Miro rated over 80% of the Passes as Fails. Miro definitely needs training to align his checks with the Chief Engineer.

The %Rated both Ways chart is interesting. Bilal did not rate any of the vehicles differently between the repeat runs. This might mean that he is very consistent or he had a system of recording how he rated the parts and they were not blind. That's another conversation the Chief Engineer needs to have.

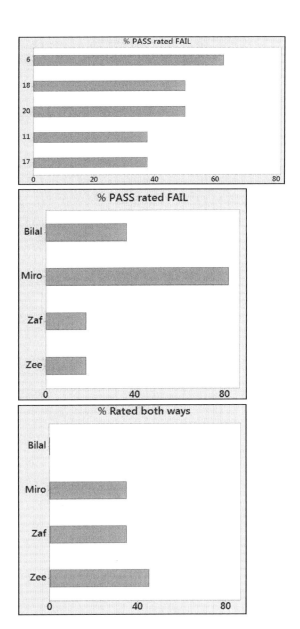

11.12 MSA Exercises

Exercise 11.12.1 Form a Gage Run Chart and then Conduct Gage R&R Crossed Study

A Gage R&R study has been conducted with 3 operators, 3 repeats and 14 parts. The study does not have a historical StDev or Tolerance. Form a Gage run chart and then conduct the analysis of the Gage R&R Study and then answer the questions shown below.

The data in File 11 MSA.xlsx worksheet Exercise1.

1) Does the Gage Run Chart indicate any particular types of problem?
2) How is the measurement system rated?
3) What is the biggest issue for the study, is it repeatability or reproducibility?
4) If there are repeatability issues who is causing them?
5) Are there any other issues?

Exercise 11.12.2 Conduct an Attribute Agreement Analysis

Data collection for an Attribute Agreement Analysis has been conducted with 3 operators, 2 repeats and 40 parts. Conduct the analysis and answer the questions shown below and then answer the questions shown below.

The data in File 11 MSA.xlsx worksheet Exercise2.

1) How is a good appraisal system?
2) Are any of the Appraisers different from the other Appraisers?
3) Are any of the part difficult to appraise?
4) Are the appraisers failing more good parts or passing bad parts?

12 Regression

12.1   What is Regression?

Regression is the name for several techniques that we use to build a mathematical model of our process. Along with regression, you will probably hear the term correlation. Correlation is about defining the strength of a linear relationship between a predictor and a response.

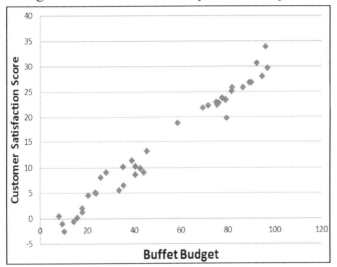
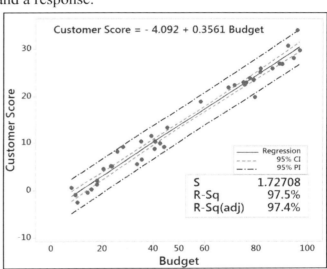

Let's say that I have been doing a project on an all-you-can-eat buffet and we have data on the buffet budget against our key output variable for the project, which is customer satisfaction score. Wouldn't it be great if I could mathematically predict what the customer satisfaction score would be for a £50 Buffet Budget? If I use regression, it will fit the line that best describes the data and give me the equation for that line using a procedure called Least Squares. I am also told the amount of variation in the data that the equation describes, that's the R-Sq (adj). And because I asked for them, I have 95% confidence and prediction intervals on the graph

For a budget of 50, I can use the regression equation to predict my customer score.
Customer Score= -4.092+ 0.3561*Budget
Customer Score= -4.092+ 0.3561*50
Customer Score= 13.7

If there were no error in the regression equation, I would get a customer satisfaction score of 13.7 for a budget of £50. The 95% Confidence Interval (CI) tells me where the mean of repeated measurements of a Buffet budget of £50 would be. The Prediction Interval (PI) tells me with 95% confidence that a single point would be within the upper and lower limits of the PI.

Simple Regression limits itself to systems with one predictor and one response. However, the main regression procedures can model systems with a higher number of predictors. When we have two predictors and one response we get to the limits of 3D space and our graphing capability as shown in the 3D scatterplot. When we start adding more predictors, we are limited with graphics but can still form the equations using Regression. We can still form graphs but we have to select the predictors we wish to vary in the graph and hold the others.

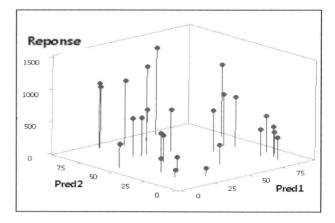

Just for a bit of revision on how we form equations if we have

$$Y = 3X_1^3 + 5X_2^2 + X_1*X_2 + 5.3$$

It is a standard convention in equations and graphs that Y represents the response and X the predictors. We have 4 terms in this equation

Term 1=$3X_1^3$, Term2= $5X_2^2$, Term 3=X_1*X_2 , Term 4= 5.3
Term 1 is a cubic term as X_1 is raised to the power of three, meaning it's $X_1* X_1* X_1$. The coefficient of Term 1 is 3.
Term 2 is a quadratic term as X_2 is raised to the power of two. The coefficient of Term 2 is 5
Term 3 is an interaction of X_1 times X_2. Both X_1 & X_2 are linear in this term as they are raised to the power of one.
Term 4 is called the constant. It is a number.

There are two predictors in the equation X_1 & X_2. We could use a 3D scatterplot to plot the 3D representation of this equation.

12.2 What are we Covering?

We would have stuck to the Assistant for this chapter but Minitab has dropped the cubic relationship from the Simple Regression routine. In order to cover cubic relationships in the 'Simple' routine we will use the classic menus.
Then we are going to move onto Multiple Regression and Optimisation using the Assistant. The Optimisation part is just an add-on to the Multiple Regression Procedure.
You can see that building mathematical models using regression can be instrumental within the Analyse step of DMAIC. In the real world, the prediction capabilities of regression are used in design, modelling, pattern recognition, artificial intelligence etc.

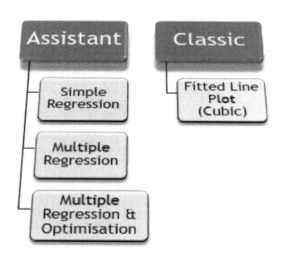

12.3 Simple Regression

Simple Regression	
Function	Produces a regression model for simple systems where there is one predictor and one response.
Sample Size	One of the assumptions for Simple Regression is having normally distributed residuals. For this not to be an issue a sample size greater than 15 is required. If a precise estimate of model error is required then a sample size greater than 40 is recommended.
Data type & Format	Numeric data is required for the predictor and the response
Considerations	Data for the study should be randomly selected to provide a cross section of the range of the predictor. Data should be recorded in the worksheet in time order. This allows for the detection of time related patterns within the data. Just because a predictor and response can be modelled together it does not mean they have a real world relationship. Minitab cannot check a real world link exists so this is up to you. A model equation of the form Y=3.14+6X may indicate that any value of X can be entered to predict the value of Y but you should only enter values of X within the range of the data used to form the equation. In other words, do not extrapolate.

Example 12.3.1 House Prices and Owner Ages

As part of her Geography project, Iqra collects data on the average age of house owners and the value of their properties in Ellesmere Port, Cheshire. Iqra feels that as a person becomes more established, they can afford a more valuable house. Iqra has two columns of data; one is the predictor called Age. The other is the response called House Price (unit of 1000£). The data is not recorded in time order.

Use the Simple Regression procedure to establish if a mathematical relationship can be found between Age of owners and House Prices.

All data for this chapter is in '12 Regression.xlsx' and the data for this example is in the worksheet called 'Houses'.

As we are happy that there is probably a link between average age of house owners and house prices, we can continue and form the model.

1. Transfer the data into Minitab. There are 2 columns of data.

2. Click *Assistant<<Regression.*

3. Click on the *Simple Regression* box which is used when there is only one predictor.

4. Enter the column headings. House Price is the response and Age is the predictor for House price.

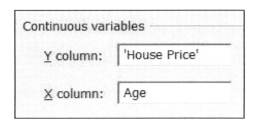

5. We can then ask Minitab to find the best model for us or we can choose between Linear and Quadratic. The Cubic model no longer appears in the Assistant. Leave 'Choose for me' as the selected option.

6. Click OK to produce the 5 page report in the Output Pane.

In the top left corner of the Summary Report, we have three decision bars. The first confirms that there is a relationship between the Predictor and the Response.

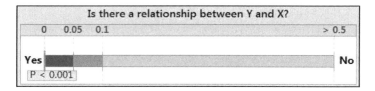

The second tells us that 85.96% of the changes in the response can be explained by changes in the predictor.

The final decision bar, which makes an appearance when the fitted model is linear, confirms whether there is a correlation between Y and X. 0.93 is the value of the correlation coefficient, the closer the value is to 1 or -1 the more strongly linear the relationship. A positive value for the correlation coefficient indicates a positive gradient of the line of best fit.

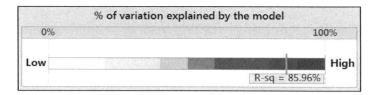

The top right of the Summary Report gives us the fitted line plot. As this is repeated later in the report, I have not shown it here. However, it is worth looking at the model equation. An equation like this indicates that the model is not limited in terms of the X values but we should not extrapolate outside the area of the study. The main reason for this is that the model may change or in this case, specific values could give you ridiculous answers. For example, an X-value of 19 years old is outside the range of the study but if you used the prediction equation, your house would have a negative value!

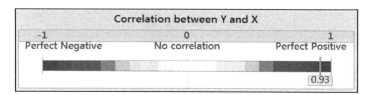

$$Y = -61.69 + 3.308 X$$

The top of the Model Selection Report shows the fitted line plot, but again as it is repeated in a slightly different format, I have not shown it here. Below that we see the data for model selection. The alternative model, which is the Quadratic, was tested as well but it was found that the Quadratic term was not significant with a P-value of only 0.655. Therefore, the quadratic term was removed. For the selection of the linear model, we see that the linear term was significant.

The Diagnostic Report shows us the value of our Residuals against the fitted values. Minitab will identify any unusual points for which we should examine the experimental data and set-up. Unusually, we don't have any unusual points to check. If you want to review information on Residuals look back to section 8.6.1 ANOVA GLM. On the right-hand side of the diagnostic report, Minitab suggests the patterns that we should look out for. One of the common ones is strong curvature in the residuals. This indicates that a higher-order term has been missed. If you see this pattern in the residuals, then perhaps Simple Regression is not the tool to use.

Statistics	Selected Model Linear	Alternative Model Quadratic
R-squared (adjusted)	85.71%	85.52%
P-value, model	<0.005*	<0.005*
P-value, linear term	<0.005*	0.002*
P-value, quadratic term	—	0.655
Residual standard deviation	19.218	19.352

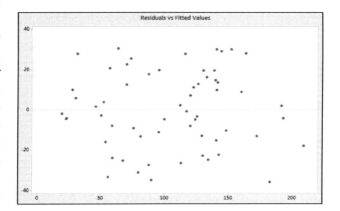

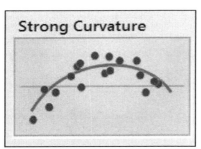

On the Prediction Report, we have the Prediction Plot, which is why I didn't show you the plotted data on two previous occasions. The prediction plot has the 95%PI. These show graphically where new data points could fall. The Prediction Report gives a list of selected X values and gives the Y value predicted by the model equation but also provides the 95%PI. For example, for an X of 27 years, the model equation predicts a value of 27.638 k£. However, due to the error, a single Y value might fall anywhere between -12.004 and 67.280 95% of the time.

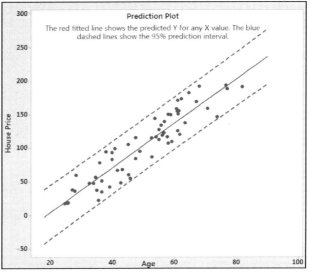

Unfortunately, the prediction report does extrapolate predictor values outside of the range of the study.

The Report Card, not shown here, gives us the all-clear on our analysis.

X	Predicted Y	95% PI
18	-2.1371	(-42.551, 38.277)
21	7.7879	(-32.343, 47.919)
24	17.713	(-22.161, 57.586)
27	27.638	(-12.004, 67.280)
30	37.563	(-1.8752, 77.001)
33	47.488	(8.2267, 86.749)
36	57.413	(18.301, 96.525)
39	67.338	(28.347, 106.33)
42	77.263	(38.366, 116.16)
45	87.188	(48.355, 126.02)
48	97.113	(58.316, 135.91)

Example 12.3.2 Pump Curve

Humzah has been asked to study the characteristics of a particular pump in a circuit. He has taken readings of various flowrates that the pump can deliver and then measured the pressure that the pump achieved at these flow rates. This is called the Pump Curve. He has been asked to model the Pump Curve and also whether the high-pressure alarm should be set to 80 pressure for a flow of 50. This means that Humzah has been asked to find out if 50 flow, 80 pressure is close to the 95% Prediction Interval but not within it as the alarm should not be sounding frequently. The data is not in time order.

All data for this chapter is in '12 Regression.xlsx' and the data for this example is in the worksheet called 'Pump'.

1. Transfer the data into Minitab. There are 2 columns of data.
2. Click **Assistant<<Regression.**
3. Click on the **Simple Regression** box.
4. Enter the column headings. Pressure is our response and Flow is the predictor for Pressure.

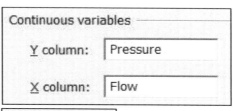

5. Leave 'Choose for me' as the selected option.
6. Click OK to produce the five page report.

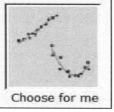

In the top left corner of the Summary Report, we have two decision bars. The first confirms that there is a relationship between the Predictor and the Response.

The second tells us that 85.57% of the changes in the response can be explained by changes in the predictor. This indicates a good model.

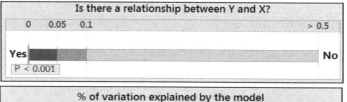

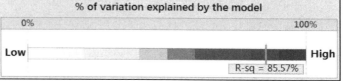

The top of the Model Selection Report shows the fitted line plot, and I have added the Regression Equation. We are shown that we have three unusual data points which can cause the regression line to be pulled away from other points and one point with a large residual which does not fit the equation well.

Below that we see the data for model selection. The Quadratic model was selected as the Quadratic term was significant with a P-value of <0005.

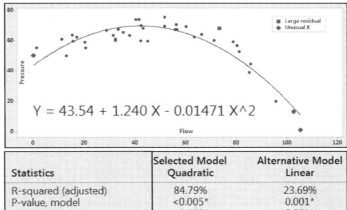

$$Y = 43.54 + 1.240 \, X - 0.01471 \, X^2$$

Statistics	Selected Model Quadratic	Alternative Model Linear
R-squared (adjusted)	84.79%	23.69%
P-value, model	<0.005*	0.001*
P-value, linear term	<0.005*	0.001*
P-value, quadratic term	<0.005*	—
Residual standard deviation	6.121	13.710

On the Prediction Report, we have the Prediction Plot and the prediction data table. I have removed the data related to a flow of 50 and put it on the chart. We see that according to the model, a flow of 50 will give a pressure of 68.78; however, individual points could be anywhere between 56.09 and 81.47. This means that our alarm setting of 50 flow and 80 pressure would be within the prediction interval. As it is within the 95%PI it would not be suitable as an alarm value as it could be sounding frequently.

Let's see if we can learn anything by changing to a Cubic model. The cubic model is the next step up from the quadratic as it contains a term raised to the power of 3. Unfortunately, Minitab has dropped the cubic model from the Assistant, so we need to go to the traditional menus.

7.   Click *Stat<<Regression<<Fitted Line Plot*

8.   Enter the column headings. Pressure is our response and Flow is the predictor for Pressure.

9.   Click on the radio button to use the Cubic model.

10. Click on the *Options* button and select the tick box for 'Display prediction interval'. Click OK.

11. Click on the *Graphs* button and select the Four-in-One Residuals Plot. The classic method relies on us to check if there are any issues with the residuals to validate our study rather than check the Report Card.

12. Click OK & OK again.

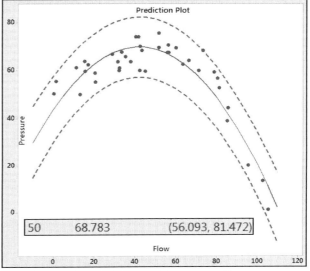

| 50 | 68.783 | (56.093, 81.472) |

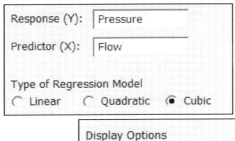

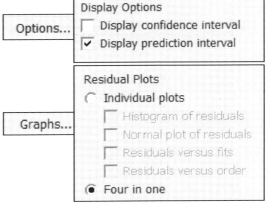

If you go to the Output Pane and locate the Sequential analysis of Variance, you can see that the Cubic term is significant.

Now go to the newly created Fitted Line Plot. At the top of the plot, you can see the new regression equation that contains the cubic term. The coefficients for the other terms and the constant have also changed. This model gives a better fit to the data as the R-Sq value has gone from 85.6% to 92.3%.

We now need to check our data point of 50 Flow & 80 Pressure and check if that lies within the Prediction Interval or just outside it.

13. Double-click on the Graph to access the Editor. Then right-click on the graph and select *Add<<Reference Lines.*

14. Enter '80' for the Y value and '50' for the X value. Then click, OK. Then Click OK to exit the Editor.

Sequential Analysis of Variance				
Source	DF	SS	F	P
Linear	1	2464.20	13.11	0.001
Quadratic	1	5756.47	153.65	0.000
Cubic	1	648.89	31.68	0.000

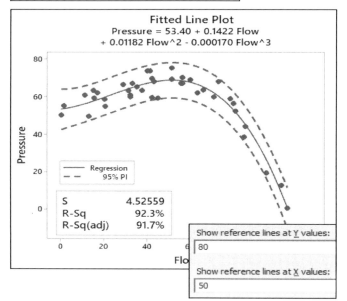

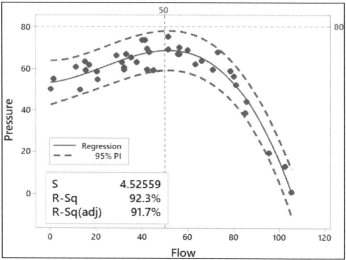

The intersection of the two reference lines is the proposed alarm setting. With the Cubic model, this is just outside of the prediction interval and therefore suitable for an alarm setting. And we have not selected it so we can use the alarm setting there is statistical evidence to support the selection of this model.

We also need to check the Four-in-One Residual Plot, as we did in the ANOVA GLM section.

The Normality plot shows that the Residuals are normally distributed, and the Versus Fits shows that the residuals are equally spaced about the zero line. All other subplots show that the Cubic study was valid.

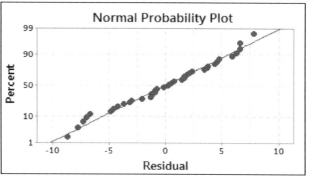

12.4 Introduction to Multiple Regression the Assistant

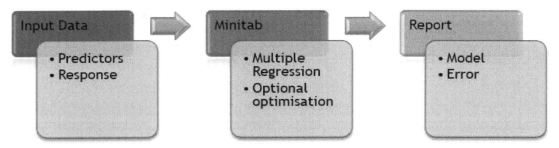

The Multiple Regression routine in Minitab 19 is a magical black box that gives the user special powers, or so it would seem. To use this magic, we enter the predictors and the response data into the worksheet and complete a relatively simple menu where we tell Minitab which are the predictors and the response. For the enchantment to work, we must have between two and five numerical predictors. We also have the option of adding a categorical predictor, which can have two or more unordered states. When we run the procedure, the Assistant will work its magic and produce the report.

The report will tell which of the predictors are significant and how they are linked to the response in terms of the Regression Equation. In this routine, Minitab will check for interactions between the predictors and can check for quadratic terms. I think this is magic as once you have gathered the data building a regression model is easy to do and is only a few clicks away.

Disclaimer-Minitab 19 does not actually perform magic.

Minitab 19 will employ a Stepwise Regression process to build up the model. It will first add the term that has the most effect on the response. It will then keep adding or subtracting terms as long as that action has the most significant effect on the response. One difference that you will see from ANOVA GLM for term selection is that a Significance value of 0.1 is used rather than 0.05 as in ANOVA GLM. The Stepwise production of the model and P-values can be seen on the Model Building report.

The Assistant will check for quadratic terms and interactions if the option is selected. The Assistant won't check for cubic terms unless the user pre-forms the cubic term in the worksheet and enters it as one of the predictors.

Rules of hierarchy apply in model selection. Let's say that we have two predictors, A & B. On the first round A is found to be significant. On the second round A*B, the interaction term, is significant, but B is not. Stepwise Regression will automatically add B to the model as it is in the significant interaction.

12.5 Multi-collinearity and Variance Inflation Factors

12.5.1 What is Multi-Collinearity

We briefly discussed Variance Inflation Factors (VIFs) in the ANOVA GLM section, but I'm afraid we have to do it here again. Multi-collinearity is when at least two of the predictors in a Regression study are correlated with each other. This causes complex issues with the matrices that are used to solve the simultaneous equations that are used to form the regression equation. Weak multi-collinearity is usually not a problem but strong multi-collinearity can cause specific problems. The most accurate way to detect multi-collinearity is to look at the VIFs in the coefficients table.

If   VIFs=1, there is no correlation between predictors

          VIF are >1 and <5, there is moderate correlation

          VIFs are >5 indicate strong correlation.

Let's look at an example of a multiple regression study, where we have 3 continuous predictors and a continuous response, and we decide to graphically examine the data using a matrix plot, we could get the following.

For Multiple Regression, it's good if our predictors look correlated with the response. There appears to be a correlation between all 3 predictors and the response.

If we are considering a multiple regression study, where we have 3 continuous predictors and a continuous response, and we decide to graphically examine the data using a matrix plot, we could get the following. The issue is that Pred2 % Pred3 appear to be highly correlated. This is **Data-Based Multi-collinearity.**

When I run the regression routine, you can see that the VIFs are well above 5 for Pred2 & Pred3 confirming strong multi-Collinearity.

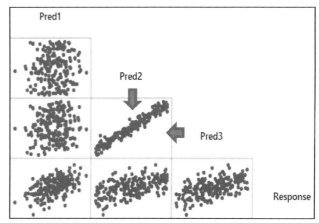

Coefficients

Term	Coef	SE Coef	T-Value	P-Value	VIF
Constant	-1.7	10.6	-0.16	0.876	
Pred1	0.5593	0.0610	9.17	0.000	1.02
Pred2	1.37	2.17	0.63	0.529	17.96
Pred3	0.324	0.175	1.85	0.065	18.03

We are using the same data from Pred1 & Pred2, which were not correlated, and the same Response data for this demonstration. Let's say that we want to include the Pred1*Pred2 interaction in the model. What does that look like in terms of the Matrix Plot and VIFs?

We knew from the previous section that Pred1 and Pred2 were not correlated, but when we add the Pred1*Pred2 interaction, it appears to be correlated to its parent terms. When it comes to high-order terms, including Quadratic terms, they are correlated to their parent predictors. I think of it as the children carrying the traits of the parents, so they will be correlated. This is called **Structural Multicollinearity.**

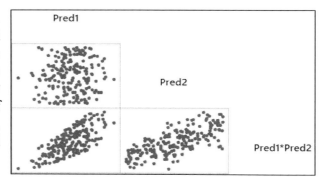

Again, when I run the regression routine, you can see that the VIFs are well above 5 for Pred1, Pred2 and the interaction term, confirming strong multi-Collinearity. Remember, the same sort of VIF values would be obtained for Quadratic terms, even though they are a single-parent family.

Coefficients

Term	Coef	SE Coef	T-Value	P-Value	VIF
Constant	-60.4	44.0	-1.37	0.172	
Pred1	1.026	0.347	2.96	0.003	32.71
Pred2	9.14	2.95	3.10	0.002	32.78
Pred1*Pred2	-0.0307	0.0231	-1.33	0.186	68.77

12.5.2 What problems can Multi-collinearity Cause

Multi-collinearity can increase the variance of the coefficients of the predicted terms, hence the name Variance Inflation Factor. The issue is that if you run the regression again with slightly different values of input predictors the coefficients of the terms may be different and you may even have terms going from not significant to significant and vice-versa. We call that instability in the model. When using the traditional menu's, we would use VIFs to detect and assess the level of multi-collinearity.

However, with reference to Jim Frost's Minitab Blog 'What Are the Effects of Multicollinearity and When Can I Ignore Them?' Multi-collinearity won't affect the overall strength of the model, and you should be able to make good predictions.

12.5.3 What can we do about Multi-collinearity

Even though Multiple Regression in the Assistant is a fantastic tool for Green Belts to use it does not mention the level of multi-collinearity within the predictors and how this affects the estimation of the coefficients of the final model, so what can we do to protect the study.

For Structural Multicollinearity.
Multiple Regression within the Assistant uses something called, Standardised Predictors, within the calculations. These reduce the VIFs produced by interaction terms and quadratics. Therefore, Structural Multicollinearity is not an issue within the Assistant (Standardising the predictors can also be employed within the traditional menu's).

Go back to section 12.5.1, where Structural Multicollinearity was being explained. Using the regression study, I have this time opted to standardise the predictors. Look at the effect it has had on the VIFs.

Coded Coefficients

Term	Coef	SE Coef	T-Value	P-Value	VIF
Constant	146.27	1.88	77.90	0.000	
Pred1	14.06	1.49	9.42	0.000	1.01
Pred2	15.25	1.49	10.23	0.000	1.01
Pred1*Pred1	0.86	1.16	0.74	0.460	1.01

For Data-Based Multi-collinearity.
1)   If we are running an initial data collection study, we could choose predictors that are not correlated. However, sometimes we are forced to study historical data and we don't get that luxury.

2)   The Multiple Regression routine in the Assistant allows 5 numerical predictors so we could check for strong correlation before we start the study. Additionally, we will be learning how to check the VIFs using the traditional menus in the next section. If strong multi-collinearity is indicated then assess whether you need both predictors in the study or can one of them be removed. The other possibility is to substitute both with a new replacement predictor.

12.6 Multiple Regression using the Assistant

Multiple Regression using the Assistant	
Function	Produces a regression model for systems with multiple predictors and one response.
Sample Size	One of the assumptions for Multiple Regression is having normally distributed residuals. For this not to be an issue a sample size greater than 15 is required. If a precise estimate of model error is required then a sample size greater than 40 is recommended for up to 3 terms and 45 for up to 6 terms.
Data type & Format	Numeric data is required for the numerical predictors and the response.
Considerations	Numerical predictors should not be correlated. Data selected for the study should be randomly selected to provide a cross section of the range of the predictors. Data should be recorded in the worksheet in time order. This allows for the detection of time related patterns within the data. Do not extrapolate the model beyond the bounds of the study data. Unusual data points and large residuals can indicate stability issues with the model. These points should be studied for unusual occurrences.

Example 12.6.1 Analysis of liquid effluent from a Paper Mill

Reinhart is leading a Six Sigma DMAIC project within a Paper Mill. The team has been asked to understand the factors influencing the Chemical Oxygen Demand (COD) within the site's liquid effluent. The team is currently in the Analyse Phase and has identified four predictors that might be linked to the COD of the liquid effluent. These predictors are Mixer Speed, Aeration Rate, Ozone Concentration and Ozone Pressure. Help Reinhart carry out a Multiple Regression exercise and confirm which predictors affect the liquid effluent COD. Form the Regression Equation and state how much of the changes in the COD can be explained by changes in the predictors.

All data for this chapter is in '12 Regression.xlsx' and the data for this example is in the worksheet called 'Paper.'

To start, we are going to check if any of the predictors are correlated.

1. Transfer the data into Minitab. There are 5 columns of data.

2. Click **Stat<<Basic Stats<<Correlation.**

3. Enter the 4 predictors so we can check if they are correlated. These are M_Speed, Aeration, Oz_Conc, and Oz_Press. Click OK.

4. Go to the Output Pane for this command to check the results.

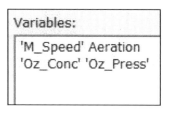

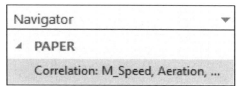

In the Matrix Plot, we can see the Correlation of Oz_Press and Aeration as a cluster of points going from the bottom left of the sub-plot to the top right. There are no distinguishable patterns in any of the other plots.

For each pairwise comparison, we get the Correlation Coefficient. The Correlation Coefficient ranges from -1 to +1. A coefficient of magnitude 1 indicates perfect correlation, 0.3 is weak, 0.5 is moderate and 0.7 as a strong correlation. Aeration & Oz_Press have a moderate to strong correlation. Aeration and Oz_Conc have a weak correlation.

We have seen statistically and graphically that two of our predictors are correlated, which may lead to multi-collinearity, which would, in turn, affect the stability of our model. We might consider removing either Aeration or Oz_Press as a predictor but before we make any decisions regarding taking out a predictor, we will examine the VIFs using the traditional menus.

To check the predictors for Data-Based Multi-Collinearity, which we will confirm by examining the VIFs, we need to roughly fit the regression model using the traditional menu's. We are not going to form the model but do a quick confirmation of whether multi-collinearity is likely to affect our model within the Assistant.

5.   Click *Stat<<Regression <<Regression <<Fit Regression Model*

6.   In the menu that opens, enter COD as the response and Aeration, Oz_Conc, Oz_Press, and M-Speed as the predictors.

7.   Click on OK to execute the procedure and find the Coefficients table in the Output Pane. I said was going to be quick!.

The VIFs are all below 5. Great! We don't have to worry about data-based multi-collinearity, and we know that the Assistant automatically standardises the predictors, so that won't be an issue either.

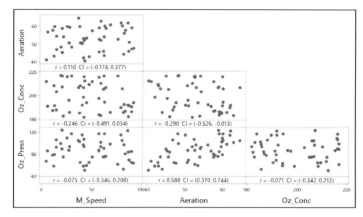

Correlations

	M_Speed	Aeration	Oz_Conc
Aeration	0.110		
Oz_Conc	-0.246	-0.290	
Oz_Press	-0.075	0.588	-0.071

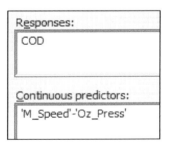

Coefficients

Term	Coef	SE Coef	T-Value	P-Value	VIF
Constant	-221.4	63.6	-3.48	0.001	
M_Speed	0.058	0.113	0.52	0.609	1.09
Aeration	-0.391	0.560	-0.70	0.488	1.71
Oz_Conc	0.964	0.259	3.72	0.001	1.16
Oz_Press	2.397	0.181	13.27	0.000	1.59

We can start to build our Regression Model using the Assistant.

8.   Click **Assistant<<Regression.**
9.   Click on the **Multiple Regression** box.
10. Enter COD as the response. Then enter all 4 of the predictor variables as the X variables. Note, the tick box to investigate higher-order terms is engaged by default.
11. Click OK to make the magic happen and produce the 5 page report.

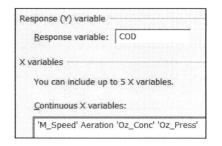

In the top left corner of the Summary Report, we have two decision bars. The first confirms that there is a relationship between the Response and at least one of the Predictors.

The second tells us that 87.43% of the changes in the response can be explained by changes in the predictors. This indicates a good model.

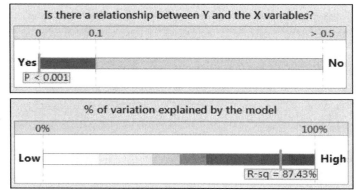

At the bottom of the Summary Report, we are given 4 scatter plots. These are for each of the predictors against the Response, COD. M_Speed is greyed out as changes in M_Speed were not affecting COD.

We can see that Oz_Press has a strong positive correlation with the Response.

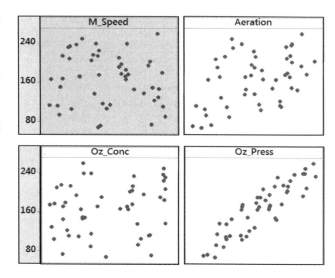

In the Comments section in the top right of the Summary Report, we are told that there are four terms in the model. Three predictors and the interaction between Aeration and Oz_Press.

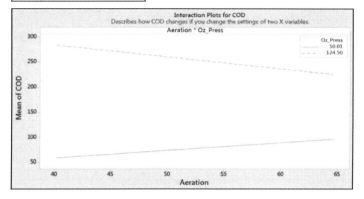

Next, we are going to move onto the Effects Report, which you only get to see if you have an interaction term in the model. This contains the Interactions Plot and Main Effect plots. We learned how to produce these plots in the Traditional Menu's when we covered ANOVA GLM.

At the top of the Effects Report, we have the plot of the Aeration*Oz_Press interaction. This shows that if Oz_Press had a low value (50), increasing Aeration from 40 to 65 would increase the value of COD. However, if Oz_Press has a high value (124.5) then increasing Aeration from 40 to 65 will have the opposite effect and reduce the value of COD.

Below that, we have 3 Main Effects plots, one for each predictor. The effect of each predictor is isolated and shown against the effect on the response. The same Y-axis scale is used for each plot so we can compare how unit changes in the predictors affect the Response. We can see that on its own Aeration is hardly having any effect on the Response as the line is almost flat. Oz_Conc has a moderate positive effect but Oz_Press is having the strongest positive effect.

On the Diagnostic Report, not shown here, we are shown the Residuals Vs Fitted values plot and told that we have 2 points with large residuals. These two points are not too far away from the rest of the data, and we would expect around this number of points to have large residuals so I am not going to take any action based on this finding.

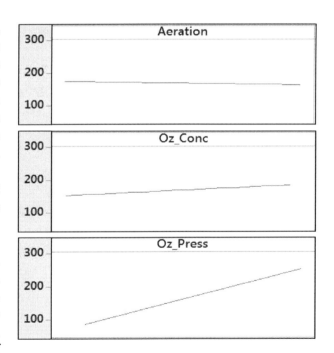

On the Model Building Report, we get to the heart of the Multiple Regression procedure.

At the top centre we get the Final Model Equation. As stated in the Summary Report, it contains the 3 predictors and the interaction term. It does not contain M_Speed as this was not significant to the Response.

On the Left, we have the Model Building Sequence as generated by the Stepwise Procedure. Initially, Oz_Press was added to the model as this was having the most effect on the Response. Then Oz_conc was added, it still had a P-Value of 0.000 but did not have as much impact on the Response. Then Aeration was added and as you can see that it had a P-Value of 0.381 which is above the Significance level of 0.10. However, this had to be added as the interaction term Aeration*Oz_Press was significant. This is one of the rules for building a hierarchical model. You can't include higher-order or interaction terms without including the parent predictors.

On the top right, we have a bar graph showing the Incremental Impact of the predictors on the response. M_Speed is greyed out as it is not included in the model.

Below that, we have a bar graph showing the impact of each term regressed on all other terms.

The Report Card, not shown here, gives us a warning about the unusual data points and tells us that our sample size was sufficient for a precise estimate of the strength of the relationship and large enough, so we don't have to worry about the normality of the residuals.

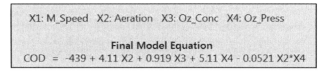

X1: M_Speed   X2: Aeration   X3: Oz_Conc   X4: Oz_Press

Final Model Equation

$COD = -439 + 4.11\ X2 + 0.919\ X3 + 5.11\ X4 - 0.0521\ X2*X4$

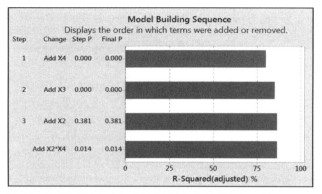

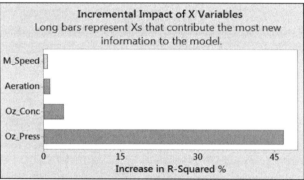

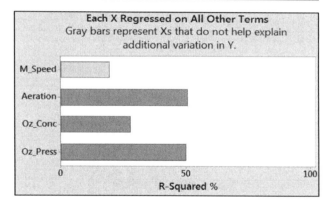

Example 12.6.2 Optimisation of Solar Cells

Woody is leading a Six Sigma DMAIC project for a solar cell manufacturer. The team wants to assess the technologies available for solar cells and reach a target of >54% energy conversion to electricity. After initial studies, the team has narrowed down the inputs to two continuous predictors which are glass purity (Purity) and array conductivity (Conductivity). There is also a categorical predictor with three levels; this is the actual photovoltaic material (PVM). The team has used the following designations for the categories A=Mono crystalline silicon, B=Gallium Arsenide & C= Cadmium Telluride. Help Woody form the Regression equation and then find the optimum settings to achieve >54% energy conversion. Display the settings on a contour plot. All data for this chapter is in '12 Regression.xlsx' and the data for this example is in the worksheet called 'Solar'.

To start off we are going to check if any of the predictors are correlated.

1. Transfer the data into Minitab. There are 4 columns of data.
2. Click **Stat<<Basic Stats<<Correlation.**
3. Enter the 2 numeric predictors so we can check if they are correlated. These are Conductivity and Purity. Click OK.
4. Go to the Output Pane for this command to check the results.

Variables:
Conductivity Purity

Correlations

	Conductivity
Purity	-0.240

The Pearson Correlation Coefficient indicates only a very weak correlation and it is not deemed significant. This should mean that we can conduct the analysis without any worries of poorly estimated coefficients.

5. Click **Assistant<<Regression.** Click on the **Optimize Response** box.
6. Enter Efficiency as the response. We can choose a target for the Optimisation, select 'Maximise the response' from the drop-down menu.
7. Enter Conductivity and Purity as our two continuous predictors.
8. Enter PVM as the Categorical X Variable.
9. Click OK to run the procedure and produce the 6 page report in the Output Pane.

Response (Y) variable

Response variable: | Efficiency

What is your response goal? | Maximize the response

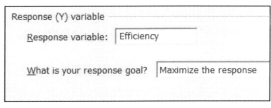

X variables

You can include up to 5 X variables.

Continuous X variables:

| Conductivity Purity |

Categorical X variable: | PVM

In the top left corner of the Summary Report, we have two decision bars. The first confirms that there is a relationship between the Response and at least one of the Predictors.

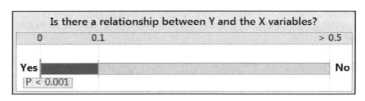

The second tells us that 60.94% of the changes in the response can be explained by changes in the predictors. This indicates a reasonable model.

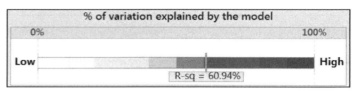

At the bottom of the Summary Report, we are given 3 scatter plots. We have two for the continuous predictors against the Response. It looks as though Purity has a stronger linear correlation with the response than Conductivity. We also have a scatter plot of the categorical predictor against the response. It can be seen that the middle level, B, gives the highest values of the response.

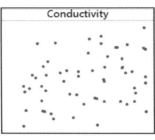
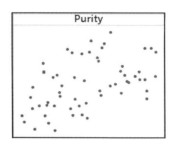

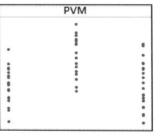

In the Comments section in the top right of the Summary Report, we are told that there are four terms in the model. The three predictors and a quadratic term for purity.

X1: Conductivity
X2: Purity
X3: PVM
X2^2

On the Diagnostic Report, not shown here, we are shown that we have one point with a large residual. It's not too far from the rest of the data, so I am not going to take any action.

Previously, on the Model Building Report, we had the final model equation at the top centre of this report, but as our model contains categorical variables, we have to wait until the next page before we see the equations.

On the Left, we have the Model Building Sequence as generated by the Stepwise Procedure. Going from top to bottom, you can see the order that the terms were added to the model with the quadratic term being the last added to the model.

On the top right, we have the bar graph showing the Incremental Impact of the predictors on the response. We see that in terms of R-Sq%, the terms had almost the same incremental impact on the model.

On the Models Equations Report, we finally get the model equations. We get three equations one for each of the levels of the categorical variable.

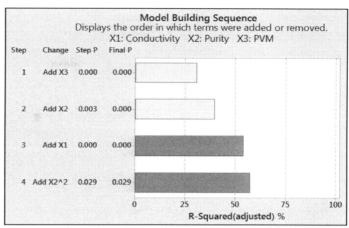

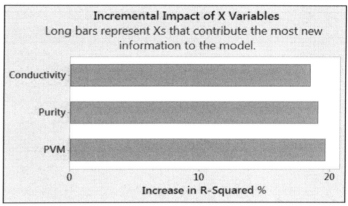

PVM		Final Equations
A	Efficiency	= 22.90 + 0.1442 X1 + 0.1673 X2 - 0.000523 X2^2
B	Efficiency	= 30.20 + 0.1442 X1 + 0.1673 X2 - 0.000523 X2^2
C	Efficiency	= 23.52 + 0.1442 X1 + 0.1673 X2 - 0.000523 X2^2
		X1: Conductivity X2: Purity X3: PVM

Next, we are going to move onto the Prediction and Optimization Report which is added if you select the Optimization option.

Initially, we wanted to maximise the response, so right at the top of the report, we are given the highest predicted level of efficiency that we can achieve, which is 55.06%. Next to that, we have the settings we need to get 55.06%. Keep in mind that the first panel you make could have an efficiency anywhere between 44.34% and 65.78%. Eventually, after enough panels are tested the average should settle down to 55% using those settings.

Goal: Maximize Efficiency

Predicted Y	55.0615
95% PI	(44.346, 65.777)

Solution: Optimal Settings

X1: Conductivity	79.536
X2: Purity	159.876
X3: PVM	B

Below that, we have 3 optimisation plots showing the optimal setting in the form of a dashed line. I have to say that the Response Optimizer in the classic menus is much better, as it is dynamic. You can move the predictor settings around and see the effect on the response.

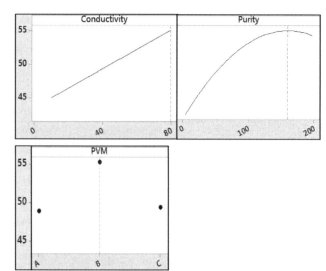

On the bottom left, we are given the top five alternate solutions. Note that all of them involve panel type B.

The Report Card, not shown here, gives us a warning about the unusual data points and tells us that our sample size was sufficient for a precise estimate of the strength of the relationship and large enough, so we don't have to worry about the normality of the residuals. It also says that once we have settled on the optimal values, we should conduct 20-30 test runs to validate the results. This is good practical advice.

X1	X2	X3	Predicted Y
78.318	131.962	B	54.4736
62.233	197.058	B	51.8503
77.974	76.029	B	51.1470
54.239	190.437	B	50.9307
57.64	114.666	B	50.8274

The final part of the task was to form the Contour Plot. This must be done in the traditional menus. There are two ways of navigating to the contour plot. The route shown below is better as it will automatically pick up some parameters from the regression model.

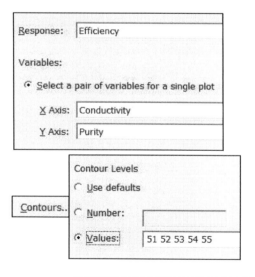

10. Click **Stat<<Regression <<Regression <<Contour Plot**

11. You should find that the Response and the Variables have the relevant data columns auto-filled. If not, enter the data as shown.

12. Click on the **Contours** button. We are going to change the contours on the plot to focus on the region we are interested in and not be spread evenly over the map. Select the radio button for 'Values' and then enter '51 52 53 54 55'. Placing a space between each number.

13. Click OK and return to the root menu.

14. Click on the **Settings** button. We need

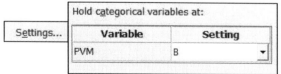

to lock in a value for PVM of material B. Select 'B' from the drop-down menu. Then click OK and OK again to form the contour plot.

I have added a flag to show you where an efficiency of 55% can be achieved.

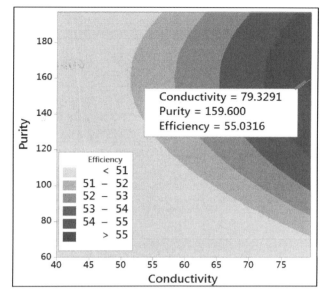

12.7 Regression Exercises

Exercise 12.7.1 Simple Regression Study

Data has been collected on a process where a single predictor affects a continuous Response variable. The data has not been collected in time order. Conduct the appropriate Regression analysis and answer the questions below.

The data in File 12 Regression.xlsx worksheet Exercise1.

1) What order of equation best fits the data and is significant?
2) How much of the variation in the Response can be explained by changes in the Predictor?
3) Are there any unusual data points in the study and are they an issue?
4) Using this process could we reasonably expect a data point to appear at 60 for the predictor and 200 for the response?

Exercise 12.7.2 Multiple Regression Study

Data has been collected on a process where four predictors are thought to affect a single continuous Response variable. The data has not been collected in time order. Conduct the appropriate Regression analysis and answer the questions below.

The data in File 12 Regression.xlsx worksheet Exercise2.

1) Are any of the predictors correlated?
2) Are all the predictors significant?
3) How much of the variation in the Response can be explained by changes in the Predictors?
4) What terms are present in the model?
5) Are there any unusual data points in the study and are they an issue?
6) What are the top solutions to obtain a value of 200 in the Response?

13 Design of Experiments

13.1   What is Design of Experiments

Design of Experiment (DOE) is a lot like Regression where we have a response variable, and we want to link it mathematically to two or more predictors. Except we now call the predictors, factors. We can still include interaction terms and higher-order terms in our model as well. The difference is that with DOE we plan the series of experiments that we are going to conduct and we pre-plan the levels of the factors we are going to use. Whereas in Regression, it's usually the case of grabbing pre-existing data and throwing it all into the Regression Calculation. As DOE is meticulous in the planning stage, it is often more efficient in terms of the number of experimental runs that are required to obtain the same information. Therefore, where runs are difficult or expensive to conduct DOE is the preferred choice.

There are many different types of experimental design, each with its own specialty. There are screening DOE's used to reduce a large number of possible factors to the ones that are affecting the response. Modelling designs that allow you to optimise the factors to give your required output. There are designs used to look for curvature, reduce the effects of noise variables and deal with mixtures. DOE could be a three-book trilogy becoming a four-film quadrology in itself. The classic menus allow you to run all these types of DOE. The Assistant, on the other hand, takes the most commonly and easily used elements and guides you through screening to modelling to looking for curvature. However, if you don't want to do a screening experiment, you can go straight to modelling. It provides a really useful tool that you as a Green Belt will find valuable and easy to use.

13.2 DOE Terminology

Let's say we are conducting an experiment to see if a gas conforms to the ideal gas law. We have a sealed chamber with a set mass of gas. We can change the pressure and the temperature and we are going to be measuring the volume as the response. Pressure and Temperature are our factors. In this particular DOE, we are going to be testing each of the factors at two levels, a high level and a low level. It's called a 2 Level Factorial Design.

Compared to the predictor versus predictor scatterplots generated in regression, the scatterplot produced by plotting the predictors in a DOE study is much neater. Additionally, with this type of

Pressure	Temperature	Volume
20	15	
40	15	
20	40	
40	40	

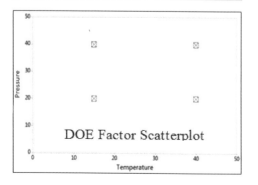

DOE Factor Scatterplot

experiment, there is no correlation between the predictors and therefore no multi-collinearity. We say that we have an orthogonal design. Bear in mind that not all DOE studies are orthogonal.

For now, we have only looked at the set-up of the gas experiment. I will conduct the investigation and write the results into the table.

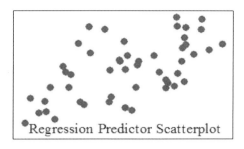

Regression Predictor Scatterplot

Pressure	Temperature	Volume
20	15	108
40	15	81
20	40	125
40	40	90

Having conducted the experiment, I can produce the Main Effects (ME) plot. We have produced these before and we know that the ME plot isolates the effect of each factor. The Y-axis on the ME plot is the response and the scale is common to both factors. What is not common is the units for the X-axis. Minitab uses the same horizontal distance to represent the change between the high and low levels for each factor not the units of the factors or their values.

The change from the low level to the high level for Pressure produces a longer steeper line than temperature. For this reason, we say that Pressure is having more of an Effect than temperature. Also, when Pressure increases the response decreases so we say that it is having a negative effect.

We need to understand the term 'Effect' as the Assistant uses it when reporting the power of the experiment. Let's have a look at how we actually calculate the effect of a factor.

Effect of Factor = Average of responses at high levels - average of responses at low levels.

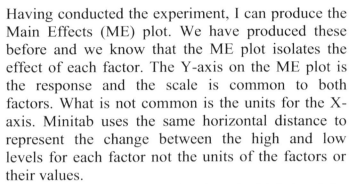

$$Pressure\ Effect = \frac{90+81}{2} - \frac{108+125}{2} = -31$$

If the line were horizontal, then the factor would not be having an effect on the response. We still need P-values to tell us if the effect of the factor is significant.

Finally, with a 2 Level Factorial experiment, we have to assume a linear response between the high and low levels of the Factors. We can look for curvature, in the form of quadratic terms, but when we do this, we need to add more points to the study.

Term	Effect
Constant	
Pressure	-31.00
Temperature	13.000

13.3 The DOE Flowchart in the Assistant

We will work through the complete flowchart when we go through the detailed examples. The DOE procedure in the Assistant has to start with the creation of a worksheet. The created worksheet tells the experimenter at what levels to conduct the experiment and in what order. The created worksheet tells the assistant that it is dealing with a DOE study. If you want to reduce a large number of factors to a significant few, you should start with a screening DOE. If you find there are between 2 & 5 significant factors when you analyse your screening DOE Minitab can then create a Modelling worksheet for you. Once the Modelling DOE has been analysed you can look at the settings required to optimise the response to your requirements or if curvature is detected add additional points to fit a quadratic model. On occasion, you may have enough data to go straight to the quadratic model without further experimentation.

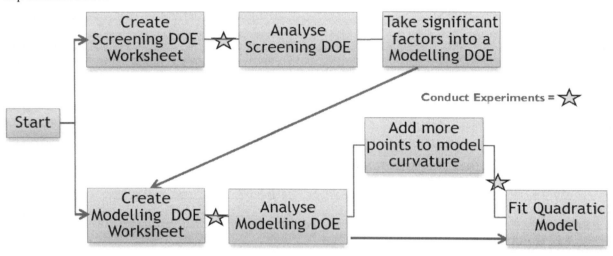

13.4 DOE Considerations

Whenever we have used the Assistant before we have used it to conduct distinct studies. For DOE the Assistant offers a sequential process. This means that the intention is that the user performs a series of smaller experiments to reach an overall conclusion. The advantage is that a series of smaller studies will be more efficient in terms of the number of experimental runs that we need to do. The reason for this is that a lot of the insignificant factors will be removed in the screening design and won't be carried through the entire study.

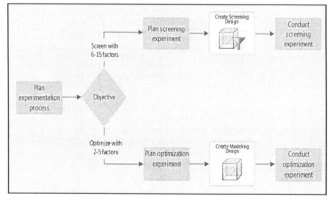

Before you go into the DOE, you will have identified your single response variable and a number of factors that you feel could be affecting the response variable. If you have between 6 and 15 suitable factors you should use a screening DOE to reduce the number of possible factors to between 2 & 5 significant factors. 'Suitable' means that the factors are controllable and that the high and low levels identified for the experiment can be set independently of each other. You will have confirmed the measurement system for the response already, if you were following DMAIC, you may want to check your measurement systems for the factors prior to starting the experiment. The high and low levels for the factors should not be extreme but set to the levels that experience tells you will change the response. When you have finalised the factors and their levels, you can then choose the number of runs within the experiment. Increasing the number of runs used in the screening design will improve the detection ability. Once you have selected the number of runs you can then create the screening design.

This will generate a worksheet with four of what I call DOE 'Admin Columns' and then the columns showing you the levels that the factors need to be set in order to get data on the response. Each row on the worksheet represents one experimental run. The worksheet can be printed and used as a record sheet. To save yourself some typing it is worth saving the worksheet, even though there is no response data, at this stage. The reason for this is that the worksheet is automatically randomised to minimise noise factors affecting the experiment. The first two of the 'Admin Columns' are StdOrder and RunOrder. StdOrder is the non-randomised order for the experiment and RunOrder is the random order for conducting the experiment. To get around the randomisation issues for the examples I sort the columns on StdOrder so we all get the same worksheet.

On creating the worksheet Minitab generates a Summary Report and Report Card which summarises the design. On the bottom right of the Summary Report, we are given information on the detection ability of the experiment. This is very different from the power bars we have seen previously and takes a bit of interpretation. In the example shown we are being told that for our experiment to achieve a power of 80% the minimum effect that we will be able to detect is 1.06 StDevs. We looked at how to calculate the effect in section 13.2. The StDev being referred to here is of the response when the factors are held. Therefore, only if you have historical data on the response can you establish the minimum effect that you can detect whilst achieving an 80% power. However, there is some advice below the power bar on the relative size of the effect that can be detected. With our 1.06 StDevs at 80%, we should be able to detect a small effect.

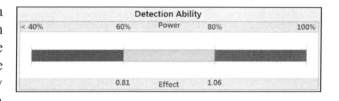

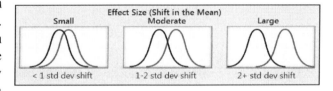

At this point, you conduct all the experiments and enter the results into your saved Worksheet. The screening DOE will look for main effects only. This means that at this point, it is not looking for interactions. The Assistant also uses a significance level of 0.1 and not the usual 0.05. Personally, I think it is a shame that the Assistant does not allow you to select a user-defined significance level. If you remember, going from a significance level of 0.1 to 0.05 will select more terms as being significant but it also increases the chance of a Type 1 error from 5% to 10%.

The point of a screening design is to reduce your initially selected 6 to 15 factors to between 2 and 5 factors to allow modelling and optimisation of the factors. It is unlikely that you will get more than 5 significant factors but if you do consider holding the levels of what you perceive are the least significant factors so that you can go into the next phase. If you get less than 2 significant factors, repeat the brainstorming exercise to establish if you have missed any significant factors. If you have one significant factor and a good fit, it may be the case that the relationship is only dependent upon a single factor. You can then use Simple Regression to model the relationship.

Once 2 to 5 significant factors have been identified, you can go into the modelling design. When you select Assistant<<DOE<<Analyse & Interpret and then click on the Create Modelling Design button Minitab will give you the option to change the factor levels that you are using. But as far as possible Minitab will auto-complete the menu for you, which is nice as there is less typing to do. You also get the option of stating the purpose of the study, is it optimisation to a max, min or for stated response level. You also specify how many replicates you want to run. Replicates are repeat runs of the experiment which will improve accuracy and will on occasion allow you to look for curvature straight away.

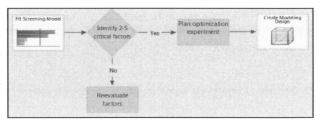

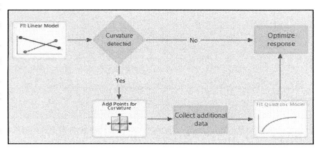

Once you have selected the number of replicates to be used in the study, you can print the worksheet. Again, always save the worksheet.

Once you have the results for the modelling experiment you fit the linear model. This looks for significant main effects and interactions at a 0.1 significance level. If curvature is detected, you will be given the option to add additional runs to the modelling design or you will be able to look for curvature straight away.

We will now go to the examples and see how the sequential process works. We will go through screening to looking for curvature in the examples. As the DOE procedure in the Assistant does not display the regression equations, we will even form the regression equations using the regression routine learned in chapter 12.

13.5 DOE Examples

Example 13.5.1 Bacterial Growth Screening DOE

Dr Foster has identified a number of factors that could be significant to the growth rate of a bacteria he is attempting to culture. Some of the factors relate to the agar jelly which the bacteria feeds upon and others are concerned with environmental conditions. Create a worksheet for the screening DOE and hand this over to Dr Foster so his team can conduct the recommended experiments.

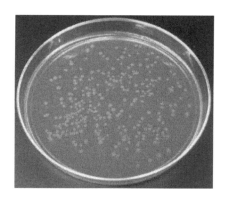

When Dr Foster has run the experiments for the Screening DOE analyse the results and establish which of the factors are significant to the response, GrowthRate. Then wait for further instructions.

The screening DOE factors are listed below using the following format 'Factor Full name (Column Heading, Lo setting, Hi Setting)'.

Lipids concentration in feed (Lipids, 1, 10)
pH (pH, 2, 8)
Sugar concentration in feed (Sugars 5, 100)
Temperature (Temperature 6,25)
Micro Enzymes in Feed(Micro_Enzms 1,100)
Light Levels (Light 1, 100)
Mutagen concentration in feed (Mutagens 1, 100)
Humidity (Humidity 10, 1000)
Percentage of Nitrogen in atmosphere (%Nitrogen 1, 100)

We can't start this sequential DOE process without creating a worksheet, so the first thing we need to do is create the Screening DOE Worksheet. We are starting with a screening design as we want to reduce the 9 possibly significant factors to between 2 and 5. Even 1 significant factor is acceptable as long as the model error is low.

To create the worksheet, we don't need to import any data into Minitab.

1.   Start with a new project and then click ***Assistant<<DOE<<Plan and Create.***

2.   Click on the ***Create Screening Design*** box.

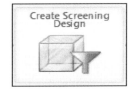

3. We need to set-up the worksheet in the menu that opens. Enter 'GrowthRate' as the response variable.

4. Dr Foster has given us 9 factors so we will enter '9' as the Number of factors.

5. We then need to enter all the factor details. We need to enter the short factor name, the data type, and then the high and low levels to be used for the factors in the experiment. Note, we can use categorical factors with two levels as well. However, for this experiment, we only have continuous factors. Note, only 8 factors are visible at a time. You will need to use the slider or tab button to make space to enter the 9th factor.

6. The minimum number of runs required for the screening DOE is 12. However, Dr Foster has decided that it would be beneficial to be able to detect a smaller effect and has decided to increase the number of runs by folding the design. Select '24 (fold design)' as the number of runs.

7. Click OK.

In the Data Pane, we have created a worksheet that tells us how to conduct 24 experimental runs in 24 rows. It has 13 columns, the 4 DOE admin columns and then 9 columns showing the factor settings. The 14th column, with heading GrowthRate, is where we will enter the response data when the experiments have been completed.

In the Output Pane, we get some instructions on how what to do with the results when the screening experiments are completed. We can also review the best practice tips for running the experiments under 'View the Pre-Experiment Checklist'. We can also print the data collections forms, which would be a good idea if we were going to do the experiments.

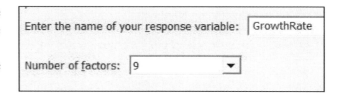

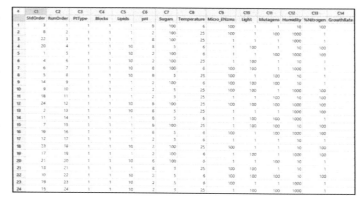

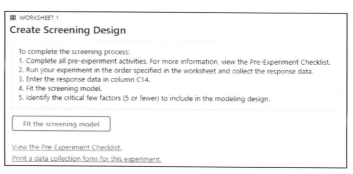

Below that we have a 2 page Create Screening Design report. Let's have a look at the Summary Report that was created for the screening experiment. In the top left, we are reminded of the goal of screening designs.

Experimental Goal

Reduce the number of factors down to the critical few that have the greatest influence on the response.

And below that, we are given a summary of the design. We are reminded that the base design was 12 runs but the 24 run option was used.

Design Information

Response	GrowthRate
Base design	9 factors, 12 runs
Total runs	24

On the right-hand side of the Summary Report, we get information on Effect Estimation and Detection Ability. We are told that this design will estimate the linear effect of factors, but won't do interactions. As we don't know if all our factors are significant yet we are quite willing not to get any information on interactions at this point.

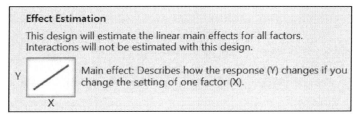

Effect Estimation

This design will estimate the linear main effects for all factors. Interactions will not be estimated with this design.

Main effect: Describes how the response (Y) changes if you change the setting of one factor (X).

On the bottom right of the Summary Report, we are given information on the detection ability of the experiment. The power bar shows us that to achieve a power of 80% the minimum effect that we will be able to detect is 1.07 StDevs. In the guidance given below, we are told that we will be able to detect down to small to moderate effects of the factors. I can tell you that had Dr Foster not added the extra runs we would only have been able to measure effects down to 2.3*StDev.

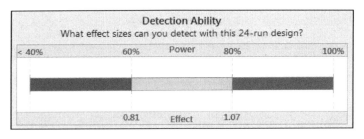

Detection Ability
What effect sizes can you detect with this 24-run design?

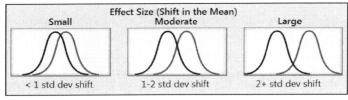

Effect Size (Shift in the Mean)

Dr Foster and his researchers work hard and complete all the experimental runs and the data is recorded in 13 DOE.xlsx worksheet 'Bacteria Screen'. As the auto-randomisation will create worksheets where everyone's StdOrder is different, the Excel worksheet has been sorted on the StdOrder column. This means we can't just copy the response column into Minitab. We need to copy the entire Excel worksheet and transfer it into Minitab.

8. In Minitab highlight column C1 to C13 from row1 to row24. Do not delete the title row.

9. Right-click and then left-click on 'Delete Cells'. This will clear the Minitab worksheet leaving only the column headings.

10. Go to the Excel worksheet 'Bacteria Screen' and copy cells A2 to N25.

11. Paste those cells into Columns C1 to C14 directly under the title bar. That brings the complete screening DOE, including the response data into Minitab. We can now analyse the screening DOE.

12. Click *Assistant<<DOE<<Analyze and Interpret.* Click on the *Fit Screening Model* box. Even though you have just indicated you wish to fit a screening model, you get a pop-up menu that asks the same thing again. Click 'Yes'. Or the easier way is to click on **the Fit the Screening Model button** but in the Output Pane.

The Assistant creates a new command in the Output Pane. At the top, it has a summary of the results from the Screening DOE and further instructions on the next steps. We also get a 4 page report from the Screening DOE.

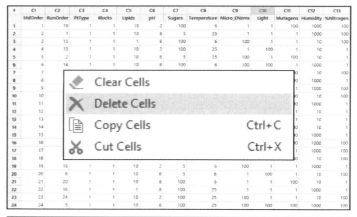

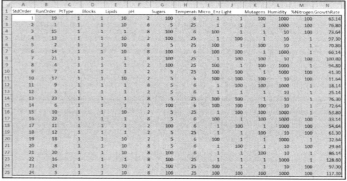

Navigator ▼

Create Screening Design

Fit the screening model

⊞ WORKSHEET 1

Fit Screening Model

Your screening experiment identified 4 critical factors, which are represented by the blue bars in the Pareto chart. You can now use those factors in a modeling design to create a predictive model for the response. When you set the factor levels in the modeling design, it is common practice to set them closer together than in the screening design. This can increase the chances of identifying optimal settings for the critical factors.

The top left of the Summary Report has the Pareto Chart of Effects. This shows which of the Main Effects or Factors were found to be significant. These are the effects that extend past the dashed line, which indicates significance at the 0.1 level. We see that Sugars, Temperature, pH & Light were significant factors.

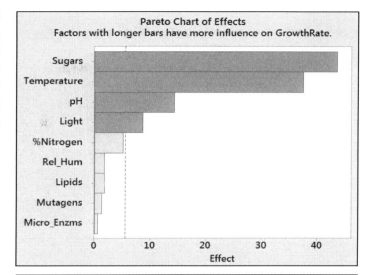

We are told that changes in these four factors explain 94.68% of changes in the response. Which is a very good fit.

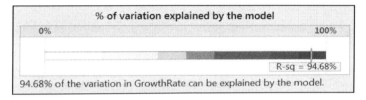

On the Effects Report, we have the Main Effects plots for all the factors. The non-significant factors have been greyed out. Light is the only factor that has a negative effect on the response. We can also see that Sugar has the largest effect followed closely by temperature.

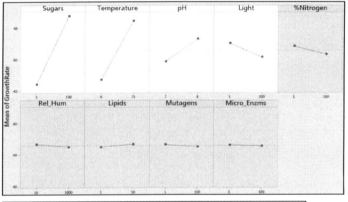

At the top of the Diagnostic Report, we have the Residual Vs Fitted values plot. We have one point with a large residual. It is not that isolated from the other data. Therefore, no action will be taken.

The plot below that is the Residual Vs Observation Plot, not shown here. This loses it's impact as the results of the experiments were sorted and are no longer in time order.

The Report Card, not shown here, only warns us of the point with the large residual.

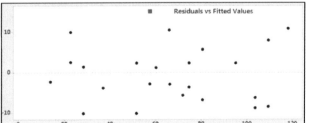

Example 13.5.2 Bacterial Growth Modelling DOE

Now that Dr Foster has the results of the screening DOE, he wants you to create a worksheet for a Modelling DOE. He advises you that he wants to maximise GrowthRate, leave the factor levels where they are and that he is happy to increase the runs in the experiment to improve the effect that can be observed.

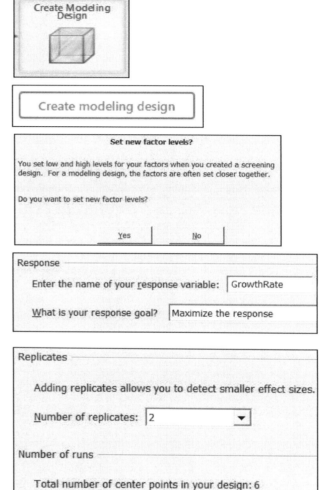

13. Click *Assistant<<DOE<<Analyze and Interpret.* Then *c*lick on the *Create Modeling Design* box. Or click on the *Create modeling design* box, that should be at the top of the Output Pane.

14. A menu box will appear and ask you if you wish to enter new factor levels. Click on No, and you are taken to the Modeling Worksheet Creation Menu.

15. Type in 'GrowthRate' as the response.
16. From the selector for 'What is your response goal?' Select 'Maximise the response'. Minitab will have already selected our significant factor and their levels, saving us some typing.

17. For 'Number of Replicates' select 2. We could have had a design with only 19 runs, but to detect smaller effect sizes, we have opted to double the number of runs.

18. Click OK.

In the Data Pane, we have created a worksheet that tells us how to conduct 38 experimental runs in 38 rows. It has 8 columns, the 4 DOE admin columns and then 4 columns showing the factor settings. The 9th column, with heading GrowthRate, is where we will enter the response data when the modelling experiments have been completed.

In the Output Pane, we get some instructions on how what to do with the results when the screening experiments are completed.

On the bottom right of the Summary Report, we are given information on the detection ability of the experiment. The power bar shows us that to achieve a power of 80% the minimum effect that we will be able to detect is 0.9 StDevs which is equivalent to small effects.

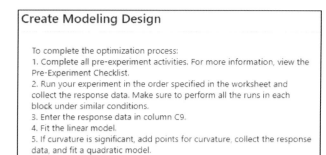

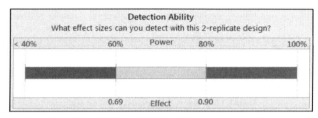

Dr Foster and his team complete the experiments for the Modeling DOE. They return the results in Excel worksheet 'Bacteria Model'.

19. Go to the Minitab worksheet where our modelling DOE worksheet was created. Delete everything but the title bar and then transfer the data from the Excel worksheet into Minitab. It's the same as we did for the screening model but the cell references are different.

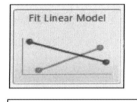

20. Click **Assistant<<DOE<<Analyze and Interpret.** Click on the **Fit Linear Model** box. Alternatively, just click on the **Fit the linear model** box that should be at the top of the Output Pane.

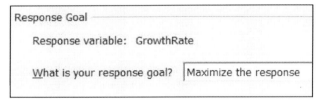

21. A menu for the Response Goal opens. If the goal is not listed as 'Maximize the response' change it to that. Click OK. This will produce a five page report in the Output Pane.

Starting at the top left of the Summary Report, which has the Pareto Chart of Effects. We see that Sugars, Temperature, pH & the interaction between pH and temperature were significant factors at the 0.1 level. Light is no longer a significant factor.

Sugars and Temperature still have the greatest effect on the response.

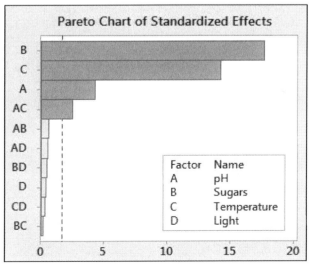

Again the model is a very good fit and we can explain 94.25% of the changes in the Response through changes in the main effects and interaction term.

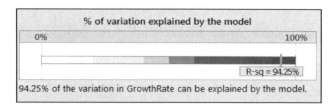

On the top right of the Summary Report, we are given the Design Information for our experiment, not shown here. Below that we have the factor settings that we should use to get the highest response value possible, which as a single value is 114.354.

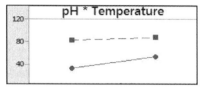

On the Effects Report, we are shown all the interaction plots and main effects for the factors. Only the significant factors and single significant interaction are highlighted and all the others are greyed out.

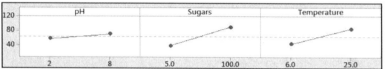

At the top of the Diagnostic Report, we have the Residual Vs Fitted values plot. We don't have any unusual data points, so I have not shown the chart here.

Below that we have the Residuals Vs Observation order chart. It's worth noting that Minitab will automatically split this experiment into two halves, as each is a repeat of the other, and it will compare the two halves to check if there was a significant difference between the two halves or Blocks. Minitab is checking to see if anything changed when you did the experiment. You can manually change the split between the Blocks if you feel like investigating a noise variable in your experiments.

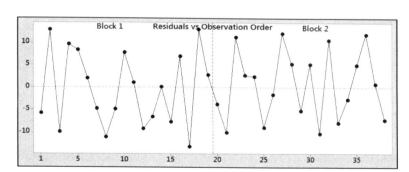

Next, we have the Prediction and Optimization Report. This is added to reports to tell us what settings we should use to achieve our aim with the response.

Dr Foster wants to maximise GrowthRate so right at the top of the report, we are given the highest predicted level of GrowthRate that can be achieved, which is 114.345. The prediction interval for single experiments is 95.98 to 132.73. Just on the right of that, we are given the settings that should be used to achieve the maximum GrowthRate.

Dr Foster notes that the maximum response is achieved at the upper limits of the three factors and that in future projects it would be worth using even higher levels of the factors to check if GrowthRate could be further increased.

Below that we have 3 optimisation plots showing the optimal settings in the form of a dashed line.

On the bottom left, we are given the top five alternate solutions.

The Report Card, not shown here, does tell us that Blocks were not significant. This means there were not any unexpected changes which affected the results between the first repeat of the experiment and the second. The Report Card also tells us that there was no sign of curvature detected. This is a really useful insight and tells us if more experimental runs might be helpful in improving the model.

Dr Foster is excited with the results so far. As curvature was not detected in the linear model, it would not be advisable for Dr Foster to conduct more experimental runs trying to find curvature. Dr Foster and his team will now look at conducting experiments with the significant factors at higher levels in the future.

The Report Card also advises that 20-30 confirmation runs should be completed at the settings which were listed to obtain the Maximum Growth Rate, to verify the solution.

Goal: Maximize GrowthRate	
Predicted Y	114.354
95% PI	(95.977, 132.73)

Solution: Optimal Settings	
A: pH	8
B: Sugars	100
C: Temperature	25

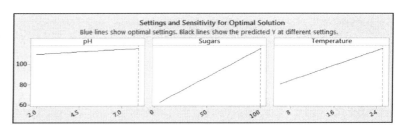

Settings and Sensitivity for Optimal Solution
Blue lines show optimal settings. Black lines show the predicted Y at different settings.

Top Five Alternative Solutions			
A	B	C	Predicted Y
2	100	25	108.979
8	100	6	79.4485
5	52.5	15.5	64.1513
8	5	25	61.7292
2	100	6	59.0735

Example 13.6.1 Fuel Efficiency Screening DOE

Zaf is not someone who is in denial regarding mankind's impact on the environment and feels that he can conduct an experiment to improve the fuel efficiency of his 5.0 ltr EM 5 car. He brainstorms 7 factors that he thinks will have a significant effect on fuel efficiency. These factors are listed below. TEL, Ferrocence & MMT are all fuel additives. Fuel Magnets are powerful magnets used to align the molecules in the fuel lines before combustion. The type of tyre is Eco or Normal, where Eco indicates a fuel saver tyre which is ecologically friendly.

The efficiency tests are conducted on a rolling road to reduce noise variables.
Help Zaf and his team save the environment by generating a Screening DOE design. Pass the design to Zaf and then analyse the data that he gives you. Continue this process through to the Modelling DOE up to a quadratic model. Zaf will advise you on the number of runs he is willing to support.

The screening DOE factors are listed below using the following format 'Factor Full name (Column Heading, Lo setting, Hi Setting)'.

Air pressure in the tyres (Tyre_Press, 25, 35)
TEL (TEL, 1, 3)
Ferrocence (Ferrocence, 1, 3)
MMT (MMT, 2,5)
Generic Type of Tyre (Tyre, Eco,Normal)
Fuel Magnets (Fuel_Mag, Off, On)
Air Conditioning (Air_Con, Off, On)

We start the sequential DOE process by creating a Screening DOE Worksheet. We want to reduce the 7 possibly significant factors to between 2 and 5.
To create the worksheet, we don't need to import any data into Minitab.

1. Start with a new project and then click **Assistant<<DOE<<Plan and Create.**

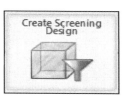

2. Click on the **Create Screening Design** box.

3. We need to set-up the worksheet in the menu that opens. Enter 'Efficiency' as the response variable.

Response and factors

Enter the name of your response variable: Efficiency

Number of factors: 7

4. Zaf has generated 7 usable factors for an experiment so we will enter '7' as the number of factors.

5. We then need to enter all the factor details. We need to enter the short factor name, the data type, and then the high and low levels to be used for the factors in the experiment. Note that Tyre, Fuel_Mag and Air_Con are categorical factors. The high and low levels must be typed in exactly as shown for the procedure to run without an error.

6. The minimum number of runs required for the screening DOE is 12. However, Zaf has decided that it would be beneficial to invest in the extra runs and be able to detect a smaller effect. He has decided to increase the number of runs to 24 by folding the design.

7. Click OK.

Enter your factor names and settings:

Name	Type		Low	High
Tyre	Categorical	▼	Eco	Normal
Fuel_Mag	Categorical	▼	Off	On
Tyre_Press	Continuous	▼	25	35
Air_Con	Categorical	▼	Off	On
TEL	Continuous	▼	1	3
Ferrocence	Continuous	▼	1	3
MMT	Continuous	▼	2	5

Adding runs allows you to detect smaller effect sizes.

Total number of runs in your design: 24 (fold design) ▼

In the Data Pane, we have created a the Screening worksheet. It tells Zaf how to conduct 24 experimental runs in 24 rows. It has 11 columns, the 12th column, with heading Efficiency, is where Zaf will enter the response data when the experiments have been completed.

In the previous example, we covered a lot of the information that is in the Output Pane and Summary Report so we won't repeat it here.

The crucial piece of information on the bottom right of the Summary Report is the detection ability of the experiment. The power bar shows us that to achieve a power of 80% the minimum effect that we will be able to detect is 1.06 StDevs. In the guidance given below, we are told that we will be able to detect down to small to moderate effects of the factors. This is a similar level to the last example.

Design Information

Response	Efficiency
Base design	7 factors, 12 runs
Total runs	24

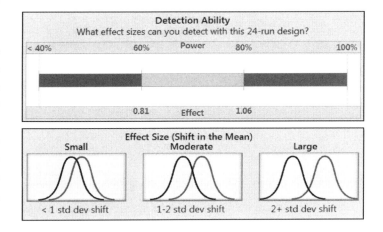

Zaf and his team of modders have a great time collecting the data and complete all 24 experimental runs. The data is recorded in 13 DOE.xlsx worksheet 'Efficiency Screen'.

As the auto-randomisation will create worksheets where everyone's StdOrder is different, the Excel worksheet has been sorted on the StdOrder column. This means we can't just copy the response column into Minitab. We need to copy the entire worksheet in.

8. In Minitab highlight column C1 to C11 from row1 to row24. Do not delete the title row.

9. Right-click and then left-click on 'Delete Cells'. This will clear the worksheet leaving only the column headings.

10. Go to the Excel worksheet 'Efficiency Screen' and copy cells A2 to L25.

11. Paste those cells in Columns C1 to C12 directly under the title bar. That brings the complete Screening DOE, including Response into Minitab. We can now analyse the screening DOE.

12. Click **Assistant<<DOE<<Analyze and Interpret.** Click on the **Fit Screening Model** box. Even though you have just indicated you wish to fit a screening model, you get a pop-up menu that asks the same thing again. Click 'Yes'. Or the easier way is to click on **the Fit the Screening Model button** but in the Output Pane.

This will produce a 4 page report on the results of the report on the Screening DOE in the Output Pane.

The top left of the Summary Report has the Pareto Chart of Effects. This shows which of the Main Effects or Factors were found to be significant. These are the effects that extend past the dashed line, which indicates significance at the 0.1 level. We see that we have only two significant factors and these are Ferrocence and Tyre. Some factors are almost significant but they miss the 0.1 level.

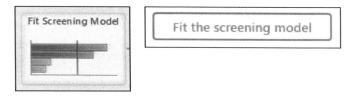

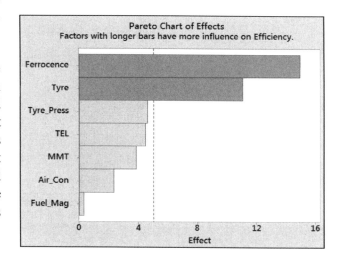

We are told that changes in these two factors explain 65.72% of changes in the response. This is an okay fit. It does warrant a conversation with Zaf to ask him to review if there could be a missing factor that was not in the experiment.

On the Effects Report, we have the Main Effects plots for all the factors. The non-significant factors have been greyed out. We see that increasing the Ferrocence additive increases the efficiency and the Eco tire also increases the efficiency.

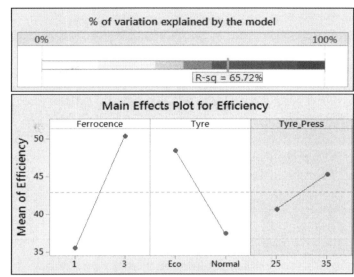

At the top of the Diagnostic Report is the Residual Vs Fitted values plot. We don't have any unusual points.

As we have sorted the data the Residual Vs Observation Plot, not shown here, is not relevant.

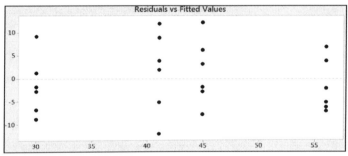

The Report Card does not give us any warnings that we need to be concerned over. The Report Card does tell us that for our 'Next Steps' we can create a modeling experiment using the two significant factors. Strangely enough, that's precisely what we are going to do.

Example 13.6.2 Fuel Efficiency Modelling DOE

With these results, Zaf is keen to get started with the Modeling DOE. Create the worksheet for a Modelling DOE. Zaf advises you that he wants a fuel efficiency of above 50 mpg. This means you need to target 50 mpg and then tell Zaf the factors he can change if he wants to go above 50 mpg. Zaf also advises that he does not want to change the factor levels and that he is willing to go up to 25 experimental runs at this stage.

13. Click *Assistant<<DOE<<Analyze and Interpret.* Click on the **Create Modeling Design** box. Alternatively, just click on the **Create Modeling Design** button in the Output Pane.

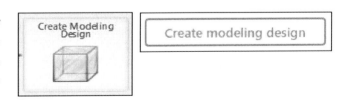

14. A menu box will appear and ask you if you wish to enter new factor levels. Click on No, and you are taken to the Modeling Worksheet Creation Menu.

15. Type in 'Efficiency' as the response.
16. From the selector for 'What is your response goal?' Select 'Achieve a target value' from the drop-down menu. As per Zaf's requirements enter a target of '50'.
17. For 'Number of Replicates' select '4'. This will create an experiment with 24 runs. If we select 6 replicates then that would give us 36 runs which is more than Zaf is willing to accept at this stage.
18. Click OK.

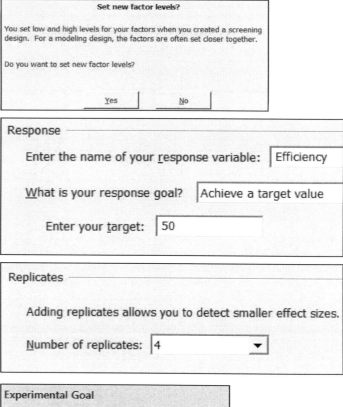

In the Data Pane, we have created a the Modeling DOE worksheet. It tells Zaf how to conduct 24 experimental runs in 24 rows. It has 6 columns, the 7th column, with heading Efficiency, is where Zaf will enter the results of the Modeling experiments.

On the top left of the Summary Report for Model creation, we are given the experimental goal. Strangely we are told that the goal is 'Construct a quadratic model..'. This is strange as we were expecting a linear model. Also, in the bottom left, we are told that this design will model curvature. As the curvature can only be associated with the numerical factor and not the categorical factor, it does not take a great many runs to investigate the single factor for curvature. We get that investigation as a bonus within our specified runs.

Zaf and his crew complete the experiments for the Modeling DOE. They return the results in Excel worksheet 'Efficiency Model'.

19. Go to the Minitab worksheet where our modeling DOE worksheet was created. Delete everything but the title bar and then transfer the data from the Excel worksheet into Minitab. It's the same as we did for the screening model, but the cell references are different.

20. Click *Assistant<<DOE<<Analyze and Interpret.* Click on the *Fit Quadratic Model* box. Or click on the **Fit Quadratic model** button in the Output Pane.

21. A menu for the Response Goal opens. If the goal is not listed as 'Achieve a target value' change it to that and then enter the target as '50'.

22. Click OK to produce the five page report for the Quadratic DOE.

Starting at the top left of the Summary Report, which has the Pareto Chart of Effects. The terms that extend past the red dashed line are significant. We see that Ferrocence and Tyre are both significant, but the Ferrocence quadratic term is also significant. The interaction term between Ferrocence and Tyre is not significant.

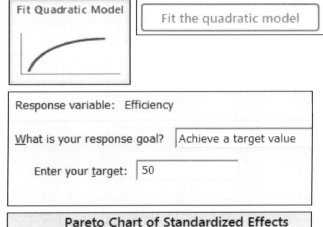

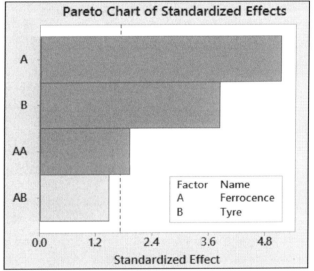

The model fit has improved by a few percent and is now up to 69.16%.

On the top right of the Summary Report, we are given the Design Information for our experiment, not shown here. Below that we have the factor setting that we should use to obtain the target response value of 50. To get Efficiencies higher than 50, we would have to increase the level of Ferrocence. There will be more on that later.

On the Effects Report, we are shown the interaction plot for Ferrocence*Tyre. This is greyed out as it is not significant and it is not shown here.

The ME plot for Ferrocence shows a curve which is typical of a quadratic term. The ME plot for Tyre shows that the Eco tyre was more fuel-efficient than a normal tyre.

At the top of the Diagnostic Report, we have the Residual Vs Fitted values plot. We don't have any unusual data points and there are no patterns that we need to worry about so I have not shown the chart here.

Below that we have the Residuals Vs Observation order chart which shows how the experiment was split into two blocks. Again, as we had to interfere with the run order, these are not worth examining.

Let's have a look at the Prediction and Optimization Report. In the top centre, we are given the 95% prediction interval we can expect to achieve when conducting runs at the settings given to achieve an average mpg of 50.

Goal: Target Efficiency at 50	
Predicted Y	50.0000
95% PI	(39.219, 60.781)

Solution: Optimal Settings	
A: Ferrocence	2.63503
B: Tyre	Eco

We are then shown the settings that we need to set to achieve our target response using main effects plots. We can tell Zaf that a Ferrocence level of 2.635 will achieve his minimum target value. Increasing the Ferrocence level up to 3 will further improve fuel efficiency. We don't predict what happens above 3 as that would be extrapolation and as good Six Sigma practitioners, we don't do that.

On the bottom left, we are given the top five alternate solutions. Some of these solutions even attempt to use the Normal tyre. However, as can be seen from this data even using the hi-level of Ferrocence of 3 a response level of 50 would not be achieved with the Normal tyre.

The Report Card, not shown here, does tell us that Blocks are not significant.

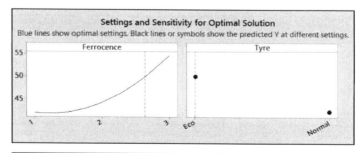

Top Five Alternative Solutions		
A	B	Predicted Y
3	Normal	47.0612
3	Eco	54.7081
2	Eco	44.3816
1	Eco	42.1606
2	Normal	36.7347

Example 13.6.3 Fuel Efficiency Regression Equation

We thought that the results of the DOE would keep Zaf happy, but we were wrong. Zaf has realised that ECO tyres are more expensive than normal tyres by £9.55 per tyre and that Ferrocence cost £0.5/ltr. Zaf is willing to do the maths but he wants us to give him the regression equations for this DOE so that he can understand the costs associated with his fuel economy.

23. Click *Assistant<<Regression.*

24. Click on the **Optimize Response** box. We could have selected the Multiple Regression option but the selection that we used gives us additional verification that the model used in DOE and Regression within the Assistant is the same.

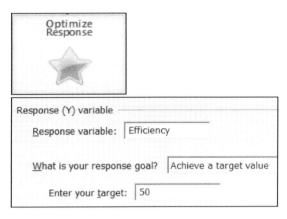

25. The Optimize Response menu opens. Enter Efficiency as the response. Set up the menu to tell Minitab we want to achieve a target of 50.

26. Enter Ferrocence as the continuous predictor variable and Tyre as the categorical predictor. Note, the tick box to investigate higher-order terms is engaged by default.

27. Click OK to run the procedure and produce the 6 page report.

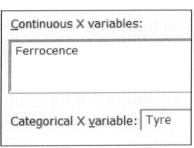

We are going to go through this report very quickly as we only want two things. The first is that we want to confirm the regression model is the same as the DOE model, and then we want the Regression Equations. Unfortunately, the regression equations do not appear in the DOE report.

Let's go to the Summary Report first and check the R-Sq value. It is 69.16% which is the same as the DOE report. Great!

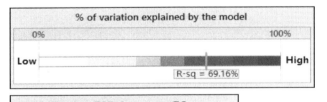

Next, we are going to jump to the Prediction and Optimization Report which is added if you select the Optimization option.

The settings to achieve a response of 50 and the 95% PI are the same as the DOE model. This means we can conclude that the models are the same.

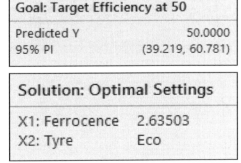

Now let's go to the Model Equations Report. This is where we find the two regression equations that we need to give to Zaf. Zaf said he would do the maths but let's just think about what he needs to do. For the tyres, he needs to work out the life of the tyre and the cost of petrol the tyres would consume in their life. Then work out if the extra cost of Eco tyres is less than the cost saving in fuel. The same type of arithmetic needs to be done for Ferrocence as well.

Tyre	Final Equations
Eco	Efficiency = $48.05 - 9.94 X1 + 4.05 X1^2$
Normal	Efficiency = $40.40 - 9.94 X1 + 4.05 X1^2$

X1: Ferrocence   X2: Tyre

Apart from the next exercise, this brings the book to a close. I hope that you found it useful and that you learned a lot from it. Please leave a quick review as it helps authors reach a greater audience if users leave reviews. Please take a couple of minutes and complete the feedback form that can be downloaded within the Chapter 1 area. This will significantly help me improve the next book.

If you have any quick questions you can email me at admin@rmksixsigma.com, there is no charge for this.

Also, if you think your company would benefit from receiving this book in the form of a training course, please drop me a line at admin@rmksixsigma.com or if you want more detailed help.

13.7 Sequential DOE Exercise

13.7.1 Starship Engine Power

You are helping Jock, the Chief Engineer, increase the engine power of the Starship Emoji. Jock has identified 8 factors and level that he wants to be investigated. Your mission is to boldly identify significant factors and maximise the response, Power, using a Screening DOE. Once significant factors have been identified, run a Modeling DOE with the intention of maximising the response using existing levels. If curvature is detected, conduct additional runs to characterise the curvature.

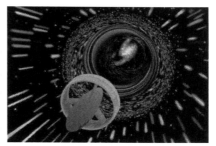

The screening DOE factors are listed below using the following format   Factor Full name (Column Heading, Lo setting, Hi Setting).
Engine Temperature (Temp, 9k, 12k)
Magnetic Field Density (MFD, 180, 230)
Magnetic Field Flux (MFF 26, 49)
Scones, Cream or Jam (Scones 0,1) Categorical
Reaction Initiation, Crank or Fusion (Initiation 0,1) Categorical
Core Wavelength (Wave 13k, 21k)
Plasma Input Angle (PIA 14, 26)
Plasma Input Flux (PIF 80, 120)

14 Detailed Contents of the Black Belt Edition

1 INTRODUCTION

2 MEASUREMENT SYSTEMS

02.1.1 Review Introduction
02.1.2 Graphical breakdown of Measurement Error
02.1.3 Gage R&R Review
02.2.1 Gage R&R
02.2.2 Gage R&R Example, Bicycle Frame Measurement

02.3.1 Gage R&R Expanded
02.3.2 Gage R&R Example, Further Bicycle Frame Investigation
02.3.3 Gage R&R Exercise, Temperature Changes

02.4.1 Type 1 Gage Study Intro
02.4.2 Type 1 Gage Study Example, DC Current PT14
02.4.3 Type 1 Gage Study Exercise, DC Current PT17

02.5.1 Gage Linearity and Bias Study Intro
02.5.2 Gage Linearity and Bias Study Example, 200kg Dosing Vessel
02.5.3 Gage Linearity and Bias Study Exercise, 500kg Dosing Vessel

02.6.1 Attribute Agreement Analysis Intro
02.6.1 Attribute Agreement Analysis Metrics
02.6.2 Attribute Agreement Analysis Example, Movie Certification
02.6.3 Attribute Agreement Analysis Exercise, Marking Scheme

3 PROCESS CAPABILITY

03.1.1 Review Introduction
03.1.2 Review Overall and Within Process Capability
03.1.3 A further summary of Process Capability within the GBE
03.2.1 Normality of the Underlying Data

03.3.1 Process Capability for Non-normal Data Intro
03.3.2 Process Capability for Non-normal Example 1, Invoice Payments.
03.3.3 Process Capability for Non-normal Example 1, Nuclear Fuel Pellets
03.3.4 Process capability for non-normal exercise movie streaming services

4 ANOVA

04.1.1 Review of ANOVA

04.2.1 Intro to General Linear Model
04.2.2 ANOVA GLM Example 1, Khanicci Pizzeria

Printed in Great Britain
by Amazon